DARE
TO THINK
DIFFERENTLY

DARE TO THINK DIFFERENTLY

How Open-Mindedness Creates
Exceptional Decision-Making

Gerald Zaltman

STANFORD BUSINESS BOOKS
An Imprint of Stanford University Press
Stanford, California

Stanford University Press
Stanford, California

Special discounts for bulk quantities of Stanford Business Books are available to corporations, professional associations, and other organizations. For details and discount information, contact the special sales department of Stanford University Press by emailing sales@www.sup.org.

ISBN 978-1-5036-4429-8 (cloth)
ISBN 978-1-5036-4502-8 (electronic)
Library of Congress Control Number: 2025027447

Library of Congress Cataloging-in-Publication Data available upon request.

Cover design: Jan Šabach
Cover art: Rawpixel

The authorized representative in the EU for product safety and compliance is: Mare Nostrum Group B.V. | Mauritskade 21D | 1091 GC Amsterdam | The Netherlands | Email address: gpsr@mare-nostrum.co.uk | KVK chamber of commerce number: 96249943

*This book is dedicated to my wife, Ann,
for her advice and great patience during
my long preoccupation with this book.*

CONTENTS

PREFACE

Why do some decision makers consistently out-innovate, out-manage, and out-perform their peers? The answer I've uncovered is deceptively simple: *because they have open minds.* Open-minded leaders actively question the validity and reliability of what they know and how they think about it—a process that has never been more necessary than it is in today's complex and volatile world.

A recent report from the Rand Corporation underlined the stakes. "History is full of great powers that hit a peak . . . and then stagnate and eventually decline," it noted.[1] What separates the ones that recover and thrive, it continued, is the vitality of their thinking, which can be revived by "open-minded learning and adaptation."[2] As I will show you, there are six universal actions of mind that when engaged wisely can help ensure that learning and adaptation occur. In brief, open-minded learning demands that you engage in serious play, befriend your ignorance, ask the right questions, indulge your curiosity, use panoramic thinking, and embrace ambiguity. These actions enable and encourage unorthodox thinking. They stress self-training and learning over conventional notions of intelligence.[3]

Becoming open-minded, of course, is just the first step toward the restoration of a healthier, more prosperous society. But it is a step with a very long stride. Without it, innovation and other renewal efforts simply won't happen. Fortunately, it is a skill that anyone can learn.

AN INNER VOICE

I've long wondered why people think and act as they do, and I addressed the question directly in my books *How Customers Think* (2003) and *Marketing Metaphoria* (2008). This book draws on exercises I've used with great success with my Harvard MBA students and consulting clients, some of which are also presented in these pages.

The research I undertook for this latest volume was profoundly enriched by interviews that my colleagues and I carried out with hundreds of creative and forward-looking executives, artists, academics, and thought leaders, who generously shared their thinking styles with us. In various ways, each told us that they are guided by an inner voice, one that ceaselessly reflects upon and challenges their assumptions while seeking out new perspectives and ideas. As one put it, it is as if there is a "reminder angel sitting on your shoulder asking questions." I call that angel the mind's "inner voice." Among its questions are variations of these:

- Am I engaging in serious playfulness to ensure novel thinking?
- Am I asking bold enough questions?
- Am I allowing my curiosity to lead me to unfamiliar domains?
- Am I willing to learn the languages spoken by other disciplines?
- Am I viewing ambiguities as sources of opportunities?
- Am I identifying what I don't know?

All of these Am I? questions and their Are we? siblings must be asked and answered and asked again, because open-minded learning and adaptation is a process that never ends. And as you'll see, your mind is not only yours—it is shaped by others, as well. It never operates without being in a context. Of course, the fact that other minds impact our own also applies to me. While I like to think that at least some of my ideas are unique to me, it is also the case that handprints belonging to many others are present when I dare to think differently. A brief elaboration will help you see that this book is the product of these influences.

First, a great many people identified in the acknowledgments have advised me in the course of preparing this book. But there is an even larger, more varied community of bold, innovative thinkers who have a major presence in these pages. One group is the many executives and leaders in other fields I've interviewed, which I will have more to say about later. Another major group is the authors of the extensive multidisciplinary research literature cited in this book, whose thinking augments, clarifies, verifies, and renders more useful the ideas I derived from the interviews.

Second, I have had the enormous good fortune to have as mentors and colleagues some of the world's foremost thinkers. They taught me many things, such as being willing to regard the gaps in my knowledge as opportunities rather than something to hide or hide from. They taught me to dare to think differently, not for the sake of being different, but because of what thinking differently can produce. They also taught me the importance of being prepared for and finding value in resistance to my thinking, to view my encounters with pushback as a valued friend, a way to make my ideas even better. Sometimes being wrong is the requisite condition for being right later on.

What strikes me as I reflect on my career thus far is that it has led me to places where people dare to think differently about how they create, share, and apply their knowledge, and for whom the half-life of knowledge is always short. Here are some examples of those environments.

While a doctoral student in sociology at The Johns Hopkins University, I worked for and with world leaders in the sociology of education and the sociology of science. During an interim appointment as a research associate at the American Institute of Physics, I studied the communication behaviors in the field of theoretical high energy physics.

My first position after receiving my doctoral degree was in the Marketing Department at Northwestern University's Kellogg School of Management. While there, I became the co-director of the Center for the Study of Science and Technology as well as the research director at the Kellogg School. I couldn't have asked for better mentors and colleagues. Later, I joined the Katz Business School at the University of Pittsburgh, where I was codirector of the university's Center for the Study of Knowledge Use. As director of the school's doctoral program, I worked to create a community of thought leaders.

Subsequently, I joined the Harvard Business School, where I was surrounded by open-minded thought leaders who dared to think differently, both at HBS and the larger university. During this time, I obtained three U.S. patents, one of which became known as ZMET, a research tool that is taught and used around the globe. Additionally, I was invited to join the university's select Mind, Brain, Behavior Initiative and served on its steering committee. With Stephen M. Kosslyn, a leading cognitive neuroscientist, I cofounded the HBS Mind of the Market Laboratory, where we conducted the very first neuroimaging study in marketing. Another major initiative was the launch of a long-running series of ZMET interviews about how leaders solve difficult problems. Those interviews, which continue today, inform much of this book.

It is hard to overestimate how much I've learned from the outstanding people at the many institutions I've been connected with, going all the way back to my undergraduate work in government and economics at Bates College and my MBA education at the University of Chicago. The faculty there encouraged me to consider an academic career, an idea which I tested by teaching at the University of Alaska, where I was encouraged to write my first book, *Marketing: Contributions from the Behavioral Sciences*.

Most importantly, my careers in both academia and global consulting have given me the privilege of teaching and mentoring others. Many of my students and clients went on to become CMOs and CEOs, among other important positions. A great many have become very highly respected scholars who are boldly shaping their respective fields. And others have endowed professorships, hold or have held positions in professional associations and at leading journals, and have received major professional awards. Because of this track record, I'm often asked about my "secret sauce" for mentoring. Most interviewers are surprised to learn I don't have one. But as a learner, you do have a recipe. Successful learners examine their thinking, change it as appropriate, and are inventive in adapting new ideas to their special needs. Intelligent ownership of ideas is your secret sauce, and I strongly encourage you to apply it liberally to the contents of this book.

My role as author is to help you improve your thinking. But doing so is a lot like teaching someone to swim, ride a bike, whistle, or blow a bubble with bubble gum. Describing what to do is important, but at the end of the day, what matters most is providing the support, encouragement, and confidence you need to place your personal stamp on what is offered. I've placed my own stamp on these lessons. Now it's your turn.

What you do with these lessons is up to you, but I can promise you this: if you apply them diligently, your approach to challenging problems will change for the better. You'll have a more open mind and an eagerness to take intelligent ownership of important ideas, qualities that are closely and positively related to sound decision-making, cognitive flexibility, the use of imagination, respectful consideration of others' viewpoints, a science orientation, and the ability to separate reliable from unreliable information.

The executives, researchers, colleagues and students I've admired and learned from embrace the excitement and inspiration inherent in their not knowing.

They do so with courage and confident humility driven by curiosity. I'm certain this describes you, since you have chosen to read this book.

I look forward to hearing from you any time in our journey. And remember: while I am the author of this book, you are the author of what you do with its ideas. So, let's get going. Our future depends upon what each of us does right now.

ACKNOWLEDGMENTS

An African proverb tells us it takes a village to raise a child, and this applies to bringing *Dare to Think Differently* to fruition. Foremost among the "villagers" are the many interviewees whose thinking informs this book. I hope I have done justice to all the instruction they offered.

Many other practitioners and academics shared their ideas and constructive critiques and advice. Writing is a deeply personal experience. In my case, it is how I discover what I think and do and do not know. And, like first-time parents whose child is the world's most beautiful baby, assessing your own ideas and their expression is sometimes difficult. Many villagers are needed to provide reality checks and other forms of guidance. In my case, these villagers included:

Vincent P. Barabba, Andy Baron, Cassandra Bates, Arigun Bayaraa, Tim Bradley, Katja Cahoon, Lou Carbone, Robin Coulter, Nancy Cox, Jeffrey Fisher, James Forr, Cindy Haroonian, Bill Harvey, Dawn Iacobucci, MaryGrace King, Philip Kotler, Jess Kukreti, Andrew Lazzaro, Gary Massel, Lynn Massel, Horace Maxcy, Joe Meth, Christine Moorman, Jerry Olson, Christian Petredis, Bianca Philippe, Joe Plummer, Nicole Raynard, Stephen D. Rappaport, Randi Rossi, Ivan Sanchez, Rob Scalea, Kathy Shaw, Sanya Shikari, Stephen Silverman, Diana Luisa Simion, Shelby Smith, Brian Sternthal, Anne Thistleton, William Totten, Alice Tybout, Bruce Weinberg, Kelly Willis, Charles Young, and Lindsay Zaltman. As the development of this book was protracted, there are undoubtedly many other contributors, and I apologize for their inadvertent omission.

Nearly all my colleagues at Olson Zaltman have contributed to this book in one way or another. The topic, for instance, was explored in various OZ retreats and examined by various project teams. Having the support of such talented colleagues was highly motivating. A special shout out goes to my long-time partner and cofounder of OZ, Jerry Olson. Whenever I became stuck on an issue, he was always present to help bail me out.

Two of the most talented developmental editors I've ever worked with helped me bridge the gap between being in an author's shoes versus those of a reader. One is Francesca Forest and the other is Arthur Goldwag. Both are amazingly perceptive and knowledgeable. They were also adept at making me feel humble and good at the same time. Each one is a highly accomplished, published author which likely contributes to their abilities to see things through both a reader's and author's viewing lenses. I feel privileged to call Francesca and Arthur close friends.

Other villagers also had a helping hand in this book. One is my literary agent James Levine, a principal in Levine Greenberg and Rostan Literary Agency. Jim immediately grasped the importance of the book in today's world. He contributed to its structure and content and provided seasoned guidance in selecting the right publisher. That process resulted in my working with Richard Narramore and his colleague Natalie Rovero at Stanford University Press and its Business Books division. They helped improve the book's content and flow. I've worked with many senior editors in the past. None surpass their value added and ease of collaboration.

A special thank you goes to the Harvard Business School's Division of Research. Their generous and unhesitating support throughout my career there made many things possible. The resources required for interviewing so many leaders would not have been available anywhere else. There is one particular person at HBS I need to single out, my HBS assistant Luz Velazquez. This book also draws upon a large and varied research literature. Luz was instrumental in helping me access it, often in response to "needed today" requests. I marvel at her persistence and patience.

DARE
TO THINK
DIFFERENTLY

ONE

What Is a Mind, Anyway?

AND WHAT IS IT FOR?

This chapter elaborates on my goals for this book, clarifies the term *the mind*, and identifies the six actions of an open mind. It also explores the value of open-mindedness as a response to our world's most pressing changes and challenges, including artificial intelligence. It closes with my suggestions for how to make the best use of the book's many ideas and practices and the hope that as you absorb them, you will be inspired to cultivate them to achieve wiser, more fluid thinking.

We begin with a set of Am I? questions. Hopefully, your answers to each of them is yes.

- Am I ready to invest in the practices and exercises that will open my mind?
- Am I searching for ways to apply flexible thinking in a changing world?
- Am I willing to cultivate serious playfulness, befriend my ignorance, indulge my curiosity, ask the right questions, use panoramic thinking, and embrace ambiguity?
- Am I excited to learn what actions of an open mind entail, even if they challenge me to think in new and sometimes uncomfortable ways?

My interest in the mindsets of imaginative decision-makers and creative problem-solvers is long-standing. Those who repeatedly make the right calls, I've found, have open minds. Meaning they are willing, even eager, to evaluate and change the ways they think. I first noticed this decades ago, when I began teaching at the Harvard Business School using its legendary case method. Cases typically present what appear to be routine problems, but they frustrate formulaic thinking. The students who repeatedly came up with the most creative solutions were the ones who were the most willing to examine and then revise their default thinking patterns. I have witnessed the same thing again and again as a management and marketing consultant.

My goal in this book is to help you become a better decision-maker by becoming a more open-minded thinker, especially when you confront challenging or messy problems. To do so, you must use each of the six key actions the business executives, scientists, artists, and other creative thinkers we interviewed described. The actions themselves are not novel. What is special, however, is *how* they actively engage in them to challenge or question their conscious and especially unconscious or hidden thinking.

Those interviews were carried out using a theory-in-use technique I developed and patented that draws on such varied fields as cultural anthropology, cognitive neuroscience, clinical psychology, art therapy, narrative analysis, and linguistics to probe subjects' thinking and surface their unconscious thoughts and feelings. The Zaltman Metaphor Elicitation Technique or ZMET, as it is called, requires both a trained interviewer and an interviewee assured of confidentiality to encourage deep and frank thinking. ZMET is featured in textbooks, taught in classrooms, and used by market researchers all over the world. It is described in depth in appendix 2.

The key "actor" in a ZMET interview is always the interviewee, not the interviewer.[1] To prime our subjects, we ask them to find pictures or objects that capture the emotions, thoughts, and feelings that especially challenging or messy problems arouse in them. They are asked to bring these items to the session. In the final part of the interview, we ask them to create an assemblage or collage that reflects both the conscious insights they expressed during the interview and the many unconscious ones the interview elicited. Metaphors, we'll see, are a universal and generative meaning-making tool based on analogical thought, drawing on lived experience, culture, and our bodies, to grasp and express abstract ideas.

Allow me to share a serendipitous discovery. A great many interviewees remarked that they were unaccustomed to being questioned about how they think. As one jokingly put it in a follow up note, "Usually when I'm asked about how I was thinking, it is an expression of disapproval, not curiosity." Interviewees were unaccustomed in their work life to being asked to reflect deeply and describe the reasons why they acted in certain ways and the processes involved. As intrusive and probing as our interviews were, most found them refreshing, challenging, and very worthwhile.

Interviewees were diverse in age, gender, nationality, and professions. Virtually everyone, from a world leader in neuroscience teaching at the Harvard Medical School to the CEO of a major European telecommunications company, practiced the same six actions of an open mind. Though their descriptive language varied, they all:

- Cultivate serious playfulness
- Befriend their ignorance
- Ask the right questions
- Indulge their curiosity
- Use panoramic thinking
- Embrace ambiguity

I will devote separate chapters to each action, but as you'll see, when they are undertaken and combined in the right way, they form a complex adaptive system that is greater than the sum of its parts.

Open-minded thinking demands humility, courage, and discipline. It also takes hard work and study. This is why I address the six actions individually in sequence. We'll move step by step toward the ultimate object of this complex system, which is to not only practice the actions habitually, but wisely choose when and how to apply them in each situation. The result is a way of fluid thinking that serious problems require. This is described more fully in chapter 9.

Serious thinking always entails both implicit and explicit processes, especially when a problem is particularly knotty or challenging. Metaphor elicitation is a powerful way of uncovering people's *theories-in-use*, which are mental models of what they don't know they know along with what they feel they do know.[2] Once uncovered, those ideas may be inspected, improved, and shared. Of course, every reader is unique, and some of what works well for an interviewee may require adaptation or not work at all for you. But all of their insights warrant serious attention and will hopefully inspire you to think critically about your own mental models.

Psychologists sometimes talk about two different systems of thought—System

1, often associated with unconscious processes, and System 2, often associated with conscious processes—as if they were independent. They are not. As David Melnikoff and John A. Bargh point out: "[This] dual-process typology is a convenient and seductive myth, and we think cognitive science can do better."[3] There is just one mind, not two. The distinction between two independent systems has been attributed to Daniel Kahneman but goes back to Freud and even earlier. However, as John A. Bargh and another of his colleagues Ran R. Hassin point out, Kahneman himself stated that System 1 and System 2 were merely "fictitious characters," intended only as a useful heuristic in the context of making decisions.[4]

Distinguishing between the unconscious mind and the conscious mind as independent of each other is mistaken.[5] There is no "the" there.[6] There are only degrees of and occasions for being unaware and aware. As noted by Vinod Venkatraman and John Wittenbraker, the former an academic and the latter a practicing executive:

> Human decision making is governed by a much more complex and nuanced process than a simple binary switch between two modes of thinking. We are flexible and dynamic in the way our decision processes unfold such that we can adapt our behaviors and outcomes to fit the environment or context we are in. Multiple processes ranging from more mindless and automatic to a more mindful and controlled cascade in any given problem or focal choice situation. And all of this is influenced by our context, goals, sensations, emotions and prior experience and memory.[7]

Having an open mind requires a more holistic approach to thinking, one that consciously seeks to uncover inductive and deductive thinking among practitioners. Sometimes this thinking is fully conscious, but most of it occurs below awareness. Surfacing unconscious operations of mind enables us to inspect and improve upon them using other sources of knowledge. In short, we need to uncover our own or others' mental models—their "pictures" or "stories" about how an aspect of their world works and what they do about it and why.

THE MIND'S JOB

What is a mind for? Let's begin by addressing the seemingly simple question. Then we'll move on to a much harder topic, which is what a mind might be.

The mind's purpose—its job—is to enable its owner to make meaning.[8] For most readers of this book a special kind of meaning is involved, which is to anticipate or predict the outcomes of alternative actions in challenging situations and thereby reduce the likelihood of making errors. To that end, a mind's special job for our purposes is to predict, that is, to ask and try to answer basic questions about the consequences of choices. It does this in varied ways and with exceptional speed—typically faster than the time it takes to go from *this* to *that* as you read this sentence. Nature favors actions that are successful and can be harsh when they are not. In other words, it rewards what works, which is not always the same thing as what is true, as Donald D. Hoffman points out in his book *The Case Against Reality*.[9] The actions of an open mind as introduced here, practiced wisely and internalized to become habits, favor social and economic well-being.

For a mind to achieve its purpose, the six actions must work as a team of specialists. These members are highly dependent on one another, like a dance troupe engaged in an intricate performance. Each action potentially impacts and is impacted by the others, and the patterns constantly change as learning occurs. There is no inherent sequential order among them except what you, the choreographer, choose in light of your goal.

Every open-minded action has both a conceptual and practical dimension. The conceptual dimension defines, describes, and reflects on the qualities of an open mind. It helps us understand what we're looking for, so we'll know it when we see it. The practical dimension is all about putting those open-minded actions to work in real-world situations to achieve workable solutions. My goal in this book is to make the importance of each action salient to you in conceptual and practical terms—just as they became salient to interviewees and me during our conversations. As you read, reflect on your experiences to see where the qualities of an open mind appear in your life and how you can employ them more intentionally.

So far, I've been referring to a mind as if its nature is well understood and widely agreed upon. It is not. So, let's address that topic next.

WHAT IS THE MIND?

Questions about what the mind is, who and what has one, its purpose, and how it works are so contentious that they are often ignored or assumed away. As a result, people are generally left with the burden of inferring what someone means when they use the term *mind*. Metaphors can help us understand. Here's a small sampling of some of the common metaphors people use to express certain features of the mind. You've probably used all of them at one time or another. I know I have.

COMMON METAPHORS FOR THE MIND
A mind is a:

- Surface: What is *on* your mind?

- Container: What do you have *in* mind? Are you *out* of your mind?

- Traveler: Is your mind *wandering?*

- Force: She is *strong/weak* minded.

- Sponge: His mind *absorbs* everything.

- Text: I can *read* your mind.

- Malleable thing: I can/can't *change* his mind.

- Movable object: Have you *lost* your mind?

- Resource or tool: Put your mind to *work.*

One definition of the mind that has found some consensus is a predictive enterprise requiring the collaboration of different ways of knowing.[10] This view is rooted in the predictive activities a mind undertakes for us. However, a definition I am most comfortable with is somewhat broader. It views a mind as a set of distinct capacities that work together cooperatively, much like the ingredients that go into a handshake. Although we use our minds to predict outcomes, not every action that contributes to that task is always used in a predictive way.

A handshake is a physical action involving people's hands, the neurological and muscular systems that bring them together, and a host of abstract elements. These elements include the emotions it conveys and the social and cultural norms that dictate when a handshake is or is not appropriate. All those elements operate together to create an action that has a certain meaning.

Just as a handshake requires two participants, our minds are shaped in part by the minds of others—whether via education and socialization or by formal collaborations. This is very important.[11] Minds, like team sports, are collective enterprises. Success or failure depends on how its parts work together.[12]

Building on all this, I define the mind as:

A highly versatile, blended force emerging from a joining together of (1) the external context, that is, physical environments and settings of life, (2) its social and cultural environment, (3) individual, body-based actions, and (4) neuronal activities in the brain. These forces or "hands" grip one another in an all-for-one handshake, their respective causes and effects accommodating one another as they work together (as illustrated in figure 1.1).

FIGURE 1.1   The Metaphoric Handshake of the Mind.

DESIGNED BY SANAYA SHIKARI.

Within the great grip of this handshake, the nexus of its varied forces, lies your mind which is both similar to and yet different from someone else's. That is why, for instance, different readers may have different takeaways upon reading this book. That makes for a very healthy world.

Discussions of the mind customarily pay the greatest attention to the brain. This is understandable, as a brain is a tangible object (*very* tangible: the average adult brain weighs about three pounds, accounts for about 2 percent of total body weight, and consumes about 20 percent of our daily energy), while a mind is not and so is much harder to discuss objectively.[13] Thomas Nagel, author of what may be the most frequently cited article in philosophy, "What Is It Like to Be a Bat?," highlights the challenges of understanding another's mind but even our own as well.[14] An unfortunate consequence of this focus is that the impact of the external environment on the daily functioning of the mind is often overlooked in favor of brain structure and functioning.[15] As the leading cognitive psychologists Steven Sloman and Philip Fernbach remind us, "The brain and the body and the external environment all work together to remember, reason, and make decisions . . . *the mind is not in the brain. Rather the brain is in the mind.*"[16] Harry Collins, a leading sociologist of science and knowledge, makes a powerful argument about the importance of social and cultural forces as a foundation for mind: "Nearly all of what we know comes not from 'thinking,' but from where we are born and how we are brought up and, mostly, what we know seeps in unconsciously."[17] How social arrangements "get under the skin" is also discussed by neuroscientist Michael L. Platt in his book, *The Leader's Brain.*[18] It is a process that begins early in life's social and economic experiences, which have long-lasting consequences.[19]

WAYS OF KNOWING

All these influences support four basic ways of knowing: science, reason, educated intuition, and purposeful imagination. The neuroscientist and philosopher Iain McGilchrist stresses that while each path has its own distinct virtues and vices, gifts and dangers, "any world view that [does not pay] due respect to all four of these is bound to fail."[20] Now, the four pathways are not hard and fast ways of learning and discovery. Nor do they occur independently of one another. However, throughout this book I'll remind you that imagination must be present for any of the other pathways to work well. Imagination, we'll see, powers all six of the actions I attribute to an open mind. Without imagination we can't create meanings, and without meanings we can't make useful predictions.

Reason and science are self-explanatory. By collecting and organizing data, carrying out experiments, and drawing logical conclusions, our conscious minds can make useful sense of the world. But imagination, our capacity to envision missing and even nonexistent information, and educated intuition, a form of understanding that bypasses logic and seems to be grounded in our guts rather than our brains, are more mysterious. They occur when unconscious and conscious thinking whisper to one another. This back-and-forth also enables us to deliberately challenge what might otherwise remain automatic or unconscious. None of these four modes of knowing are infallible; all are susceptible to bias. That is one of the reasons frank conversations within teams are so important: they can encourage open-mindedness.

There is one more observation I'd like to make about imagination that will help clarify its use in this book. Often, people use the terms *imagination* and *creativity* interchangeably. I make an important distinction between them. I define imagination as the ability to see or envision what is missing when problem-solving. I view creativity as the successful articulation or bringing into being what is perceived as missing. If imagination is the vision, creativity is the off-ramp that leads to vision's actualization.[21] This is an important distinction, as our focus in this book is more on imagination than creativity, though both are important and are discussed.

A vivid example of this comes from Garrett M. Graff in *When the Sea Came Alive*, a recent oral history of the Allied invasion of Normandy in World War II. The invasion planners faced a seemingly intractable problem: the absence of a suitable harbor along the French coast that could be readily captured by surprise and immediately deployed to meet the urgent resupply needs. The invasion's success required such a harbor. No harbor, no invasion.

At the end of yet another fruitless meeting to solve the problem, Commodore John Hughes-Hallett of the Royal Navy remarked, some thought flippantly, "Well, all I can say is, if we can't capture a port, we must take one with us."

This was not a considered thought; it was more an expression of his frustration. But it took an immediate hold on him, and he spent the entire night assessing its potential feasibility. The next day he was able to provide enough detail about his vision to convince the others that it was at least somewhat plausible. Absent any other alternatives, it gained immediate buy-in. Bringing it into being—the creative off-ramp—required endless cycles of "imagine then create" among an extraordinary variety and number of skilled people.[22] The result was what were called Mulberry harbors, sixty-one ships and caissons that were either towed or sailed across the channel under their own steam and then sunk into place to act as breakwaters and piers.

I emphasize the role of imagination because our world demands immediate and prolific output, but output without vision seldom succeeds. I encourage you not to dismiss your own or others' imagination as fanciful. Its role is no less important than science, reason, and other ways of knowing.

WHAT IS AN OPEN MIND?

I'd like to propose that an open mind is one that actively thinks about how it is thinking and is willing to make improvements as necessary.[23]

Open-mindedness is also commonly used to mean a willingness to encounter, consider, and possibly adopt new ideas and experiences. That is certainly a valuable trait, and various psychological tests exist to measure it. But it cannot be cultivated successfully without a willingness and ability to think about thinking, which is sometimes called "metacognition" or "critical thinking." The first term underlines the higher level of awareness that thinking about thinking requires, while the second stresses the use of reasoned judgments. I like to put the emphasis on the *open mind* rather than on these other labels because the mind is where the process happens. And, practically speaking, it's easier to interest colleagues in the concept of an open mind itself than metacognition, critical thinking, or even thinking about thinking.

Viewing open-mindedness as a set of six practical actions encourages their being cultivated to form habits. Thus, being open-minded is not a static quality that comes about in a vacuum. It can—and must be—continually developed. When this occurs, it results in greater imagination and creativity.[24]

Individuals and groups with open minds are willing to pause and examine how they approach challenges and assess the outcomes they achieve. Those with closed minds, in contrast, are prone to minimizing or avoiding thoughtful examinations of how they think and act so they can proceed directly to a solution. This is the "fire first, then aim" way of thinking that is all too common today. Can you think of a few times that you've followed or witnessed this approach? What did you notice before, during, and after the situation occurred? How did it make you feel? Maybe you saw it coming and felt powerless to respond. Or maybe you spoke up, only to be met with the other party's stubborn resistance. Or maybe you only saw it in hindsight. What behaviors would have had to change to make this an example of an open-minded approach? How would the outcome have differed?

It's in decision-making that we're most likely to see the consequences of unreflective thinking. When we approach a decision with a closed mind, we're unlikely to take full stock of all the surrounding circumstances. In contrast, when we approach a decision with an open mind we are aware of our ignorance but use it as a goad to acquire new knowledge and not as a reason to double down on what we think we already know. The result is better decisions. Maintaining an open mind does not guarantee successful outcomes, of course. But having a closed mind comes close to guaranteeing poor ones.

Open-minded thinkers take more responsibility for their thinking and consequently have greater agency. The following scenario illustrates this: Imagine that you are tasked with conducting one-on-one interviews with two characters, an open mind and a closed mind. Your first question to each is: What word stands out to you in the aphorism "Luck favors the prepared mind"?[25] Now imagine their replies. Most people think an open mind would choose "prepared" and a closed mind would choose "luck."

When I conduct this thought experiment with executives, I ask them to describe the reasoning they imagine each mind state would use to explain its choices. They usually describe the open mind as thinking proactively while the closed mind has a reactive reasoning stance. The open mind's operations include a regime of critical self-assessment, as it is constantly carrying out pre- and post-mortems with the goal of improving outcomes. "Good enough" works fine for the closed mind, so it has fewer ideas with which to innovate or experiment and only changes its approach when hindsight reveals the better way not taken. Most of the time it is on standby.

THE OPEN MIND AS AN ANTIDOTE TO THE PERMACRISIS

The World Economic Forum's 2024 Global Risks Report notes, "The world is undergoing multiple long-term structural transformations," some of which represent potential "existential threats to humanity."[26] It identified the following as the top ten:

- Extreme weather events
- Critical change to Earth systems
- Biodiversity loss and ecosystem collapse
- Natural resource shortages
- Misinformation and disinformation
- Adverse outcomes of AI technologies
- Involuntary migration
- Cyber insecurity
- Social polarization
- Pollution

How urgent are they? Of the 1,490 experts surveyed, 84 percent expect the next two years to be bad. When the timeline was extended to ten years, the percentage rose to 92 percent. Chaim Oren, a colleague, aptly describes this enduring, problem-laden world as a "permacrisis."

Each problem area—and there are a great many beyond those noted above—is a breeding ground for business challenges. A few are: ensuring reliable access to essential raw materials, finding and cultivating skilled personnel, adapting to regulatory actions, understanding changing customer needs and preferences, being competitive in developing new production and distribution technologies, and adapting to new information technologies. Most are not amenable to the rote decision-making used to handle more routine problems.

Encouragingly, the World Economic Forum notes that "the actions of individual citizens, companies, and countries—while perhaps insignificant on their own—can move the needle on global risk reduction if they reach a critical mass."[27] Unfortunately, the report does not discuss the type of thinking that will produce those move-the-needle decisions. It is highly doubtful that the same kind of thinking that created these problems can also solve them.

Nimble thinking is demanded when responding to problems that

- exist on the fringe of awareness (we sense something is wrong without knowing exactly what),
- are recognized but poorly understood,
- are understood but lack clear, workable solutions,
- need an urgent resolution, or
- have a major emotional impact on the decision-maker.

When leading executives and other professionals describe challenges like these, their choices of metaphors reveal strong emotions. Many evoke devastating forces of nature such as hurricanes, earthquakes, and floods and describe feeling intimidated, overwhelmed, victimized, angry, frightened, or enslaved. Feelings about failing to solve important challenges are described by images such as an exploding bomb, a deflated hot-air balloon, being burned at the stake, being caught naked in public, being left waiting at the altar, and a captain treading water as his ship sinks.

Success in wrestling with messy problems elicits a powerful set of positive metaphors. Examples include: reaching the top of a mountain after an arduous climb, experiencing the jolt of smelling salts, watching the birth of a child, going to the ballet, having a dream come true, scoring a winning touchdown, being unshackled, surviving a near drowning, being born again, and the fresh-start promise of a sunrise. Taken together, they elicit the deeper metaphor of a transformational journey.[28]

The impact of our permacrisis world on executives is sobering. Their metaphors show us that they care deeply about the seismic implications of their successes or failures. One expert in the area of corporate wellness informs us that 53 percent of corporate leaders feel burned out, and 80 percent feel they are unprepared for their leadership roles.[29] Those are staggering numbers. And there's more. The same authority reports that 56 percent of employees believe their boss is toxic, and 75 percent believe their boss is a source of stress.[30] These are not conditions leaders knowingly choose. So, what is going on?

First, let's rule out a couple of things. Most leaders know that systems thinking and divergent thinking are important. We can also rule out insufficiencies in general intelligence. As we've all observed, being smart does not guarantee effectiveness. Robert J. Sternberg, a leading scholar on intelligence, recently challenged a group of topic experts with this important question: "If intelligence is truly important to real-world adaptation, and IQ's have risen 30+ points in the past century (Flynn effect), then why are there so many unresolved and dramatic problems in the world, and what can be done about it?"[31]The Flynn effect refers to a thirty-point rise in average intelligence scores since about the 1930s. Certainly, huge advances have occurred over recent decades in many spheres of living. Still, threatening problems persist and are worsening.

So, why do most smart people, like the 80 percent of corporate leaders, feel so unprepared and inadequate? My approach in this book is to learn from the 20 percent who do feel well-prepared for a permacrisis world. What do they do when confronting major challenges? More exactly:

- What stands out in their thinking?
- Is there a pattern to it?
- Is it replicable?

I've already foreshadowed what independent research reinforces, namely that their intuitive and deliberative judgments rely on common principles. These principles are derived from the two kinds of inner-directed questions they ask.[32] These were mentioned earlier but now is a good time to clarify them.

The first set are Am I? questions. These questions require critical, candid self-appraisal with respect to the six actions. The second set I call Are we? questions. These require similar critical, candid appraisals, but this time of a team's or group's thinking involving the same actions. Both create positive climates for decision-making. Both involve consciously assessing what otherwise goes unnoticed or is unconscious. When leaders are known to critically self-examine their own and their team's thinking in this way, they are unlikely to be viewed as toxic. Provided the questions are timely, respectful, and actionable, they greatly improve the odds of a firm doing the right thing and at the right time to solve a problem. Am I? and Are we? questions are important tools for routinizing and refreshing the major actions of an open mind. A leader from an agricultural con-glomerate noted, "Critical thinking is not a 'one and done' affair. You need to keep at it. Always."

What does this look like in practice? Box 1.1 shows what fluency in the prac-tices of open-mindedness allowed one of our European interviewees to achieve. I hope that her example inspires you to consider what these habits would look like in your own life as you grapple with your own unique challenges—or in all of our lives if we adopt this mindset to confront the world's greatest global risks.

The sheer magnitude of a challenge—the feeling of vastness or awe it evokes—can provide a powerful emotional incentive to address it. Here we need to stop and acknowledge a topic in decision-making that is all-too-frequently ignored: emotion, which can stimulate us to open our minds or drive us to close them.[33] All emotions are physical in nature, and awe is no exception. Endorphins, dopa-mine, oxytocin, and serotonin are released in our systems when we experience it, manifesting such physiological effects as goosebumps and chills.[34] These dynam-ics also influence the mind's operations.

Here I particularly want to address the emotion of awe, which is only now receiving the attention it deserves.[35] Awe can be positive or negative: the meta-phors executives often use—hurricanes, volcanoes, and floods—convey vastness, but also destructiveness and their helplessness in the face of it. I won't go into the evolutionary explanations for our ability to experience and accommodate vastness.[36] Suffice it to say that our capacity to feel awe aids in our survival and so has been passed down through the millennia, shaping our views on such varied topics as science, religion, and ethics.[37] As we approach even the messiest prob-lems, we need to listen to awe and other emotions and use them to guide our actions.

THE VALUE OF AN OPEN MIND

Recently, I posed a single, open-ended question to sixty well-known executives, scholars, and other professionals: Why is having an open mind valuable? Given how busy they were, I was surprised when nearly all of them replied, some more than once to share their relevant afterthoughts. Box 1.2 contains a sample of their responses. Though I invited them to reframe the question as they felt appropriate, few did.

I had three takeaways from their replies. First, nearly all agreed that open-mindedness is important for personal, organizational, and societal success. Second, they see it as being in scarce supply. And third, many suggested that

BOX 1.1   Gabriella's Challenge

Gabriella (not her real name) is a global brand manager for a European cosmetics firm. When we met, she had just inherited responsibility for a brand that was experiencing an erosion in consumer loyalty. Gabriella and her team were under intense pressure to stanch the bleeding.

Befriending her ignorance and *using panoramic thinking* to fill the gaps, Gabriella *asked the right questions* and zeroed in on the most relevant answers. Critically, she learned that a change in manufacturing methods had compromised the product's quality, especially its perceived purity. Having addressed the issue, senior executives anticipated a rapid rebound in sales, but it didn't happen. Gabriella's recommendation that they feature the changes they'd made in an advertising campaign was rejected. Doing that, one executive said, would only remind consumers of why they had stopped buying the firm's products.

Gabriella believed they could "talk" with consumers about product purity without reminding them (or her bosses) of their past missteps. In a spirit of *serious playfulness*, she ventured outside the accepted marketing disciplines and *indulged her curiosity. Thinking panoramically,* she read widely in philosophy, architecture, religious studies, and psychology, from which she learned that visual simplicity inspires thoughts of purity and the temptation to touch. With that in mind, she proposed a radical redesign of the product's packaging.

But as Gabriella would learn, going outside the received wisdom of a field is not for timid people or lazy minds. Senior leaders resisted the *ambiguity* and uncertainty of her solution, not to mention its expense. Resistance also arose within her team, whose members were unfamiliar with the concepts she wanted to apply. Inculcating her insights into the entrenched thinking within the firm was nearly as messy a problem as her brand's decline. But in time she prevailed, and sales rebounded. Industry pundits gave credit to the new packaging. Gabriella also credited it for helping to correct a problem of longer-standing—getting the senior executives in her firm to be more consumer-centric.

Though Gabriella and her team were ultimately successful, they learned that integrating new ideas into existing thought and practice requires courage and grit. It wasn't enough for them to open up their own minds; they had to change their company's ways of thinking as well.

BOX 1.2 Why Is Having an Open Mind Valuable?

[It leads you to] become more knowledgeable and empathetic, your relationships strengthen, and you are better at solving problems.

It . . . is essential for addressing systematic biases.

It enables an upside: you can spot opportunities in a changing world.

It is contagious. Very much so.

If we are incurious about how our mind works, we can't very well cooperate or collaborate with other minds.

I hate being wasteful. If I don't have an open mind, I'm not using its full potential.

The very concept of democracy depends on an open mind.

Open minds facilitate and encourage . . . appreciation of [a] wider array of perspectives. Having an open mind allows someone to have empathy as well as sympathy for others.

An open mind enables me to see how the parts make up the whole.

If our minds are closed, we stagnate . . . The world around us changes, and we're left behind.

[Maturity] is the essential ingredient . . . Some individuals achieve [it] early in life while others never achieve the openness of mind to question and act to change the situation.

Perhaps there is not as much downside for an individual having a closed mind as there is downside to a group or a society having a closed mind.

To change, one needs to have an open mind, [and] the ability to change is essential.

An open mind is key to insight . . . It seems to be [an] . . . evolutionary adaptation that is key to our success as a species.

There is no immediate reward or incentive for keeping an open mind, particularly in middle management. However, blessed is the keeper of messy problems whose senior leader does possess both the desire and permission to make bold or provocative decisions and grants the time needed to explore the messy problems.

Open-mindedness is one of three tenets of Jainism. It is called *anekanatvada* and it literally means tolerance for alternative perspectives.

It is hard, hard work, but no pain no gain.

I think it can be taught. Should be, anyway.

Having an open mind is valuable because it is essential to learning.

An open mind offers the possibility of learning and evolving to a more complete understanding of the world in which we live . . . As such, an open mind serves the goals of agency and communion in a positive, forward-thinking manner.

It helps reduce naysaying [and] . . . stresses the constructive part of your mind.

An open mind is two-thirds of the battle for a winning strategy.

cultivating an open mind is both a courtesy and an obligation we owe to others, especially if they are impacted by our decisions. I found this last point especially important. I will speculate here that feelings of courtesy and obligation are not really separate, that they dwell together in that special space where self-respect and respect for others merge. This brings us to the overall impact of having an open mind on our sense of well-being.

OPEN MINDS AND WELL-BEING

One result of an open mind is its positive impact on feelings of well-being, a well-documented benefit in higher education and among medical practitioners.[38] This same connection became very evident over the course of our interviews. In retrospect this should not be surprising, especially when viewing business organizations as learning centers. For instance, there has been a special call for major changes in business education including teaching critical thinking to help improve the well-being of business practitioners and the larger public they impact.[39]

Issues of causality, of course, arise in any adaptive system of thinking such as having an open mind. For instance, does an open mind directly produce feelings of well-being among managers as it does among instructors and their students in higher education and among medical service providers and their patients? Is it the reverse with well-being encouraging open-mindedness? Or is something else going on? The evidence in the interviews reported here is that while open-mindedness and feelings of well-being reinforce one another, open-mindedness has greater impact on well-being. For instance, asking the Am I? and Are we? questions integral to each open mind action creates feelings of progress and confidence which contribute to general well-being. These same feelings, in turn, encourage asking tough questions, stimulate curiosity, encourage befriending of ignorance, and so on. Moreover, when executives publicly reflect on their thinking, they directly or indirectly grant permission to their colleagues to do so too. This, in turn, enhances everyone's job satisfaction and produces a resilient work climate that encourages individual creativity.[40]

As you read on, you'll discover the many specific ways the actions leading to an open mind contribute to personal confidence, satisfaction, pride, and resilience. Stated a little differently, thinking about thinking creates a warehouse of rewarding decision-making experiences that underwrite general well-being. This sense of well-being is very likely a source of mental and physical wellness too.[41] We'll see this in appendix 1 where we explore Aha! Spas as safety zones for encouraging open-minded thinking.

ARTIFICIAL INTELLIGENCE AND THE OPEN MIND

Artificial intelligence (AI) is already having a substantial impact on decision-makers, as indicated by its frequent mention in our most recent interviews. In many ways it renders even more important the topics and ideas covered in the remainder of this book. Remember, it is you—the individual reader, not AI—that has a special capacity to recognize and adapt the variations in knowledge that occur across different times and contexts.[42] AI cannot mimic your implicit and explicit thinking as you imagine and create meaning.

Most parties with a vested interest in AI agree that vigilance is required in its use, that such vigilance requires open-mindedness, and that both are in short supply.[43] As Shirley Larkin reminds us, "In a future artificial intelligence world where we can no longer trust the veracity of what we see or hear it will be even more important to know and understand ourselves."[44]

These concerns were very much in evidence at the 2023 CHI Conference on Human Factors in Computing Systems in Hamburg, Germany.[45] Researchers from the MIT Media Lab and Cornell University presented a paper in which they cautioned that:

We are increasingly exposed to massive amounts of AI-mediated information that can be potentially deceptive, misleading, or strictly false. In such cases critical thinking becomes an important skill to reliably process the information we encounter and integrate it with our existing beliefs and behaviors.[46]

The same authors also commented:

[The dissemination] of falsehoods is especially concerning when AI systems are used in conjunction with humans as people *have a tendency to blindly follow* the AI decisions and *stop using their own cognitive resources* to think critically.[47]

Whether those deficits in thinking about thinking are present because the skills are never acquired, because of our tendency to suspend them, or a mix of both, it is a matter of serious and urgent concern.

In a recent communication, my colleague Charles Young, founder of the global advertising research firm Ameritest, raises concerns about aligning AI systems with our core values, noting:

In the rapidly evolving landscape of artificial intelligence (AI), the question of how to align AI with human values has never been more critical. As we develop increasingly sophisticated AI systems, it is essential to ensure that these technologies serve humanity's best interests. . . . AI alignment refers to the process of ensuring that AI systems act in ways that are consistent with human values and ethical principles. This alignment is crucial because AI has the potential to profoundly impact every aspect of our lives, from healthcare and education to communication and governance. Misaligned AI could lead to unintended consequences, including privacy violations, biased decision-making, and even threats to democratic processes.[48]

The six actions of an open mind, I believe, express those values and principles. As we teach AI how to think, and especially as we rely upon it to complete more and more tasks, we must encourage it to think open-mindedly, in a way that reflects our fundamental values. Until then, humans retain the burden and joy of thinking with an open mind.

My own view is that developments in artificial intelligence, machine learning, and deep learning will be of continued great value, but cannot replace our tacit knowledge and its constructive use. In fact, technological advances will make even greater demands upon what I call the "necktop computer."[49] Two Carnegie Mellon University researchers, Trent Cash and Daniel Oppenheimer, have recently reached this same observation in a slightly different way: "Human experts' domain knowledge is deep, efficiently structured, adaptive and intuitive—whereas generative chatbots' knowledge is shallow and inflexible leading to errors that human experts would rarely make."[50]

Everyone can benefit from maintaining their necktop, but it's especially important for those in power. This is why findings by Mihnea C. Moldoveanu and Das Narayandas are so disturbing. In *The Future of Executive Development*, they caution that executive education programs are not providing today's leaders with the self-awareness and reflective thinking skills they need to survive.[51] In many ways, this book is a response to their call for action.

"THINKING AS" VERSUS "THINKING LIKE": AI-PROOFING YOUR VALUE

A growing concern expressed in various business forums is that AI will eliminate management jobs.[52] It is helpful to view this perception through two different lenses or thinking postures. They involve a distinction between "thinking as" and "thinking like." Let's start with the latter.

Thinking *like* another decision-maker involves imitating that party with little exercise of independent thought. I call it proxy thinking. Those who engage in it are justified in feeling threatened by AI. This book doesn't ask you to imitate anyone one. That is not what taking intellectual ownership of ideas entails.

Thinking *as* means taking ownership of ideas by applying your original and imaginative thought generated your way using your explicit and implicit thinking. It involves *constructive idiosyncrasy,* that is, the application of what is distinctive about you. That is your secret sauce in taking intellectual ownership of the ideas shared in this book. It means thinking *as* yourself, not someone else.

Just how distinctive (or idiosyncratic) are you? Consider what Robert M. Sapolsky, professor of neurology at Stanford University, has to say on this topic:

> To make sense of human behavior, you have to factor in what your neurons did one second ago, the environmental triggers of that 30 seconds ago, what your hormone levels were like this morning, and what neuroplasticity you've done over the last two seasons, and what your adolescence was like and your childhood, and your fetal experience and your genes, and what sort of culture your ancestors were inventing centuries ago because that influenced the way you were raised and what things you value, and what things your amygdala does and doesn't respond to.[53]

These factors, he argues, are far from exhaustive. Moreover, they are "utterly intertwined."[54] They make you who you are as distinct from someone else or something else like AI—if, of course, you dare to let your special qualities "speak."

Thinking "as yourself" instead of like someone else provides the grist for your conscious and especially unconscious thinking. Yes, it may be as simple as adding a twist to someone else's idea so it fits your needs. But it may also be quite complex such as using others' thinking as a gateway to something far, far better. To quote the Carnegie Mellon researchers again, "Generative chatbots lack access to critical metacognitive capacities that allow humans to detect errors in their own thinking and communicate this information to others."[55]

The several actions of an open mind we explore will improve your metacognitive capacities. They will help you put your personal stamp on the ideas encountered. In doing that you'll also be taking a major step toward AI-proofing yourself. Unless you choose otherwise. Hopefully not.

HOW TO READ THIS BOOK

You will develop your own unique ways of practicing the actions of an open mind. Add to them, subtract from them, and modify them as you deem fit. The ideas you'll encounter in each chapter are simply a starter kit as you work to create your own recipes.

CHAPTER SEQUENCE

The six core actions are a complex system more than a linear sequence, and chapters may be read in any order you prefer. Because serious playfulness is an important attitude or outlook as well as a significant action on its own, I have chosen to start with it. You also may be puzzled as to why embracing ambiguity is the last action discussed. After all, isn't the presence of ambiguity often the first clue that a difficult decision is at hand? Although it is, I noticed in many interviews that executives continually embrace ambiguity in the course of being open-minded. In this way, they constantly winnow down that initial ambiguity. Asking the Am I? and Are we? questions discussed with each action is one of the ways they do this. Still, at the end of the day, some ambiguities remain, and they need to be addressed. Doing so is only partly about reducing ambiguity. It is also about *embracing* it.

ASKING AM I? AND ARE WE?

Each chapter begins with a summary of what's to come and a set of Am I? questions to consider as you read. Others arise within the chapter. And a different set of questions concludes each chapter. Remember, it is your mind—your ways of engaging information—that is the primary case example featured in this book. The self-referencing "I" and "we" (in group decision-making) asking these questions is a fictitious character emerging from cross talk happening among the forces in the Common Metaphors of the Mind list earlier in this chapter.[56] The Am I? probes are tools to help you to ground key ideas in your daily work and experience. Only you can decide where they best fit. The Are we? questions are for you and your colleagues to pose to each other or your teams.[57] The inclusion of both sets of questions—Am I? and Are we?—simply reflects the fact that minds reside in both individuals and in informal and formal decision-making teams.[58]

Am I? prompts are featured so prominently for another reason. We found that a great many of the executives we interviewed talked about hearing an inner voice that was wise, strategically oriented, and very practical. It guided them to better decisions by asking them a steady stream of Am I? questions.[59] It is how they addressed their actual and perceived states of not knowing by surfacing and challenging their conscious and unconscious beliefs. Sometimes the questions were stated explicitly. More often they were implicit. This is not surprising. After all, questions lie behind every answer even if they are not the most relevant question to address.[60]

One final note about the Am I? and Are we? questions: they are built to encourage accurate personal and team self-awareness. The benefits of self-awareness are many. They include increased resilience, more successful decisions, professional advancement, reduced stress and anxiety, greater interpersonal sensitivity, an improved ability to adjust to uncertainties, openness to learning and novelty, and feelings of well-being. These, rather than IQ, are the strong indicators of being wise. My goal in this book, as in my teaching and work with clients, is to help you and your team cultivate your own query-oriented inner voices. As the anthropologist Claude Levi-Strauss famously put it, "The wise man doesn't give the right answers, he poses the right questions." Thus, most of what we explore together in the following chapters describes how successful leaders engage in several actions when they confront the uncertainties posed by major challenges. These actions help decision-makers minimize unpleasant surprises. (Readers familiar with Karl Friston's work on "free energy" will find these actions as essential behaviors for limiting the upper boundary of surprise.[61])

WARM-UPS

Each chapter begins with a warm-up exercise. They are intended to raise your awareness of your mind's unconscious operations while enhancing your social cognition skills. One lesson they impart is that our minds like to play tricks on us and so require special vigilance.[62] Observe where your mind goes and what it does during these warm-ups—what you notice will teach you more about how you think.

A TWO-PRONGED READING STRATEGY

Your workdays are likely long and overscheduled. Keeping that in mind, I recommend a two-pronged reading strategy. First, read just one chapter a day, preferably early in the morning. That way its exercises and insights will be top of mind for practicing at work. After you read the chapter on being comfortable with not knowing, for example, pay special attention to how you react to information voids. Notice, too, how your colleagues respond to their own encounters with their "don't know" buckets. As you do, think about which core learnings in that day's chapter might help them. Next, treat your reading time as a constructive escape, a productive, hopefully enjoyable, break. There is sound evidence that time spent reflecting on *how* you think improves *what* you think.[63] Additionally, improved awareness of your thinking enhances your understanding of others' thinking, an essential leadership requirement.

LET'S GET STARTED

A fitting beginning point for the remainder of this book is offered by Wisława Szymborska, winner of the 1996 Nobel Prize for Literature. In her acceptance speech, "I Don't Know," she reminds us that inspiration belongs to everyone. It is "born from a continuous acknowledgement of '*I don't know.*'" A seemingly small act, it carries great power. In her words:

> *It flies on mighty wings.* It expands our lives to include spaces within us as well as the outer expanses in which our tiny Earth hangs suspended. If Isaac Newton had never said to himself "I don't know," the apples in his little or-chard might have dropped to the ground like hailstones, and, at best, he would have stooped to pick them up and gobble them with gusto.[64]

The ideas of a great many inspired decision-makers inform this book. Each in their own way confront what they don't know. And their remedy is to engage in actions to overcome that challenge. This leads to wise and fluid ways of thinking. Their insights are augmented with my own and those of others whose research appear to embrace "I don't know." Ultimately, of course, it is your "mighty wings" bringing you on this journey. And, as the preface notes, I'd like to hear from you during your travels through this book.

TWO

Serious Playfulness

WHY YOU NEED CONSTRUCTIVE MISCHIEF

In this chapter, we explore what happens when we approach our problems and challenges with unconventional, flexible tools like mind maps and collages. We also explore how stepping into the shoes of Wizards and Clairvoyants can unlock new strategies and solutions. A visit to a circus illustrates serious play in action through the discipline, courage, and humility of its young performers. Finally, we explore how serious playfulness can transform our own thinking when we embrace it in the workplace. An important outcome from reading this chapter is to further incline your "inner voice" to ask questions like these:

- Am I nurturing a culture in which serious play—with its emphasis on imaginative exploration, bold experimentation, and learning from failure—is embraced as a catalyst for innovation and growth?

- Am I leveraging the power of storytelling, roleplay, and visualization to challenge assumptions, reframe problems, and unleash the untapped potential of my team's collective creativity?

- Am I embodying the principles of serious play in my leadership, demonstrating the vulnerability, resilience, and openness needed to inspire a culture where diverse perspectives are sought out, and the joy of collaborative problem-solving drives continuous improvement?

- Am I nurturing a culture where imaginative exploration, bold experimentation, and learning from failure is embraced as a catalyst for innovation and growth?

- Am I suspending judgment and truly listening when serious play brings a challenge to my perspectives and worldview?

This chapter, then, is about something human beings do naturally, even unavoidably: we play. Strange as it may sound, play can be serious and productive. We invited our interview participants to indulge in one of the oldest forms of play—storytelling—when we asked them to describe their decision-making processes. There is more to serious playfulness than storytelling, of course, but storytelling and your natural ability to engage in it underscore the importance of serious play throughout this book. Serious playfulness has a very positive impact on open-mindedness in general through its impact on overall well-being, healthy team collaborations, and innovative thinking.[1] For these reasons, it is the first action to be addressed.

People have an inborn instinct to construct narratives, in part because when we are looking to explain a mystery or solve a problem, they allow us to supplement the scant information we have at hand with assumptions and other cues in our subconscious. But as you will see, our storytelling instincts can also lead us badly astray.[2]

WARM-UP

I've shown the picture in figure 2.1 to audiences around the world. Nearly everyone who sees it responds in the same way. Let's see if you do, too.

Give both of these questions some thought before you proceed:

1. Which monster is bigger?

2. What is happening in the scene?

Most people quickly say that the monster on top is bigger. Usually, after a bit of hesitation, they also say something like, "The big monster has an angry look and is chasing the smaller monster down the hallway. The smaller monster has a frightened look and is running away." Is that pretty much how you responded?

Now, take a ruler and measure the two monsters. Or, look at the image that

FIGURE 2.1 What Is Happening?

SOURCE: ROGER N. SHEPARD, "TERROR SUBTERRA," IN
MIND SIGHTS (W. H. FREEMAN CO., 1990).

appears at the end of this warm-up. As you'll see, the monsters are exactly the same size. Now, look closely at their faces. They too are identical.

BASIC IDEA

Assuming you reacted as I predicted, what made you suppose the monster on top was bigger? Probably you didn't even think about it; you just knew. How? Because of the way your unconscious processed the visual data. Your eyes didn't just perceive two monsters, but also a long hallway. And you've learned something about objects in hallways—the further back an object is, the smaller it appears. Based on this knowledge, your mind automatically concluded that since the monster further back looks bigger than the monster up front, it must be a *lot* bigger. This is an illusion, of course. Placing the two monsters in the hallway creates a 3-D experience for us. It fools us into seeing them as different sizes.

As for the expressions on the two monsters' faces, it is an artifact of our unconscious storytelling. We suppose the "bigger" one is angry since it appears to be chasing the "smaller" one. Anyone being chased by a big monster with an angry look ought to be scared. So, we "see" a frightened look on the "smaller" monster's face.

The hallway encourages us to make these assumptions. Interestingly, when the picture is shown to indigenous people in undeveloped parts of the world, who don't have a lot of experience with hallways, they just see two identical monsters.

SO WHAT?

We have many different "hallways" in our minds that shape how we think and behave and it doesn't take much to activate them. I remember an incident that occurred when I was a child. My mother had taken me with her to a grocery store. A little kid (not me!) brought a bag of candy to his mother and asked her to put it in the cart. She just blew up. "Put it back now! Do it!" she shouted at the top of her voice. I thought, "What a mean mother!" But my mother said, "That poor mother. I bet that kid has been nothing but trouble."

My mother and I were seeing those two strangers in different "hallways," which produced two very different stories about the scene we had just witnessed. I absolutely knew that the kid was well-behaved but had a really mean mother. She was the pursuing monster in the hallway. My mother was equally convinced the kid was pure trouble. He was the pursuing monster.

So, two questions we need to ask in any situation are: What is our hallway? and How does it impact us? The fact is, we are always in "hallways."[3] They may be simple or highly embellished, but they define our expectations and responses, and for this reason are often called scripts, schema, frames, mind maps, and theories-in-use. Knowing we are in a hallway and even having a clear understanding of that are not enough. We need to engage it in constructive ways, and serious play appears to be the best way to do that.

After looking at the image in figure 2.2, return to figure 2.1. Does one monster still look bigger than the other? If you are like most readers, the illusion persists: you still experience the one on top as bigger, despite knowing they are the same size.

FIGURE 2.2   Dissolving the Illusion.

SOURCE: ROGER N. SHEPARD, "TERROR SUBTERRA," IN
MIND SIGHTS (W. H. FREEMAN CO., 1990).

DEFINING SERIOUS PLAY

The coupling of the words *serious* and *play* may induce a mental hiccup. In the popular imagination, *serious* is a word that is used to describe sober, sometimes boring activities. Adults are serious. So is work. *Play*, on the other hand, is for children, and so it is seen as inconsequential.

And yet think what a serious business children's play is. Through play, children learn and practice all the social, emotional, and practical skills they will need as they grow up. Play demands a high level of imagination and creativity, both of which can be very effortful. It also elicits a wide range of emotions ranging from elation and joy to anger and despair. It's not surprising, then, that managers who describe their work environments as places that discourage imagination, experimentation, brainstorming, and risk-taking—all of which are required for rewarding play experiences—rarely describe their work as enjoyable, purposeful, or productive.[4]

In his book *Growing Young,* anthropologist Ashley Montagu argues that playfulness is essential to open-mindedness.[5] He and many others who study play offer readers this important message about playfulness: *don't leave childhood without it.* Or, more helpfully, *don't go to work without it.* Stuart Brown, a physician, behavioral researcher, and founder of the National Institute for Play, judges play to be "largely responsible for our existence as sentient, intelligent creatures."[6] It is central to problem-solving, and premature dismissal of it can often prolong having to live with a problem as the cartoon in figure 2.3 suggests.

For my purposes, serious playfulness is as much an attitude as an action. I define it as: engaging in waywardness or mischief with constructive intent or purpose by challenging one's own and others' thinking.

Serious play is an essential requirement in volatile environments, where learning needs to be speedy and flexible, and organizational strategies need to be both reactive and anticipatory as unpredictable opportunities emerge.[7] The phrase "Let's get serious" has always struck me as incomplete; it is missing ". . . and play

FIGURE 2.3   Play Versus Work Mindsets.

SOURCE: MARKETOONIST, LLC.

hard." As we'll see in this chapter and elsewhere in this book, serious play is essential. It is the foundation for the generative thinking leading to imagination. It helps us address a crucial question: What has to happen to solve a problem or avoid a dilemma?

Serious playfulness describes the attitude we bring to puzzles (How does this work?), riddles (What else fits?), and paradox (How can that be?). Serious playfulness combined with a spirit of mischief nurtures the boldness we need to enter the "no-go zones" imposed by conventional thinking.

Note that I modify *mischief* with *constructive intent*. Serious play is not about pranks. The mischief or waywardness it engenders should never humiliate or belittle people, though it can—and should—introduce discomfort to routine thinking. Unlike humiliation, those metaphoric hiccups are actually beneficial.

Serious play is active rather than passive; it is not mindless phone-scrolling or vegetating in front of a screen. It can and often does involve watching, listening, and taking in stimuli, but doing these activities consciously and fully.

SERIOUS PLAY WITH MENTAL MODELS

One of the most important, even essential, areas of serious play involves our "hallways." These are the mental models that shape our understanding and responses to nearly every situation. They are sometimes called mind maps, schema, frames, and theories-in-use. My colleagues and I call them consensus maps as they summarize the shared thinking of a specific group, such as executives, a customer segment, opinion leaders, and so on. They typically operate below awareness and require serious play to surface, understand, and alter them. Recognizing them and understanding how they matter and how they can be improved through reengineering was a major theme among nearly all the executives we interviewed. Most often they were concerned with the mental models of their customers and colleagues.

REENGINEERING CONSENSUS MAPS

Consensus maps, then, are the core constructs—thoughts and feelings—that define in a skeletal way what most people in a group of interest think and feel about a topic. The topic might be a brand, a new product concept, employee reactions to a proposed merger, voter positions on a proposed public policy, and so on. The goal of drawing a consensus map is to describe that target audience's behavior in a way that is intuitive, visual, and actionable. These maps have some plasticity. Thus, using various marketing tools such as advertising, package design, or even choice of distribution outlet, they can be altered to better accommodate an action plan. For many leaders unaccustomed to working with consensus maps, they appear as a madman's version of connect the dots. This merely reflects the reality that visual representations of difficult challenges can be visually messy.

However, there is a brief, playful, and effective mental exercise or metaphor to use prior to introducing these maps. This exercise, described in Box 2.1, takes only a few imaginative moments.[8]

BOX 2.1   A Metaphor for Consensus Maps

Using your mind's eye, imagine an ocean pool containing several octopuses, each representing an important idea involving the issue at hand. (The ideas are those of customers, distributors, employees, or some other group whose thinking is of interest.) Many octopuses in this pool communicate with one another. That is, the tip of at least one arm of one octopus connects with that of another octopus. Some octopuses have direct connections with several others. In this way, octopus arms are conduits similar to neural pathways along which messages are sent and received. Collectively, an information network is established among members of this particular pool.

Messages sent directly from one octopus to another are often passed along by the receiving octopus to yet others not within direct reach of the originating octopus. And, much like the famous telephone game you played in grade school, the message one octopus sends may be altered by the intermediaries passing it along. (On a technical note, the arms of an octopus contain about two-thirds of their total neurons, suggesting an independent brain within each arm.)

Now, imagine you are an octopus trainer. Your job is to train members of this pool to act in your preferred ways. Specifically, you may want to alter the communications patterns among them, encouraging direct hand-holding where it doesn't exist and discouraging it in other cases. You may also want to encourage acceptance of a new octopus (a new entrant idea) to the pool and remove an existing one. Or you may want to rearrange them relative to one another to create more productive conversations.

Much like the octopuses, certain thoughts held by your target group are connected to other thoughts, behaviors, and emotions. By exploring their linkages, that is, by noting which octopuses are holding hands, you can clearly follow the pathways of thinking that are commonly held within your interest group.

Let's set this exercise in motion with an example before describing the other ways in which you can use consensus maps.

A PARADOX INVOLVING SAFETY AND EFFICACY

A research project focused on the marketing challenges of weed killer. The core challenge was to discover what was stifling sales. The team set out to listen to consumers and understand their thoughts and feelings about weed killer to better position its marketing. The team used consensus mapmaking to draw out how the identified thoughts and feelings were connected. I can assure you that their maps were thorough, daunting, and yet very, very valuable. For the sake of simplicity and playfulness, we will be using octopuses instead.

The team discovered that the consumers' minds were split into two "pools"— one concerned with the safety of the weed killer, and the other with its efficacy. In the safety pool dwelt octopuses like "Protect my family and pets" and "I make good decisions." In other words, consumers wanted to know that the weed killer they were using was gentle and safe, which caused them to feel responsible, proud, and protected (other connected octopuses).

In the efficacy pool, the constructs (or octopuses) included thoughts like "Effective product kills weeds in one go" but also "I worry about toxins, health risk." In the efficacy pool weed killers were perceived as weapons of war. The more effective they were, the more anxious the consumer felt about their negative effects (figure 2.4).

This brings us to the major business challenge: How can a consumer who worries about toxic chemicals be a "victor" in the war against weeds if they use only the gentlest and hence least effective option? The clash between their safety and their efficacy mindsets leaves consumers feeling overwhelmed and unsure. These pools reveal a paradox—a set of conflicting thoughts that somehow co-exist. Paradoxes are important, as a product or service that can resolve them is likely to be a major success. It's like having your cake and eating it too.

At first glance, it might seem like these two pools of thought are entirely separate and therefore irreconcilable. However, it pays off to notice which octopuses peer over the edge of their pools and link up in unlikely places. It turns out that the "I am responsible, protective" and the "I feel safe and protected" octopuses link up over these pools. This connection between thoughts is the place to pin-

FIGURE 2.4   Connecting Opposite Pools of Thought.

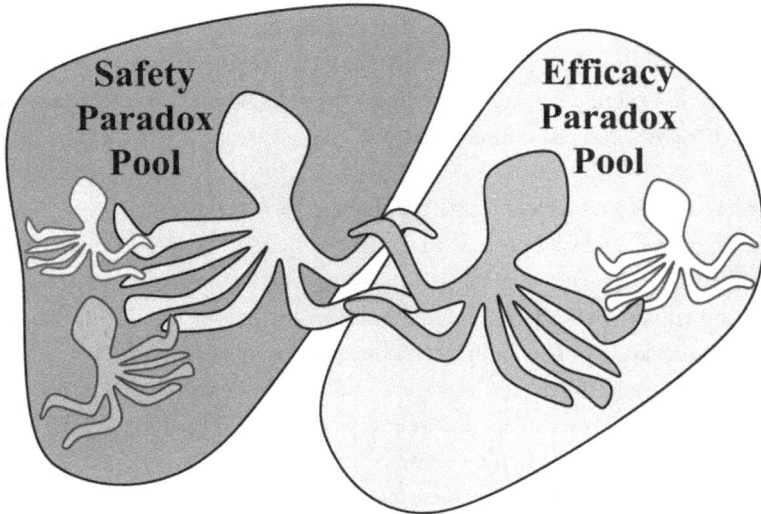

DESIGNED BY MARYGRACE KING.

point how to tell a marketing story that bridges these seemingly opposite ideas and speaks more closely to the heart of what the consumer wants.

The team explored the reengineering or What of it? questions and role playing. The result? They chose to move away from the "weed killer as a weapon of war in a battle against weeds" mindset and tell a story that could bring both sides of the map together. This new marketing story came with a new hero: a doctor! The weed killer was presented as a doctor who treats the "patient" or lawn *effectively yet safely* against the chronic disease of weeds. Communication recommendations followed from this reframe. The new marketing strategy, which was a major success for the client (though it might have caused environmentalists no end of agita), encouraged the hand-holding between "I am responsible, protective" and "I am safe, protected" octopuses.

Reflecting upon this example, when would such a consensus map work for you in your endeavors? Ask yourself:

- Am I creating space and time for flexible approaches such as building mental models, roleplaying, following "what if" trains of thought, and *playing* with ideas within projects or teams?

- Do I let methods evolve or do I try to stick to only what has worked before?

Consensus maps not only can tell us what key stakeholders such as customers, employees, and managers think, but why; as such, they can serve as *strategic playgrounds* for engaging and reshaping their thinking. My colleague Jerry Olson describes this kind of play as having two stages. The first asks, What is it? and the second, What of it?

The What is it? are the key ideas or constructs—the specific thoughts and feelings—most people in a specified group have about a topic. The constructs by themselves may have little meaning, but the consensus map or model shows their causal associations, that is, how they are linked together in a system of relationships. Again, the specified links are those made by most members of the group. The emphasis on "most" simply reflects the fact that no one group member represents in every way all other members of that group.

While consensus maps can feel overwhelming to view or create at first, you should feel empowered to pull out an electronic or literal pen and mark them up, comparing and contrasting your own thinking to that of the stakeholder group of interest. We literally "play around with" the key thoughts and feelings and their associations with one another and entertain new possibilities—first on paper through a consensus map, and then in practice with new policies or actions. To do this, you must ask several questions. For example:

- What important thoughts (constructs/octopuses) are missing on this map that we wish were present?
- How do we insert them? Which existing thoughts and feelings can be "mentors" for introducing new thoughts and feelings?
- Among existing constructs, which do we want to reinforce? Make even more salient? Less salient? Even have disappear?
- Are there associations or connections between the thoughts we'd like to create anew? Strengthen? Lessen? Eliminate?

OTHER WAYS OF PLAYING WITH MAPS

To think even more playfully, approach the exercise as a conversation with the map itself. Ask it, What are you telling us? and How can we change your connections? to help surface new ideas. Since a consensus map represents stakeholder interests, these are not idle questions. It is equally important to notice what stakeholders are *not* saying that you might have expected to learn. Then ask, where in a consensus map does it belong?

Alternatively, you might think of consensus maps as a stage play or movie.

The constructs are the characters' roles, and the nature of their interactions is set by the script you provide. As scriptwriter, you should constantly ask yourself, How can the basic story be improved to enhance everyone's experience?

This "discover and then invent" approach to mental models or consensus maps mirrors what goes on in a child's mind when they construct a drama with their stuffed animals, as it involves perspective-taking, dynamic thought, and even roleplaying. After all, what is the difference between a toy and a tool if they both move you toward new thoughts?

Approaching consensus maps with serious play not only helps you see what is but also what isn't—where there are spaces to innovate or create something new. The following example illustrates this.

TWO PLAYMATES

During brainstorming exercises involving consensus maps, I encourage teams to imagine the presence of two special characters: the Wizard and the Clairvoyant.[9] These characters dwell in every mind, though some use them far more often than others. Both are very curious, though they focus their attention on different types of issues.[10] Both are especially adept in identifying blind spots, or what one interviewee calls "ignorance potholes."

> **Wizards** channel their curiosity into sensing, diagnosing, and solving problems. They are excellent detectives, skilled in cause-and-effect reasoning, and have wide cognitive peripheral vision, meaning they have broad experience and an awareness of how comparable problems have been solved in other settings.

> **Clairvoyants** are skilled at asking and answering questions like: What could go wrong with a decision or action? What are we most likely to regret? What are we ignoring? They are attentive to cues about the future that others can't foresee and to missed opportunities in the present.

The invention of Post-it Notes is a good example of the application of clairvoyance: When 3M scientist Spencer Silver created an adhesive that stuck only lightly to surfaces, it seemed to be exactly what the company didn't need. But a colleague, the scientist Art Fry, realized the invention's potential while he was in choir practice and wished he could mark his hymnal with slips of paper that would stay put but that could later be removed without damaging its pages. Fry's clairvoyance led to a multibillion-dollar product line and, in his words, "a whole new way to communicate."[11]

Both characters recognize that ideas like "success" and "failure" contain the seeds of their opposites; neither rests on their laurels but always asks, What opportunities are we still missing?

Here is a business example of Wizards and Clairvoyants working together in serious play. A facial tissue brand was suffering from declining sales. A group of marketers convened to discuss ways to reverse the trend. They began the meeting by isolating some of the most important constructs associated with the brand, concepts like "soft" and "gentle."

The Wizards in the group, who like to fix things, focused their attention on ideas or constructs that might explain why sales were flagging. They asked:

- Do managers' and consumers' views of the brand differ? Are consumers saying one thing while managers are hearing something different? If so, how can managers' listening and comprehension skills be improved?
- Should we attempt to change the way a construct is understood? For instance, is there a dimension of "soft" that could be further emphasized in our advertising?
- Does the connection between "soft" and "child friendly" need more emphasis? Is there a better way to express it that we've overlooked?

Clairvoyants are usually focused on what is missing that could be added. They asked these questions:

- What might further research reveal?
- What constructs have consumers not considered but should?
- What is the best way to introduce new constructs into our current mental model for facial tissues?
- Can the construct "good parent" be introduced and connected to "child friendly"?
- Is there an overlooked social trend or emerging technology that requires reengineering relationships among constructs? Should, for example, there be a new emphasis on "climate friendliness"?
- Does competitor intelligence suggest a need to reposition the brand?
- Are there more compelling brand stories managers might generate using different metaphors?

Managers were tasked to think like Clairvoyants to answer what would most likely catch their attention as a near-term threat to the brand. Then they were asked to assume the role of Wizard to answer how they would fix that problem. They were also asked to identify the most pressing problems.

One outcome of these efforts was the discovery that managers and consumers had very different understandings about the connection between two constructs: "soft" and "durable." The consumer segment being studied perceived soft and durable as contradictions, that is, you could have one but not the other. Managers, on the other hand, understood the two concepts to be compatible, that is, you *could* have both. This led to a messaging effort that with some patience successfully brought consumers to that understanding as well. Intentionally embodying the roles of Clairvoyant and Wizard led to a new strategy and an ultimately successful campaign.

Ask yourself:

- Am I channeling curiosity into sensing, diagnosing, and solving problems, like the Wizard?
- Am I being attentive to cues about the future that others can't foresee and also to missed opportunities in the present, like the Clairvoyant?
- Do I put the Wizard and Clairvoyant roles into conversation in projects?
- Do I task my teammates with these roles to encourage playful perspective taking?

SERIOUS PLAYFULNESS AND EMOTIONS

Importantly, being serious does not mean being gloomy, rigid, risk averse, or displaying a negative "yeah, but . . ." attitude. Serious playfulness can lead to *hedonic happiness,* moments of pleasure, laughter, and joy, but the well-being it produces tends to be more *eudaimonic,* meaning it induces feelings of well-being, contentment, personal fulfillment, and spirituality, as well as the satisfaction, pride, recognition, and gains in confidence that come with achieving goals and being acknowledged and appreciated by others.

Because playfulness leads to satisfaction and potentially happiness, it's especially important in times of stress and crisis.[12] Sometimes sad and happy feelings occur together, producing what are called bittersweet moments.[13] As mentioned earlier, pranks and petty put-downs might feel "fun" for some, but they do not fall under the definition of serious playfulness. Nor do the recreational activities that occur outside the context of work. Serious playfulness invites one to find happiness *in* the work itself, rather than only in the respites from it.

Recently a colleague mentioned feeling this eudaimonic "flow state" during a brainstorming session. The ideas bounced back and forth easily between the participants, each of whom brought in their own perspectives based on their individual research. Bringing their perspectives together to create a consensus meaning was joyful, he said, because all of them were eager to share what they had found and to see how it would fit in with what the others had. Their disagreements never devolved into the personal but were used as tools. When they reached consensus on one point, they felt a spark of accomplishment and the motivation to move onto the next. When one of the participants looked up and saw that it was past five o'clock, they realized they had lost track of the time.

SERIOUS PLAY AND ERRORS

Daring to think differently can often produce errors, though nearly all interviewees agreed that those errors are unlikely to match a far larger error: avoiding bold, novel thinking. Serious play requires its practitioners to have the humility and courage to acknowledge their errors, which have an essential role to play in learning. It is why video is such an important training tool in athletics. It allows for conscious inspection of events occurring beyond athletes' momentary experience. Post- and premortems of managerial actions serve a similar function. Errors can be as simple as muddled thinking or poor judgment. It happens. They could be rooted in an authentic misunderstanding or, worse still (and much more rarely), someone's blatant incompetence or corruption. In most cases, catching errors provides important learning opportunities. Error-sensing should not be a blame assignment activity. Though expensive, innocent errors are best viewed as tuition payments for the staff's continuing education. Imagine learning to walk, swim, ride a bike, read, and so on if errors were allowed to inhibit learning.

VALUES AT WORK IN SERIOUS PLAYFULNESS

Three dispositions or values support and amplify the six actions of an open mind: humility, courage, and discipline. Those values also support and are supported by serious playfulness. I'd like to share a true story that shows them at work, recounted by the South African writer Mark Mathabane.[14]

A visitor to a community dedicated to living according to the principle of *ubuntu*, or shared humanity, wanted to see if he could get the community's children to compete with one another. He placed a large basket full of candy at the base of a tree. Then he assembled a group of children some distance from the tree and told them that the first to get to the basket would be awarded all its contents. The visitor then called out, "Ready . . . set . . . go!" Instead of racing to the tree as he expected, the children clustered together, conferred briefly, then joined hands and went as a single body to secure the candy. The astonished visitor demanded an explanation. One child stepped forward and replied, "How can one of us be happy if everyone else is sad?"

What is considered appropriate play depends on the players' core values. In this case, the children "inspected" the visitor's winner-take-all worldview and found it lacking. When we engage in serious playfulness, we should ask ourselves what values we bring to our play and whether we are open to unfamiliar or even conflicting values brought by others.

Now let's visit briefly with the Sailor Circus Academy, a program of the Circus Arts Conservatory in Sarasota, Florida, that works with more than a thousand young people each year. I had the pleasure of attending three of its performances as an event photographer. Each spanned three hours and involved more than a hundred performers, all of whom demonstrated the foundational open-mind values of courage, discipline, and humility.

COURAGE AND DISCIPLINE[15]

One of the pictures I took can be seen in figure 2.5. What thoughts do you think are passing through these performers' heads? I posed the question to several early reviewers of this book. One of their responses captured the essence of most of the others' responses. Perhaps it reflects yours, too: "I like to imagine them totally in the zone, concentrating with their whole selves (body-mind as one thing) on doing the moves that they've practiced so many times."

Just mounting the trapeze demands courage and daring. All the practice they did to be able to perform requires discipline. Further, these young people make it all seem easy—what the sociologist Erving Goffman described as "front stage" impression management.[16] I can only speculate about how they acquired those at-tributes. I believe, however, that they will keep them forever, along with a special brand of humility I call *quiet pride*.

QUIET PRIDE

Pride and humility may seem like opposed qualities, but when people have the quiet pride I'm speaking of, they recognize their own capabilities, but feel no need to boast. They know the hard work it took to get where they are, and they have respect for the skills they're mastering. That knowledge keeps them humble.

The young performers know things don't always go off without a hitch, but

FIGURE 2.5   Young Trapeze Performers

they're prepared to deal with that too. The Sailor Circus participants' infrequent slip-ups never interrupted the flow of their performances or their clear delight in doing their jobs.[17] Mistakes were simply taken in stride.[18]

AWE

There is more to the story of serious playfulness at the Sailor Circus. Chapter 1 introduced *awe* as a part of the complex system of open-mindedness. During the second and especially the third Sailor Circus events I attended, I was more attentive to the audience members, whose faces and body language clearly revealed their awe as they watched the youthful contortionists, fire jugglers, tightrope walkers and trapeze performers at work. I imagined them asking themselves, Could I learn that? Would I even try? Are they going to fall or miss? How can they do that!? Does that hurt?

No pun is intended, but their engagement was awesome to witness. I could see the audiences' muscles contracting in response to the performers' movements— true moments of embodied cognition.[19] It was as if they had been vicariously lifted out of their bodies.

This brings me to a last observation regarding the Sailor Circus: the performers have what might be called an implicit clarity about what is expected of them—not just their skills but their key values and qualities of mind. That clarity is something accomplished executives share and is one sign that incorporating serious playfulness into the office is not as difficult or outlandish as it might seem at first glance.

SERIOUS PLAY IN THE WORKPLACE

Serious play provides many benefits in the workplace. It introduces fresh viewpoints, leading to feelings of positivity. This improved state of mind translates into increased energy for indulging curiosity—one of the actions of an open mind—helping to stave off what one executive described as "deer-in-the-headlights responses" to the appearance of unexpected messy problems. This same executive later noted that serious playfulness helps reduce the tendency to avoid responsibility.

Creating and describing the collages that feature in our ZMET interviews certainly qualifies as a kind of serious play. The two examples below invite you to use your mind's eye to create the image being described. With your version in mind, what changes would you make so it represents your thoughts and feelings when addressing challenging problems? The first example comes from the CEO of an international management consulting firm.

> This picture summarizes my approach to handling unstructured or messy problems. Often, being at the base of the canyon, we don't look upward. We don't see the possibilities that exist above us; we are just stuck playing around in the mud. . . . [Above,] we see an image of the perfect gymnast diving into the Grand Canyon. Some might say, ' "My gosh, she's headed towards sure death," but . . . if you look carefully and closely, you are going to see the safety net below her . . . In the case of an unstructured problem, if you look long enough, and you look with the right kind of eyes, you will see an image of the future of that perfect dive which turns out to be successful. All that mucking around having fun and enjoying the dive is part of getting there. Now, moving up the canyon . . . you see this house perched on the side of the cliff. It might seem very unsafe to people . . . but then you see a bridge out into the future, out into the sunset . . . The whole challenge is to get people to decide to cross that bridge to where success is on the other side. But first you need an approach that allows them to be playful in imagining what success is and then finally a methodology . . . for building the bridge so people will feel safe and secure crossing it.

The second collage was assembled by the founder of a global design company that specializes in experience engineering. As he explains, it relates images from a bullfight to solving messy problems.

> I guess the first thing [in] looking at this picture [is taking] a perspective from up above and understanding that there is a concept, a solution, down there. It may be on the other side of the mountain or even to the sides, if you will. You may not even know what the mountain is made out of, but first you need to look at the whole thing. But you know that ultimately the goal, the challenge facing the bullfighter, [is] . . . having to do something that is concrete, that is final. There is a sense of closure that the bullfighter represents, and it's his determination, [his] ability to maintain his passion for his performance.

The ZMET collages show how liberating—and useful—serious playfulness can be. Play was involved in their creation and is evident in every image. From time to time, I would visit interviewees in their workplaces; many had framed copies of their summary images on display. They often noted that building them was the most enjoyable part of their interview. The challenge is how to nurture that spirit in the workplace. This is increasingly a challenge, as remote work arrangements discourage spontaneous face-to-face interactions, but it also represents an opportunity, as online gaming techniques can be adapted to involve employees in brainstorming.

A number of suggestions for bringing serious play into the workplace emerged from our interviews:

1. **Issue invitations to serious play.** Leaders should grant permission to engage in serious play by explicitly inviting it and, importantly, by modeling the behavior themselves. Without that encouragement, other members of a group or team may at best play "safely" rather than boldly, and breakthrough ideas are less likely to be surfaced and shared.

2. **Make spaces play friendly.** Office brainstorming rooms are open-ended makerspace—no preexisting problem or approach necessary. How and how much such space is used will vary across decision-making teams and over time. The "town hall" space in the offices of Quartz, a news outlet, includes large steps that its designer described as "as much a play structure as a platform."[20] Simple design elements, such as flexible partitions, also have potential.[21]

3. **Embrace spontaneity.** You can nurture playfulness among your colleagues by modeling the kind of playful experimentation described by "Let's just see what happens."[22] This encourages further play in the form of simulations, test marketing, and other ways of creating what Peter M. Senge calls "practice fields," where new approaches can be tried out.[23]

These questions from Harald Warmelink, an expert on game-based learning, are designed to encourage organizational playfulness:[24]

- **Are alternate realities considered?** Entertaining what-if scenarios, even improbable ones, can stimulate novel questions that lead to unexpected answers. A discussion prompted by What if instead of using cars, people got around on ostriches? led to an improved interior design for enclosed tractors.

- **Is freedom of action encouraged?** During roleplaying exercises, place as few limits as possible on who initiates a conversation or what is said. The wider the scope, the greater the variety of potential insights.

- **Does status equivalence exist?** When members of a group are "at play," status should be left at the door. To ensure this, one participant should be designated a "mind guard" and granted the power to intervene when undue deference—or conversely, the display of rank—becomes evident.

- **What is the level of engagement?** The level of engagement is usually in direct proportion to the level of passion, which depends on the seriousness of the problem and its potential consequences.

- **Is there external inconsequence?** Not every what-if question or other playful device needs to be pursued. Sometimes they help by framing the boundaries of a group's thinking.

- **Is flexibility in thinking rewarded?** Serious playfulness requires cognitive flexibility, which can be cultivated by shifting back and forth between spontaneous and controlled reflection and between generating ideas and evaluating them. Participants should be encouraged to call out inflexibility where they see it. Mind wandering should not always be discouraged, as it may be a sign that ideas are being incubated.[25]

CONCLUSION

Serious play is serious business. Fostering it doesn't require you to turn your office into a playground. The saying "Choose a job you love; you'll never have to work a day in your life"—attributed variously to luminaries such as Confucius and Mark Twain—gets it wrong: it's not *what* you do, but the values and mindset that you bring to what you do.

KEY QUESTIONS TO ASK MYSELF

1. Am I scheduling regular "imagination breaks" to question my assumptions and explore alternative approaches?

2. Am I fully absorbing lessons from play sessions, even when the format feels unfamiliar or uncomfortable?

3. Am I experimenting with storytelling and visualization techniques to reframe problems and spark novel solutions?

4. Am I finding joy in the messy, iterative process of tackling complex challenges, rather than just focusing on the end goal?

5. Am I sharing credit generously and celebrating team successes, while taking personal accountability for setbacks?

6. Am I approaching my work with constructive humility, courage, discipline, and quiet pride?

KEY QUESTIONS TO SHARE WITH COLLEAGUES

1. Are we setting clear boundaries around what constitutes productive play versus unproductive goofing off?

2. Are we normalizing healthy debate and dissent, where alternative viewpoints are evaluated objectively?

3. Are we empowering team members at all levels to initiate serious play and challenge the status quo?

4. Are we scenario-planning for unlikely but high-impact events, not just iterating on baseline projections?

5. Are we institutionalizing rituals that prompt us to surface blind spots and anticipate unintended consequences?

6. Are we engaging in serious play while imagining what has to happen for a decision to be successful and to generate potential workable solutions?

THREE

Befriending Ignorance

MAKING "I DON'T KNOW" AN ALLY

This chapter explores what it means to befriend your ignorance—to view it as a constructive partner rather than a hostile foe. Knowing how much you don't know—and how many of the things you think you know may be wrong—clarifies your thinking, leading to more intelligent decisions. We'll consider different types of ignorance and ignorance-adjacencies. And finally, we will walk through practices and questions designed to inspire you to engage with your own ignorance.

The goal is to stimulate asking yourself questions like these:

- Am I actively seeking out my ignorance, engaging in serious play and humble inquiry to surface blind spots, question assumptions, and generate creative solutions?

- Am I reframing ignorance as a source of insight and innovation, leveraging the power of wondering and "what if" thinking to explore new possibilities?

- Am I modeling intellectual humility, creating space for myself and others to acknowledge knowledge gaps and learn from them, while avoiding the traps of willful blindness and excessive data collection?

One reason serious play is so good for thinking and problem-solving is because it puts business as usual on pause. By doing that it opens a space in which we can reflect on the possibility that our minds are playing tricks on us, which they often do. We may be so certain about something that it becomes an unconscious assumption—even though it's wrong! Indeed, a great deal of our ignorance is unconscious. Here we depend on other minds to bring it to our attention. Their willingness to do that is influenced by their perception of our response and being open to their feedback. Conversely, we and our coworkers may believe something is false despite strong evidence to the contrary. This is naïve and sometimes willful ignorance. For instance, a firm concerned with being seen as a monopoly by government agencies may eschew any research on pricing. Knowledge and ignorance can play games of tag with one another, taking turns being "it." This isn't because we are stubborn or mentally lazy. Much of it has to do with the nature of human cognition, which evolved in a very different environment than the one that most of us live and work in today. Our minds were optimized for survival rather than objective understanding. This, we'll see, is an important theme in this book and a special challenge to open-mindedness.

For an example of assumed knowledge being disastrously incorrect, consider the case of a petroleum company I worked with. They believed that commercial vehicle owners regard motor oil as a commodity and so cut back on their advertising and branding efforts. When their sales plummeted, they engaged Olson Zaltman to learn why. When we interviewed professional drivers and fleet owners, we learned that, far from a commodity, they viewed motor oil as the life blood of a vehicle; all of them had great emotional attachments to their brands.

"Ignorance" has never been included on a list of qualifications in a help-wanted ad or on a résumé, but a willingness to admit to it is a trait that goes along with bold leadership and open-mindedness. The sense that there is something important that you don't know is the spark that ignites your drive to learn. Gary Ruvkun, the 2024 Nobel Prize recipient in medicine, describes the importance of ignorance this way: "*The surprises are what keep you young in science and I'm constantly surprised. My ignorance is bliss.*"[1]

Ignorance has great motivational value and great rewards when properly engaged. This is as true in the corporate world as it is for leading scientists and even for our *Australopithecus* ancestor Lucy over three million years ago. Embracing your ignorance is a necessary first step on the path to wisdom.

Ask yourself:

- Am I excited to learn more about my knowledge blind spots and areas of ignorance, or would I rather hide from these in order to look more knowledgeable?

- Am I able to dare, question, and change how I think?

The following warm-up should help you get comfortable with one common form of not knowing.

WARM-UP

Have you ever had an honest argument with someone about what was actually said or even who said it during some past event? Or who didn't say or do something on that occasion? By "honest," I mean that you and the other person had genuinely different memories of an event, not merely different interpretations of it. I imagine the answer is yes, and that you don't have to look very far to come up with examples.

Sometimes we misunderstand events or actions or receive deliberately misleading reports about them. But more often, we simply misremember them. We might even "recall" things that never happened.

The following exercise demonstrates that while your memory contains hard data that you can access and recall, much of it is reconstructed from fragmentary recollections.

PART I
Read the list of words below.

noble	castle	crown	king
royal	monarch	throne	servant
jewel	princess	purple	carriage
court	regal	tiara	jester

Done? Now cover them up. Have a drink of water or think about something else—perhaps the plot of the last TV program you watched. Take a moment and describe it out loud. Then proceed to Part II.

PART II

Write down all the words you remember from the list in the spaces below. Don't worry if you can't recall all of them. Most people can't. Then, using a 1–3 scale, rate how certain you are that each word you remember is in the list (1 = very certain; 2 = reasonably certain; 3 = not very certain).

	Words	Certainty Rating
1.	_____	_____
2.	_____	_____
3.	_____	_____
4.	_____	_____
5.	_____	_____
6.	_____	_____
7.	_____	_____
8.	_____	_____
9.	_____	_____
10.	_____	_____
11.	_____	_____
12.	_____	_____
13.	_____	_____
14.	_____	_____
15.	_____	_____
16.	_____	_____

Finished? Now check your responses against the original list.

1. Did you "remember" any words that were not on the original list?

2. Did you rate your confidence that they were on the list about the same as you did for the words you remembered correctly?

Your answers to both questions are likely "yes." Researchers have a lot of experience with exercises like this, and they nearly always see the same results: people remember words that weren't present, and their confidence that they remember those words correctly is about the same as for the words that really were on the list.

Did you write down *queen*? It wasn't on the original list, but about two-thirds of people who participate in this exercise recall that it was. That so many people may agree on the same "fact" can become reinforcing evidence for it. The belief becomes a "fact" despite being wrong.

BASIC IDEA

It turns out that the areas of the brain involved in misremembering overlap with those involved in accurate recall. That may be why we feel so confident about some false memories. Most of our memories are of events that occurred days, weeks, or years ago as opposed to just the few minutes that I gave you to distract yourself between reading the list and attempting to recall it. We have plenty of opportunities to add or subtract things from our memories without being aware that we are doing so.

"Remembering" isn't like downloading a document from a computer. It's more like reconstructing a narrative from fragments. We sketch in the missing details that seem to finish the picture, even if they don't. The overarching theme of the words listed in this exercise was royalty. That made it more likely that you would misremember a seemingly obvious word like "queen," even though it wasn't listed. I doubt that any of you added "carpenter" or "wrestler" or "pilot," as those words don't go with the story of royalty.

SO WHAT?

The message here isn't that you should never trust your memory. It's that you should be skeptical enough to always double-check it. You should also be open to the possibility that another person's memory of a shared experience that seems to confirm or contradict yours may also be wrong. We may reconstruct a past event in a different way than it occurred yet feel it is correct—indeed we may insist it is—and be unaware that we are in a state of nescience or unwitting ignorance.

An example of a false memory comes from a study of consumer experiences my firm once conducted for a fast-food chain, in which we interviewed patrons as they were leaving a restaurant. One complaint involved the many dirty dishes lying around. Interestingly, video of the restaurant showed few, if any, dirty dishes. The interviewee was either mistaken or had formed a negative impression based on a single table that had yet to be cleared. A response to this complaint would have been unproductive.

Often, we continue to make choices that are not based in fact, even when we know better. We once conducted a study investigating why, when given the choice between an expensive name-brand pain reliever and a generic, many consumers opted to purchase the name brand. The consumers we interviewed all understood that both products contained the same ingredients. So, why were they willing to pay more for the name brand? They told us they preferred to use the name-brand pills when their pain was especially bad, when they needed to control it while attending an important event, and when they had to give a pain reliever to a family member. In effect, they discarded their knowledge that the two products are identical in favor of their feeling that the more expensive one was superior.

You might not be able to prevent your gut inclinations from swaying your decisions—you may not even want to. Feelings like "it just seems right" often contain sound, relevant information. But it is important to pause and assess whether they are warranted. Now that you know that your feelings weigh at least as heavily as your knowledge, try to know which is which.

Ask yourself:

- Am I skeptical enough to double-check my memory, or open to the possibility that someone else's memory is also not perfect?
- Do I assess where my gut feelings come from and have strategies in place to counter my own assumptions?

Because the term *ignorance* has such negative connotations, some prefer *not knowing*. I like *ignorance*, as I want to encourage befriending it as a state of mind.[2] Doing so invites introspective thinking, which prevents us from becoming, in one interviewee's colorful coinage, "decision-making slugs." Regardless of what you call it, it is important that you acknowledge your uncertainties about information.[3] As one leading researcher urges: "We need to make . . . ignorance itself the object of study . . . shining light on forms of unknowing, mis-knowing, and varieties of ignorance can help us to better grapple with and work through them."[4]

It is the same with organizations as with individuals. "Knowing what is not known can be as important to organizational performance as knowing what is known," one management expert writes. "Different types and sources of ignorance require different management approaches."[5]

A CASE EXAMPLE: SELLING HALF A BEVERAGE

Let's begin with an example involving a firm that was actively open to the possibility that they were missing an important piece of knowledge. This soft drink company, which is widely acknowledged for its unrivaled understanding of its global markets, is also well known for placing immense value on discovering and addressing its "ignorance zones." So, it wasn't a surprise when they approached us with a specific challenge: to "map" the consumer experience of Brand X with the goal of getting at consumers' hidden thoughts and feelings. In effect, they were asking us to help them answer a basic question: What don't we know that we should know but haven't discovered yet?

The aim wasn't to confirm or deny an assumption about their brand. The brand was well established; it wasn't clear whether we would discover anything that had been overlooked or ignored. They simply wondered if there could be something potentially important that their brand was offering to consumers that could be further leveraged. If so, what was it?

Recall from our earlier discussion that a mind is a predictive machine. Brand experiences are shaped by what happens when the brand promise is fulfilled, that is, when the consumer's predicted or anticipated experience meets what actually occurs as the product is used or consumed.

To get at this, our research team and the client reviewed several alternative questions to ask consumers to stimulate their thinking during a picture-gathering exercise. We settled on a simple one: "What is the role of Brand X in your life?" There was concern that this could be too general, but after minor pre-testing, we discovered it was potentially quite productive and proceeded with a major multimarket study.

The resulting data produced a complex consensus map which, as anticipated, contained many of the company's previously learned insights. This was viewed in a positive way, because it validated our still somewhat new methodology, lending credence to any new, previously unknown dimensions of the consumer experience that we might discover. And we did indeed identify one. Moreover, this new dimension was arguably at least as important as any of the familiar ones.

We discovered that consumers predicted the brand would deliver—and even more importantly, that it *did* deliver—an emotional state that balanced a feeling of relaxation, calm, and serenity, even in the midst of contexts that were energizing, active, and gregarious. That state of mind was a major reason they consumed the brand. In effect, the firm discovered they had been "selling" just one-half the consumption experience, its suitability for festive social occasions, while consumers were buying the product for the whole experience.

To underscore the importance of the discovery, at a major marketing leadership meeting, the CMO arranged to have a half-filled glass of Brand X at each seat. The message was crystal clear: up until now, we have been selling half of our product. Just imagine how much more we could accomplish if we made the whole consumer experience our brand story.

Let's stay with this example a while longer, as it helps us identify different kinds of ignorance. First, there is *factive ignorance*, which doesn't allow for the possibility of unknown facts ("If it was there, we'd have seen it by now"). Fortunately, some managers, as a matter of sound practice, were willing to challenge that belief, even though they didn't expect to learn anything new. Factive ignorance is fueled by another kind of ignorance, which is misplaced confidence in one's expertise on the object of interest, sometimes referred to as *objectual ignorance* ("I know exactly what motivates consumers and it is not that"). Objectual ignorance is one reason more exploratory research isn't done.

Exploratory research focuses on what might be, as opposed to confirmatory research, which is inquiry to prove a point. Most research is of the latter sort. It favors research with clear actions. This brings us to a third type of ignorance, missing in this example, which is not knowing how to put knowledge to work ("That's all very interesting, but what do I do with it?"). This might be called *procedural ignorance*, to denote the inability to map a path from data to action. Not knowing how to use research findings is a major problem and an underdeveloped science in its own right. Later in the book we'll explore opportunities for addressing this form of ignorance. Again, that was not a problem in the beverage example.

POSITIVE METAPHORS FOR IGNORANCE

The first step in befriending your ignorance is developing a better way to think about it, much as a worried parent might be urged not to think of their challenging child as "problematic" or "difficult" but "spirited" and "determined." Consider the following approaches:

Negative space. Negative or white space, as it is sometimes called, is what surrounds and thus helps define the center of attention in a picture. Sometimes the negative space itself can become the center of attention, as with a Rubin Vase, the famous image of two faces in profile, rendered in black, that face each other across a white space that also can be seen as a candlestick or vase. Since the eye is unsure which space is negative, it switches back and forth between them.

Terra incognita. Knowledge management systems rely on the effective use of well-established knowledge to solve problems, but that has a downside. When data appears to be abundant, people are reluctant to pursue missing information. I call this an *ignorance avoidance bias*. Ignorance is the mind's *terra incognita*—its unknown territory.[6] On early maps from the age of exploration, those unknown territories often bear the warning "here be dragons." Daunting! And yet all over the world, bold spirits ventured out into them.

BEFRIENDING IGNORANCE

Changing our metaphors for ignorance can help create a mindset for accepting it. But changing our understanding of ourselves is even more important.

The most confident executives I encounter share one of the key traits that support the actions of an open mind, namely, humility.[7] Humble people don't brag, and they don't cover up their mistakes to protect their reputations. Instead, they acknowledge them openly as a way to share learnings.

Sincere expressions of humility engender trust and encourage colleagues to develop and express humility as well. One leader described his process for sharing ignorance: "We give an award each month for the biggest knowledge management error among staff, and I always start meetings with one of mine. My goal is to empower humility and learning." Staff dubbed those meetings "Mistakes Anonymous." Another organization has a digital message board called "School of Hard Knocks," an often humorous forum where employees share their mistakes and learning experiences.

Sometimes decision-makers are ignorant about their ignorance. I worked with a client once, a Fortune 500 consumer goods company, that was developing a campaign for one of its products based on the theme that it made consumers "feel good." But when the senior leaders who had green-lighted the approach were shown the sample creatives, they hated them. I suspected they construed "feel good" in a different way than their target customers did, and when we put them through the same interviews we had carried out with consumers, my suspicion was borne out. These were very affluent people, who operated in a very particular milieu, one that had little in common with that of their target customers. When they saw the gap between what they thought they knew and what they in fact didn't know, they changed their minds.

WHY IT'S DIFFICULT TO UNCOVER OUR IGNORANCE

Our brains are most impressionable during our first two-plus decades of life, so influences we receive during those formative years have a first-mover advantage in creating durable imprints.[8] The four forces that combine to create our minds (physical environment, society and culture, individual bodily behavior, and brain activity) implant *pro-knowledge* and *ignorance-avoidance* biases in our thinking that operate subconsciously.[9] As a result, we tend to be more comfortable when we feel knowledgeable and less comfortable when we feel ignorant. That is one reason it can be so hard to change people's minds.[10]

Collaboration can help overcome these biases, because it provides more diverse inputs, but the process can be contentious.[11] Team members may vary in their prior personal or professional cultures and so have conflicting criteria for evaluating the same information and insights. But with a high level of trust, those differences can be managed.[12]

But too much agreement can harm collaborations. As a species, we are prone to imitate others; it is an efficient way to leverage what they have learned without having to invest the same resources ourselves. In fact, our brains contain special cells called mirror neurons that facilitate our imitations of people who seem to know what they are doing.

That reliance on the presumed expertise or competence of others is one reason personal mentoring is so effective. But people are not always discriminating about what they choose to imitate. I have worked with many clients whose sole reason for maintaining a failing marketing program is the fact that a competitor is using it successfully. I worry a lot when I see a monkey-see, monkey-do culture. A sign of one is managers who unthinkingly adhere to industry best practices, even when they don't fully understand why those practices work and whether they apply to the situation at hand.[13]

TYPES OF IGNORANCE

While some kinds of ignorance are beneficial, all of them must be acknowledged and understood. Most fall into one of three major categories:

VIRTUOUS IGNORANCE
Sometimes denying ourselves knowledge is a good and necessary act. Double-blind trials in medical research and elsewhere in the sciences provide one example. Similarly, it can be right to withhold information from some parties in legal settings, as justice is not inherently blind.[14]

AFFECTIVE IGNORANCE
Affective ignorance is a lack of awareness of two things: (1) that you feel a certain emotion, and (2) how that emotional state affects your judgments and behavior. When biases operate unconsciously, we are unlikely to challenge them.[15]

Examples of affective ignorance include aversions to categories of people, physical settings, information sources, and research methodologies. These biases can then be passed on to artificial intelligence (AI) systems, which train on human decisions, judgments, and responses. As AI becomes more pervasive, so will this problem. Letting our feelings lead can also empower what has been called *myside bias,* in which we unconsciously favor the methods and viewpoints of our own group.[16]

Although affective ignorance causes problems, it's important to recognize that it's the *unawareness* of feelings, not the feelings themselves, that are the issue. Feelings can be constructive silent partners of formal reasoning and often provide the special guidance that distinguishes outstanding decision-makers from those who are simply good.[17] The question to ask is how well informed your feelings are. Were they shaped by sound feedback from prior experiences? Do they take into account how predictable the object of their reasoning is?

A sample size of just one can still be enough to implant a permanent bias. How likely are you to return to a restaurant where you had a bad experience? Even knowing that it was just one meal out of many, or that your waiter had a bad day, the association is still poisoned.

WILLFUL OR TACTICAL IGNORANCE

We are tactically ignorant when we choose to deprive ourselves of certain kinds of information. For example, a leader may instruct subordinates to keep him in the dark about embarrassing or incriminating information. There can be justifiable reasons not to know—for example, when the financial cost or time delay involved in collecting and processing more information is greater than any possible benefit.

But willful ignorance can reflect an unhealthy contempt or hostility toward certain kinds of information. People who align with the political right or left tend to rely on media that reflects their own point of view—*The National Review* versus *The Nation;* MSNBC versus Fox News—and avoid exposing themselves to media that might challenge it. In his book *Respecting Truth: Willful Ignorance in the Internet Age,* Lee McIntyre argues that willful ignorance may pose the greatest threat to an open mind.[18]

Willful ignorance also allows people to avoid *forbidden knowledge*—topics that a community tacitly agrees should be avoided in conversation or research. Forbidden knowledge will come up in later chapters when we discuss *groupthink* and *mind guards.*

IGNORANCE-ADJACENT ISSUES

The *big-data paradox* and the *pro-knowledge bias* aren't types of ignorance, but they help ignorance to flourish.

THE BIG-DATA PARADOX

Paradoxically, collecting vast quantities of data may inadvertently introduce ignorance.[19] Large sample sizes tend to enhance confidence in the generalizability of research findings. But unnoticed biases or flaws in a sample-collecting methodology can lead to even greater distortions. Relatedly, *statistical significance*—which large samples do tend to provide—is often confused with *substantive significance*. This confusion muddies assessments of the meaningfulness or importance of findings.

When conducting research, it is important to understand *what type* of information is being collected and *how much*. Market researchers use different methodologies to develop quantitative versus qualitative insights; bringing the methods and attitudes of one type of research to the other can lead to serious errors. Every organization must decide what the right balance of research is for them but even more importantly, must understand what it can and can't illuminate.

PRO-KNOWLEDGE BIAS AND FALSE CONFIDENCE

When someone believes they know all there is to know or all they require, they are likely to jump to wrong conclusions.[20] We see this when someone assumes they possess a deep understanding of a topic because they have read a Wikipedia entry or something similar.[21] Nonexperts' unmerited confidence in their expertise is known as the Dunning-Kruger Effect, after the pair of researchers who first identified the phenomenon.[22]

Another type of false confidence is unwarranted faith in our subjective knowledge, that is, the belief that if we feel we know something "in our guts," we truly know it.[23] Of course, none of us would ever commit that error. Or would we?

Let's examine false confidence further. Most readers know how to ride a bike, snap their fingers, or catch a ball tossed in their direction. So, if a child were to ask you to teach them one of these skills, you would likely agree. But knowing we can do something is not the same as knowing *how* we do it, as you'd quickly discover.[24] The same thing is likely to happen if you are asked to put your know-how into writing.[25]

In fact, no one can teach these skills. The best we can do is provide learners with emotional support disguised as instruction as they figure them out for themselves (the good news is that we are teaching them the importance of perseverance). In fact, it is estimated that even "experts articulate only about 30% of what they know."[26] This isn't all bad news: observing and imitating experts leads to more mastery than simply following written instructions.[27]

CONSEQUENCES OF IGNORANCE

It can be hard to befriend your ignorance, considering how daunting its consequences can be, from minor embarrassments (when you ask after someone's spouse, only to discover that they've recently divorced) to catastrophic (if you failed to learn the implications of a competitor's product launch).

Our minds are prediction-making machines. We are constantly thinking, "If I do X, I can expect Y to occur as a result." When Y happens, we are pleased to be right. When Y fails to happen, we feel surprised or dismayed.[28] Few things signal the presence of ignorance more than when something we thought would happen . . . doesn't. Even a welcome surprise, such as greater demand for a product than we predicted and prepared for, reveals flaws in our thinking. It suggests that we missed, or perhaps misused, key information that might have led to a more accurate forecast.

Open minds entertain the possibility of positive and negative surprises in advance of an action. They engage in premortems, asking, What if a decision goes bad? What might we have missed that we could have anticipated? Is the knowledge we might be missing available now? Can it be acquired in a timely way? An example of befriending ignorance by routine use of ignorance is provided below.

CASE STUDY: BEFRIENDING IGNORANCE THROUGH ROUTINE PREMORTEMS

A firm marketing specialty coffees routinely conducts premortems using metaphor elicitation techniques in their new product development process. They understand that consumer responses to coffee are rooted in multiple sensory experiences. Using that understanding, they are able to engineer the whole experience—not just its taste, but its name, scent, texture, and packaging—to ensure a positive reception. Before launching a new brand, they ask and then test in advance whether and how these features complement one another or are discordant. Conducting premortems with regularity also helps reduce how daunting it feels to confront ignorance—if it's already on the schedule or a set step in project procedure, it becomes a habit to cozy up to ignorance—and even something to look forward to. It becomes a chance to explore the blank spaces of the unknown with curiosity, instead of pointing a blaming finger at anyone for knowing less than they should. Consider where you could conduct a premortem—or better yet, where you can make it a routine step, like the specialty coffee brand's marketing team does.

Experienced, intelligent, and diligent executives often experience post-decision regret, characterized by groans of "shoulda, woulda, coulda" and a bad case of if-only. Often, it's a consequence of acting too hastily. How often have you wished for a do-over following an important decision? When I put that question to executives during our interviews, most responded with resigned laughter or an exaggerated exhale, followed by some version of "Lots!" or "Too often!" When I invited them to describe their typical decision-making process, it was generally reasonable. As one executive put it, "We always measure twice before cutting." But in retrospect, the information they used and/or the reasoning they applied often proved faulty in ways not evident at the time. Most errors are more visible with hindsight. But many turn out to have been detectable but ignored.

Attempts to avoid post-decision regret can lead executives to become entangled in "sacred excess,"[29] which Stefan Schwarzkopf describes as "too much data, too much information, and . . . too many things drawn into the abyss of the unknown because of sheer information overflow."[30] Too much data is not just overwhelming for individuals; most businesses lack the processes or skills to handle all the data they collect. Dell Technologies surveyed 4,036 global directors and decision-makers responsible for data strategies and digital transformation.[31] Most agreed that their organizations were gathering data faster than they could analyze and apply it.

Ask yourself:

- Am I mindful of the "sacred excess" of collecting too much data to digest properly?
- Do I tend to collect more data when I feel like the current data set isn't giving me what I want?

PLAYFUL IGNORANCE

On the positive side of the ledger, ignorance creates opportunities for novel thinking.[32] Playful ignorance is often a partnership or a joint venture between discovery and invention, that is, between finding ideas that already exist but have previously escaped our attention, and ideas that are new. Sometimes one partner will be more prominent, sometimes the other. Both discovery and invention walk along the four paths of knowing: intuition, imagination, reasoning, and scientific procedures.

Many of the most successful decision-makers I've been privileged to know insist on seeking out and befriending important unknowns, an approach that is much less prevalent among their less successful colleagues.

Asking and answering various what-if questions, sometimes called "miracle questions," can be like twisting a kaleidoscope—each turn produces a dramatically different view, helping transform sound strategies into excellent ones and converting failed solutions into ones that work.[33] Here is a starter set of what-if questions:

- **What if the cause of the problem is multiple rather than singular (or vice versa)?** This approach often surfaces previously unobserved causes and even manifestations of a problem, correcting for what is sometimes called a Type III Error, which is solving the wrong problem.[34]

- **What if our approach is too particularistic—or too generalizing?** For example, what if we view a market as having more or less segments than it really does? The tendency to carve markets up into increasingly finely differentiated segments can be costly. Why not try to hit a home run instead by focusing on the single most important need they all share? When resources are scarce, this type of triage is especially beneficial. If markets are segmented by age or ethnicity, for example, we may fail to recognize that each segment's purchases are driven by the same emotional experience and readily addressed by the same product feature. Or, the opposite may be true, and we may be treating groups who want our service or product to do very different jobs for them as if they were the same.

- **What if we've reversed cause and effect?** A recent article on jet lag confidently asserted that simply thinking about being jet lagged in advance of a trip greatly worsened the jet lag the passenger ultimately experienced. But the methodology it used was fatally flawed, as it did not take into consideration the fact that some people have a greater biological susceptibility to jet lag than others. People with that susceptibility naturally think about jet lag with dread prior to a journey, while people who experience it rarely or never don't. The results are the same, but the cause and the effect are the reverse of what the article suggested.

- **What if our evaluation is incorrect?** What if something we have judged to be bad is actually good? For generations, federal prohibitions against medically supervised experimentation with psychedelics were justified because of the potential for abuse. Now psychedelics are proving useful for treating such mental disorders as posttraumatic stress, depression, and alcohol dependency.[35] The risk of abuse is far outweighed by the potential benefits.

Other what-if questions could address tools, metrics, research methodologies, evidence, and bias.

EPIPHANIES

"Aha!," "I've got it!," "Now I see!," and the classic, "Eureka!" are expressions that suggest an epiphany has occurred. But what exactly has happened? Sometimes, a remembered piece of relevant information has bubbled up from the subconscious. Its arrival "out of the blue" suggests a magical, extraterrestrial, even heavenly source. An executive friend of mine once described such insights as "a collapse of vectors into knowing."

Sometimes, its source is the imagination. Many of the best managers, researchers, and other professionals I've interviewed read between the lines of the incomplete data they have and imagine what else must be present for it to make sense. A chief marketing officer described the result of such an exercise:

> [The answer] was clear as day. It didn't have numbers attached . . . it wasn't found in a transcript . . . but [it] reeked of truth. Once the idea was floated, everyone saw how all of our data supported it . . . As soon as I asked [the question], all the pieces of a very big puzzle fell into place. We all knew the answer was right.

Epiphanies never occur in a vacuum—ignorance doesn't spontaneously turn into knowing, even when it feels that way. More likely there was a known piece of information that had been ignored up until the moment of insight. Whatever the case, epiphanies only happen to minds that welcome them.

WORKABLE WONDERING

Children wonder all the time, a process that Yale University's Frank C. Keil describes as a quest for understanding. "Instead of merely asking 'What's next?' which is closer to curiosity," he writes, "wondering goes further and asks, 'Is it something like X or something like Y or Z that is next?'"[36] Early childhood is the life stage when open-mindedness is most on display.[37] As we grow older, our capacity for wondering gets rusty. Sadly, once lost, this capacity is too often never recovered. As Keil puts it, "[questions] dramatically decline during the elementary school years. Most children continue this unquestioning passivity for the rest of their lives."[38]

To restore that capacity, picture yourself at a potter's wheel trying to fashion a perfect vase. You know it's lurking in that lump of clay, and your job is to bring it out.[39] To capture the sense of engagement and open-minded imagination that creative problem-solving requires, I use the term *workable wondering*. As a form of cognitive play, it can be great fun and even addictive.

At the end of the day, what distinguishes high-achieving people from those who are simply good at what they do? Malcolm Gladwell's 10,000 hours of practice notwithstanding, it's more than putting in the hours to acquire specialized knowledge.[40] Asking and answering questions about what's missing, what's ignored, and what needs to be added is part of it, as is the judicious use of all six qualities of mind.

And there is one more quality, hinted at in a commentary on Jun'ichiro Tanizaki, a highly regarded twentieth-century Japanese novelist, which attributes the following sentiment to him: "Too orderly an exposition falsifies the ruminations of the heart . . . The truest representation of the searching mind is just to 'follow the brush.'"[41]

In far less elegant words, "Just do it." Be as mindful of your intuition and imagination (the heart's brush) as you are of reason and science. If you know better, then *do* better: act with the courage of your convictions. That is what winning business strategists do.[42]

When you have the courage of your convictions and the audacity to run with them, you may meet with disapproval; being a bridge between a messy problem and its potential solution invites being walked on. Some may privately applaud your thinking but be unwilling to support it publicly. You may experience what one interviewee described as the "heat of a cold reception." There can be good reasons to oppose bold ideas; one must be prepared to hear and address them constructively, as Gabriella in chapter 1 did. We must remember that the problem we are trying to solve is our primary foe, not our less imaginative, meeker colleagues who are also trying to solve it.

THE THREE DARES

In closing, let's briefly discuss three dares. All of them require you to make your-self vulnerable, which in organizations requires a high degree of interpersonal trust.[43] You may find that such trust is in short supply, especially when the stakes are high. However, a dare helps you approach ignorance with courage, which will give you the push toward befriending it instead of regarding ignorance as an enemy to avoid. With that in mind:

Dare to understand how you think. We are how we think. But while re-flecting on who we are may be enjoyable, we generally don't spend enough time thinking about how we got to where we are. We'd rather explain and justify what we think and who we believe we are now.

Dare to question how you think. Asking the right questions of ourselves (as opposed to asking merely convenient ones) is hard work that requires us to access our unconscious thoughts and mental operations. Our reluctance to do so is one reason so much market research is geared to confirming existing ideas rather than seeking out new ones.

Dare to change how you think. We need to be ready to perform occasional surgery on our thinking. This does not grant you permission to play the role of a naysayer where others' thinking is concerned; it requires you to challenge your own assumptions, to wonder whether they might be wrong and why, and to experiment with alternative viewpoints and information acquisition and pro-cessing strategies. To do this well, you need the cool passion of a circus tightrope artist, what I've called "di-stance," being separate enough from your own think-ing to monitor it, while also being deeply engaged in it.

CONCLUSION: TWO STATES OF MIND

In general, we celebrate knowledge and deride ignorance. But knowledge is not always deployed constructively or wisely, and it is a perishable commodity. In our turbulent world of disruption, its shelf life appears to be getting shorter by the day. Ignorance is often viewed as the antithesis of knowledge, something for knowledge to vanquish. Yet there are always frontiers of ignorance before us, as the cartoon in figure 3.1 suggests.

As an alternative to the metaphor of eternal warfare against ignorance, I sug-gest we embrace ignorance with "playful engagement." A constructive way of doing this involves the image of two koi ponds in figure 3.2. One pond is illumi-nated; the other is dark. Koi are swimming in both—and are able to cross from

FIGURE 3.1 Passing the Buck Doesn't Work.

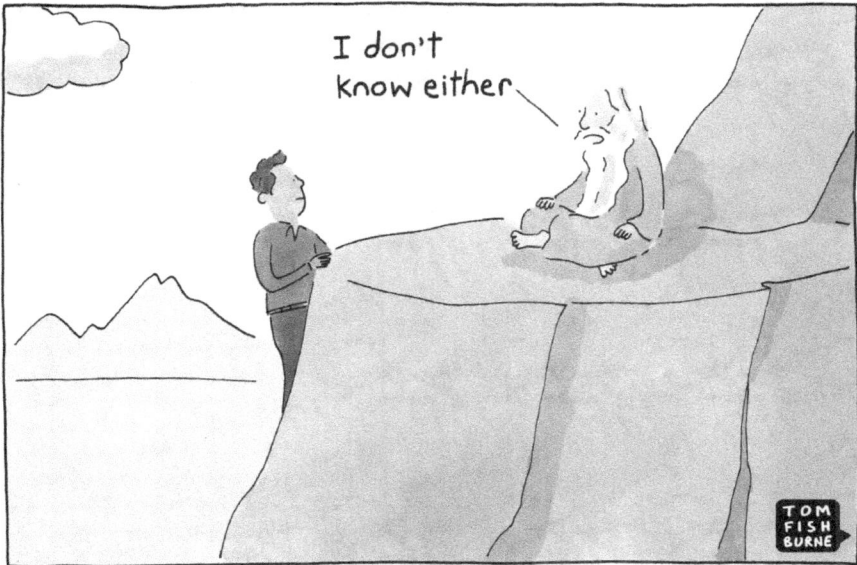

one pool to the other. As you look at the image, try meditating on the following questions and the implications of your answers:

- Which pool do you associate with knowledge? Which with ignorance? Why do you suppose you have those associations?
- Is one pool a more productive spawning ground than the other?
- Why do fish migrate between them?
- What routes do they follow? A leap of faith from one to the other? A subterranean stream?
- What emotional experiences arise migrating from one pool to the other?
- What perils or opportunities produce these emotions?
- Is it possible there is just one pool with varying depths?

Finally, befriending ignorance is one of the most challenging actions in pursuit of an open mind. This challenge is defined by the common expression, "I'm of two minds on [fill in the blank]." The prompts an interesting question: when you, me, or someone else is of two minds about something and one wins out, where does the other one go? The answer appears to be: not very far away. It like the famous illusion of a vase versus a face; we can only see one at a time, and yet the contours of one define the contours of the other. Knowledge and ignorance share mutually defining borders. It is difficult to have one without the other.

FIGURE 3.2   Which Pond Are You In?

DESIGNED BY SANAYA SHIKARI.

KEY QUESTIONS TO ASK MYSELF

1. Am I carving out dedicated time for deep reflection on my ignorance, and exploring how embracing it could catalyze my growth and impact?

2. Am I embracing ignorance-befriending practices, such as workable wondering and asking bold "what if" questions, to spark imaginative decision-making and fuel my drive to learn, even when it feels uncomfortable or counterintuitive?

3. Am I actively seeking to identify the various types of ignorance within and around me, and challenging myself to discern which to engage with versus accept?

4. Am I role-modeling humble curiosity, vulnerably acknowledging my knowledge gaps to create psychological safety for others to do the same, even when it feels risky?

5. Am I resisting the urge to make decisions without considering what critical information might be missing, while also avoiding the trap of endless analysis?

6. Am I continually monitoring and challenging my thoughts and decisions, staying alert to pro-knowledge and ignorance avoidance biases that could derail me?

7. Am I proactively conducting premortems, boldly envisioning pitfalls and unintended consequences, to stress-test my strategies and assumptions?

8. Am I leaning into the discomfort of serious play as a tool for navigating ignorance, using thought experiments and scenario planning to surface new possibilities, even when it feels silly or unserious?

9. Am I consistently asking myself and others, "What opportunities might we be overlooking?" to identify and fill gaps in our knowledge and strategies, leveraging ignorance as a catalyst for growth and innovation?

KEY QUESTIONS TO SHARE WITH COLLEAGUES

1. Are we actively celebrating and rewarding intellectual humility and vulnerability as critical leadership strengths, not just paying lip service to these values?

2. Are we consistently creating psychologically safe spaces for team members to say "I don't know," and openly share their doubts, questions, and knowledge gaps without fear of judgment or retribution?

3. Are we assessing our individual and collective expertise not just based on what we currently know, but also on our ability to effectively teach and share that knowledge with others?

4. Are we rigorously interrogating the substance and significance of our data, looking beyond surface-level metrics to uncover potential biases, limitations, or faulty assumptions?

5. Are we critically examining our data collection and analysis methodologies to uncover potential biases or flaws, resisting the temptation to blindly trust findings based solely on large sample sizes?

6. Are we critically evaluating our data collection and analysis practices, ensuring that we're not falling into the trap of "sacred excess" or analysis paralysis, but rather focusing on actionable insights?

FOUR

The Power of Surprising Yourself

ASKING THE RIGHT DISCOVERY QUESTIONS

Serious playfulness facilitates befriending conscious ignorance. Identifying ignorance enables the next step in the process of inquiry: asking questions. In many ways, questions are the unsung heroes of inquiry. We inquire when we pose a question, and the questions we pose constrain the answer we discover. In this chapter, we will ask, What is a question? to understand the purposes questions serve in different situations and build your ability to ask the right ones in the right situations. I will take you through some exercises to hone your question-asking abilities and provide you with some cautions as well, and show you what happens when you let curiosity, questions, and answers play a game of tag. By asking questions about questions, you can build your ability to craft the right question when you need it—leading to the answers you seek. There are several Am I? questions for you to practice with as you read this chapter.

- Am I asking the right questions in the right situations, crafting queries that maximize decision-making value and helpfulness of the answers?

- Am I embracing serious playfulness when asking questions, exploring the dynamic interplay between curiosity, questions, and answers to generate novel insights?

- Am I vigilantly questioning data and assumptions, implementing formal processes to identify and challenge potential errors in thinking and decision-making?

- Am I using questions as a tool to cultivate intellectual humility, embracing the opportunity to learn from others and continuously expand my knowledge and perspective?

- Am I creating a psychologically safe environment that encourages questioning, exploration, and the open sharing of ideas, valuing the contributions of all team members?

WARM-UP

We are all natural historians, constantly probing events to ask: Who did this? Why did they do it? How did they do it? When? Such questions reflect an innate, often self-reinforcing curiosity. My colleagues and I always invest considerable effort to find the "Goldilocks" ZMET question, that is, "just the right" question to satisfy a client's knowledge needs for understanding and addressing a problem.[1] There is neither too much nor too little information provided. This is the research question that guides participants' selection of images in advance of their interviews. It can neither be so abstract that it prevents detailed insights into behavior from emerging, nor so detailed that it limits the scope of the conversation and overlooks special opportunities. In one research project we conducted involving a breakfast brand, the question we finally arrived at, intended for mothers of young children, was: "What role does [brand X] play in the life of your child?" This allowed them to describe its role as a breakfast food along with its other uses in their children's lives. What emerged was that, much more than a breakfast food, it was a cherished marker of transitions. It was often the first food a child could feed to themselves. It was a celebration of the first day of school. When included in a kid's lunchbox it was a reminder of parental love. Baked in cookies, it was a welcome-home-from-school treat. As an adult breakfast (or sometimes lunch and even dinner) comfort food, it was endowed with childhood memories. Asking such a broad question uncovered many specific new opportunities, both for the brand in question and for other of the firm's products.

EXERCISE

While on the topic of youngsters, imagine that you are four years old. You are in the kitchen with your parents and the tea kettle has just started whistling. You ask a simple question: Why is the kettle whistling?

One parent automatically responds with a causal, if-this-then-that explanation: because the electric coils on the stovetop became hot and transferred their heat to the kettle. That made the water molecules get busy and produce steam. The steam tried to escape through the narrow opening of the kettle, causing a whistle.

Then, you ask your other parent the same question and the answer is: because I want a hot cup of tea. This second answer is diagnostic, as it addresses why the tea kettle is in use. Both answers are correct but assume different motivations for the question.

Now a few questions for you:

Which response would have satisfied the four-year-old you? The "how does it happen" answer or the "what purpose is served" answer? Of course, maybe you had neither answer in mind. Were you just trying to get your parents' attention?

And here's another question I can't resist asking. When you imagine the parent giving the cause-and-effect answer, did you imagine a particular gender? How about the parent who wanted tea? Might societal attitudes about gender roles and family makeup have affected your answers?

SO WHAT?

Sometimes we understand a question in terms of the answer we're most prepared to give—even if that answer isn't the one the questioner is seeking. How often have you asked a question and felt the need to respond to the answer you received by saying, "No, what I was really asking was . . ."? And how often have you had to say in reply to a question, "Oh, what I thought you were asking was . . ."?

Familiar, conveniently available answers can lead us to ask and/or answer the wrong questions. This produces explanations that are incomplete and often shallow, or worse still, incorrect. When we are crafting questions, we must be vigilant for these dangers, which means carefully assessing our thinking. We want to try to ensure people hear what we mean to ask.

THE PERFECT QUESTION CANNOT ALWAYS BE ASKED

Formulating the central question in a research project is not always straightforward. The difference between a question that elicits priceless responses and insights and one that brilliantly illuminates exactly the wrong material can be extremely subtle, and getting it wrong wastes the client's money. Exploring the Alps isn't helpful when the client has asked you to explore the Andes.

An insurance company wanted to better understand consumer attitudes about auto insurance programs that use telematics to collect data on policyhold-ers' driving habits. Safer drivers would receive benefits and discounts, while less safe drivers could expect an upcharge.

The client wanted to understand what consumers would think and feel about that potential surcharge. Would they leave the program if they had to pay one? To add to the challenge, none of the existing policy holders could be interviewed because of confidentiality issues. The population to interview would have to be people who would be open to such a program but not enrolled in one.

The research team didn't want to ask respondents how they *might* feel about receiving a surcharge, since hypotheticals typically fail to anticipate or close the "say-do" gap. So, the most direct question wasn't the best or right one. Instead of focusing specifically on car insurance, the product at hand, or even on driving, the team decided to broaden the scope of the question and ultimately settled on "What are your thoughts and feelings about dealing with setbacks?"

While the stories the participants shared were off-subject, their emotional and psychological territory that was revealed provided answers that were incred-ibly relevant to the client's issue. They were filled with insights into what leads some people to rebound from setbacks and others to give up, and what envi-ronmental conditions make it easier to persevere. Based on the patterns of these emotions and behaviors, the team was able to recommend elements to add to the client's communications about the telematics program that would encourage consumers to persist.

It took time, trouble, and imagination to craft the question, but the insights it yielded were richer and more useful than if it had been solely focused on the program's logistics.

WHAT IS A QUESTION, ANYWAY?

Where do questions come from? Idle curiosity? Mistakes? Encounters with anomalies? Do questions contain their own answers? What makes one question good and another not? What happens to questions after they've been answered? You likely have other questions to add to this list, and I hope this is one of them: Why does it feel so good when an interesting question comes to mind, making us eager to ask it?[2]

When we formulate a question that feels good or right, we reduce the tension caused by not knowing something even before we hear the answer. Sometimes we experience it as a high.[3] Having a question already is a major step toward reducing uncertainty.

A chief financial officer we interviewed called questions "the long fuse attached to answers." When we asked what lights that fuse, the CFO replied that it was figuring out the thing that the company "didn't ask about that got us in trouble in the first place." Another interviewee commented, "Knowing you've asked and answered the right question is a confidence booster."

One way to think of questions is as the sharp hook at the business end of the spear we call curiosity. Importantly, they help us detect errors. They also lead the way to corrective answers—although, as the warm-up noted, they may produce very different answers depending on the source consulted.

Let's return for a moment to the four-year-old you introduced earlier. You are already quite sophisticated. Of special note is your ability to think in terms of cause and effect. You've learned to notice associations and ponder interventions, such as What happens if I do this instead of that? You've even learned to ask counterfactuals, like What might have happened if I had done something else instead?

Often the consequences we are contemplating have to do with how we will feel. At the end of the nineteenth century, the psychologist Edward Thorndike articulated "the law of effect," which states that we decide what to do and what to avoid doing based on the felt consequences of our actions.[4] Contemplating that law, the neuropsychologist Mark Solms concludes: "Thorndike's law actually amounts to a Law of *Affect*, since it implies that behaviors which make us (and other animals) feel good are the behaviors that we repeat, and those which make us feel bad are the ones we avoid."[5]

By asking questions about causes and effects, four-year-old you is doing what our ancient ancestors did to test and further develop their mental models of the world. Questions are pivotal in the emergence of consciousness. Drawing on contemporary advances in information science theory, Solms describes how question-asking contributed to our ability to be observers of ourselves.[6] Four-year-old you already realizes that you are not the only one with a mind. Moreover, you've discovered that others' minds differ from yours and from one another's. In short, you've developed a "theory of mind."[7]

This leads to another ability you've developed: mind reading. You have learned the importance of understanding what's going on in other people's minds, and how to read their apparent causal mental models.[8] You know that if someone wants a cup of tea, they'll heat up water. You've also acquired other impressive reasoning skills, including ways of manipulating others' behaviors. For instance, you know that by asking questions, even if only to get attention, you may get others to act in certain ways.

In terms of human evolution, these skills were a long time in the making. It wasn't a straight-line affair, of course, but an overall progression of fits and starts across millennia.[9] As social and cultural practices grew more complex, there was more to read in others' minds. This resulted in the development of still more complex mental models.

The cognitive psychologist Cecilia Heyes describes questions as "cognitive gadgets," thinking tools that arise more through cultural evolution than genetic change.[10] The more valuable a cognitive gadget is, the more likely it is that it will be passed on through instruction or imitation.[11] Throughout history, innovations followed from the big questions of the day. The seventeenth century's How do I harness electricity? turned into the nineteenth century's How can we make this available on a wide scale?

Today, certain big questions evolve as businesses evolve. The guiding question for an emerging brand may be, How am I different from everything else on the market?, but as it matures it must ask, How do I share my story with new markets? As the culture of the company (and the market) changes, the questions evolve to match pace.

Questions go hand in hand with analogical thinking and metaphor, which enable us to find similarities in differences, a crucial part of thinking panoramically and metaphorically. Asking questions can lead to discoveries of connections between such varied phenomena as the preening actions of waterfowl and design of cell phone cases.[12]

ASKING GOOD QUESTIONS

We typically ask different questions of different types of people (colleagues, superiors, subordinates, customers, family members, etc.). In every case, your assumptions about and feelings toward the person you're questioning affect how you ask the question and, as a consequence, the answer you receive. A brand manager might ask a parent why they use Brand X. Or she might ask what I call a generic question that can produce an array of insights relevant for all brands.

What makes a question wrong or right is its decision-making value—that is, how helpful its answer is, not how easily its answer can be found. Sometimes a simple change in wording can yield dramatically different results in terms of helpfulness. For example, a company we worked with was contemplating offering a new service. When the brand team began testing the market, they experimented with different questions. Roughly half of those surveyed were asked: "Would you recommend this service to a friend or colleague?" A large majority responded very positively, which seemed like good news for the brand team.

The other half of interviewees were asked the same question with a minor twist: "Would you recommend this service to a friend or colleague, or not?" The addition of those two extra words "or not" led to much less positive results. Apparently, the wording granted the interviewees permission to put their negative feelings into words. This seemingly small alteration greatly improved the decision-making value of the question, as it raised new doubts about the wisdom of a full-scale launch of the service.

The decision-making value of a question is best assessed by eliciting or simulating contrasting answers in advance and deciding on what actions you would take for each. If different actions are suggested by the different answers, then the question can be judged good for decision-making. That said, it is surprising how often the same action would follow regardless of the answer. That may signal a different issue: seeking data after the fact to justify a decision that's already been made.

Almost all the executives we interviewed stressed the importance of questions, and several had unique ideas for ways of questioning that can lead to better answers. Several are described below.

SUNRISE OR RESET QUESTIONS

Let's begin with an idea shared by the CEO of a global agricultural company that I've found very constructive, both in the classroom and in my work with clients. This CEO noticed that key executives often came to him with ideas for addressing difficult problems without being able to provide sufficient detail about what inspired them. When he challenged them to describe the question that led to their recommended action, managers "seemed to reverse engineer questions to fit the answers they already had in mind." If the problem involved declining sales in a region of the world, for example, the question they would come up with was "How do we address declining sales in region X?" But the CEO wanted them to probe the problem more deeply. In his words, "I would be more [impressed] if they wondered about causes more than consequences."

So, he began pressing his colleagues for their "sunrise questions," to "expand [their] thinking to include novel, even risky ideas." In the context of the problem of declining sales in a particular global region, examples of sunrise questions might be: How can our company energize and excite our customers in that market? or How can we respond creatively to the infrastructure problems affecting sales there? To be clear, the CEO welcomed conventional questions, too, so long as they were appropriate.

I've adapted this CEO's approach when I think someone has prematurely defined a problem or its solution. Imagine if, when a difficult problem first becomes apparent, someone says in effect, "The real issue is . . ." or "The best response is . . ." Now, sometimes such statements are warranted, but typically not for truly messy problems. When I suspect things are not so simple, I find it productive to seek clarity with a situation-specific question like "What question did you ask whose answer leads you to this position?" Too often the answer is some version of, "Well, actually we didn't do that. We just assumed that . . ."

After allowing some (but not too much) silence or equivocation to occur, I follow up with questions like these: What other questions should we ask if we want to generate as many relevant, reasonable diagnoses (or solutions) as possible? and How can we be sure we are not accidentally excluding problem assessments (or solutions) that could be even more helpful or productive? Rather than the CEO's sunrise questions, I call these reset questions. Although they can still result in automatic responses, far more often they elicit bolder, more novel, and more fruitful thinking.

A GAME OF TAG

Difficult or messy problems are non-routine. As such, they often require non-routine questions to spur novel thinking. Unfortunately, many people are taught from a young age that all questions have right and wrong answers that must be chosen from among a set of established options—which is very different from seeking and even creating novel answers. This leads to another questioning approach, this time from a renowned historian of science I interviewed.

Without using the term *serious playfulness*, this historian described its presence in her own work and in her mentoring of students. She encourages engaging in an imagined game of tag with three players: the question, curiosity, and the answer. Any player can be tagged as "it." If answer were tagged, students would discuss a particular answer that had arisen in class. When they were finished, she'd ask who answer should tag next, curiosity or question? Or should the game end, reflecting a fully satisfactory answer? She noted regretfully that participants often chose to end the game prematurely. One way to avoid that is by asking students to debate the merits of tagging one or the other. Tagging curiosity means asking if you've been sufficiently curious especially about what you don't know. For instance, what isn't known that is preventing a better solution or outcome? Tagging question means exploring a different hypothetical question.

This game can be especially helpful when a decision-maker or, say, a brand team has nagging questions, vague suspicions, or doubts about something, or hunches they want to pursue. These states may signal the presence of unconscious feelings that serious playfulness can help surface and articulate.

A CASE STUDY ILLUSTRATING A GAME OF TAG

A small company is exploring what the next few years might look like as the rise of AI affects their services and how people conduct business. Like many companies their size, they want to be proactive and continue doing what they do best in an evolving, increasingly ambiguous marketplace. They don't even know the right questions to ask—yet. They decide to play a game of question-answer-curiosity tag in hopes of articulating their currently vague suspicions and nagging doubts. What are these feelings trying to tell them?

> **Question:** How will AI influence our presence in the marketplace? Answer, tag. (e.g., "You're *it*.")
>
> **Answer:** Difficult to know for sure, but it's possible that many of our current customers will turn to AI services instead ours. I'm afraid our service will become less relevant. Curiosity?
>
> **Curiosity:** To build on that . . . I wonder how our current customers will feel after a while of using AI services. Maybe they'll find them valuable. But I wonder if there's something valuable about our offering that AI can't offer. Question, tag.
>
> **Question:** In that case, my question is—What part of what we do is irreplaceable? Curiosity, back to you.
>
> **Curiosity:** That's a great question. I wonder if this includes not only our services but our relationships with customers. And—to explore further—it's important to think about the difference between how this will affect our current customers and how it will affect new customers. Maybe we need to revisit how we attract new customers. Answer, tag.
>
> **Answer:** About the relationships piece—I like the idea of developing a different strategy for new versus current customers. I think we should look into what exactly our current customers appreciate the most about us, and what pieces they consider less important. A survey or informal outreach will give us a sense of where to focus our efforts to reach new customers. Question, tag.
>
> **Question:** What happens if we discover that AI can outperform us in providing our current customers with what they want most? Tricky. Should we consider adding new services on top of what we already offer, or focus our energy on doing what we do best? Answer, back to you.

Answer: I think we need to confront that head on in our survey. But first let's make sure we don't bias our data with wishful thinking that might blind us to new ideas. We need to simulate alternative good news–bad news results before going into the field.

The game of tag continued in this case and proved very valuable. It expanded the team's imagination and opened their thinking about basic forces at play in the marketplace. This expedited their taking action on the information they developed and greatly reduced their post-survey regrets about questions they had missed or wished they had framed differently.

DIFFICULT QUESTIONS

Hard questions demand significant cognitive resources both to pose and to answer; as such, they are taxing.[13] But easy questions typically aren't as productive. Hard questions are those arising from a clearly identified area of ignorance. They are questions that often have to be asked in multiple ways to understand the small but important differences that can arise from how they are framed. All questions are hard if the learning environment doesn't reward question-asking. There is another factor that makes asking certain questions difficult. Interviewees often noted that important questions were skirted because they implied criticism of colleagues by simply asking them or because of the answers that would be found.

An easy question about a proposed decision is, What will it achieve? The answer is predictable: simply point to the problem the decision is intended to address and declare that it will make it go away. A harder question is, How will this decision achieve success? This question requires causal explanations. The answer goes from a blithe assurance of success to a more cautious "it *could* work," which is more honest and realistic.

In market research, the so-called easy question might be, What are people thinking and feeling about this particular product, brand, or company? (I say "so-called," because when pursued correctly, this question isn't easy at all!) A more difficult question might be, How can we share these thoughts and feelings with the client so they can make the best use of them to build their strategy? Answering the difficult question requires more thought partnership and trust from the client, as well as significantly more forethought, but it is much more valuable than simply providing them with data that doesn't tell them a story or offer a way forward. Ask yourself:

- Am I judging my questions by how helpful their answers are, or how easily they can be found?

MOTIVATIONAL QUESTIONS

Sometimes we pose questions or stimulate others to ask questions to draw them into a story we're telling. In the case of fiction writers, this isn't a metaphor—fiction writers quite literally put questions to their readers or stimulate them to ask questions about the story. Stephen King describes this skill in his book, *On Writing: A Memoir of the Craft*. Narratives, he suggests, need to trigger unconscious questions in their readers.[14] These stimulate curiosity, propelling them on to the next paragraph, page, and chapter for answers. The question to ask of your marketing communications, such as brand story development and advertising, is the following: Is the communication first stimulating a viewer's questions before it offers an answer?

This critical action of stimulating questions may occur so quickly that viewers are unaware of their questions. Even so, it is a major reason viewers will feel ownership of the "answers" being delivered. This is consistent with the argument that questions are themselves insights and register in similar ways.

But this process occurs in other contexts, too. A marketer for Product A asks potential customers questions that will motivate them to seek out Product A as opposed to Product B. An ad or point of purchase display may do this directly but also through cues that prompt a brand-switching question to "naturally" occur to the consumer. The questions raised in any artful narrative, be it an advertisement, a hiring notice, a feature film, a stump speech, or a Stephen King novel, emerge from a process of conceptual blending that is sometimes called cocreation, in which authors and readers jointly produce both questions and their answers.[15]

Maybe (hopefully!) you are already cocreating ways to use these examples in your own projects. I'll pose a few more sample questions for inspiration:

- What questions might your messages raise in your audience?
- When and where do you expect them to cocreate meaning, and what do those cocreations look like?
- Are they cocreating more than you expected, or something different than you would hope?

These are important questions to ask and consider when crafting your messages to your audience, whether they are consumers, coworkers, or readers.

USING QUESTIONS TO DETECT ERRORS

Causal thinking produces minds that are optimized to anticipate or forecast future consequences and their events.[16] Being able to think predictively has major survival value. But the path to sound answers is typically littered with mistakes or errors. The fear of making errors is rivaled only by the fear of confronting them. Both fears severely dampen our natural tendency to ask questions.

While encounters with errors are hardly fun, recognizing them is one of the most valuable insights you can have for moving forward. Here, an inner Clairvoyant and Wizard (you met these personages in chapter 2) are two of the best friends an open mind can have. As you'll recall, the Clairvoyant is adept at asking what may be missing from the information, ideas, or mental models under discussion, while the Wizard is adept at solving problems, especially those caused by faulty causal reasoning. The Wizard's suspicious mind is always questioning predicted outcomes.

Most executives I've interviewed spoke at length about the importance of asking the kinds of questions that can either prevent errors or repair the damage they caused. The challenge is that "errors are not prone to announcing themselves in a clear and timely way," as one put it. One question that's always helpful to ask is: Do your errors in thinking become evident before or after you implement a solution? It sounds like a trick question, but it's not. Many interviewees described how a common finding in postmortems was the presence of a "shoot first, aim later" attitude born of overconfidence, a false sense of urgency, a fear of being wrong (discouraging risk-taking), unwarranted imitation of another company's actions, inappropriate research methods, and incomplete data. Any one of those things, let alone combinations of them, can create a large potential error zone for decision-makers to navigate. These errors are what the Am I? and Are we? probes are intended to prevent.

When managers don't value error-sensing efforts, they misjudge messy problems as routine ones.[17] Those misjudgments can be costly. The executive who introduced Gabriella (see box 1.1 in chapter 1) to me summed this up nicely: "Firms will throw a lot of money at a problem before they'll change their thinking about it."

When using questions to uncover errors, two targets to lock onto are data and assumptions.

QUESTION DATA

We often hear "the data speaks for itself," especially when someone wants to shut down further discussion. This is reflected in the cartoon in figure 4.1. People tend to hold up data as beyond question, particularly when it takes numeric form. However, data is dumb; it doesn't speak on its own. Or, as the famous market researcher Vincent Barabba puts it, "Data don't say anything, only models do."[18] And models, he points out, are created by imperfect humans.

Data requires interpretation, and where there's interpretation, there's the possibility for error. Companies and individuals can go wrong with data in other ways, too, notably by delaying interpretation in favor of more data collection. Companies are always trying to improve their forecasts, which seems to justify more data collection in the hope that it will speak for itself, releasing the company from the challenging task of interpretation.[19] Finally, the method used to determine which data to collect and which to ignore may be based on erroneous thinking. This is why it is important to make time to interrogate data and data-collection methods instead of assuming they tell a complete story in raw form.

FIGURE 4.1   The Confirmation Bias at Work.

Let me ask a question that reveals exactly the answer I'd like to hear.

TOM FISH BURNE

SOURCE: MARKETOONIST, LLC.

Ask yourself:

- Am I able to imagine multiple stories emerging from the same data set?

- What do I prioritize when I interpret data—strength of pattern, what's unique, what answers my question cleanly?

- If someone with different priorities saw this data, what story might they tell?

QUESTION ASSUMPTIONS

The philosopher of science Michael Strevens once observed that the heart of scientific logic is human.[20] This subjective aspect of science is a topic of great interest and importance. Management scientists often discuss it in terms of the inevitable assumptions that support decisions, many of which are hidden below a decision-maker's level of awareness.

Any assumption underlying a decision has a chance of being wrong, which means that as assumptions proliferate, the possibility of error increases. When a decision feels right, assumptions often go unstated and therefore unexamined. They may even be used unconsciously as evidence.[21] As momentum for a "go" decision builds, unconscious individual and organizational biases arise to protect and reinforce it. This is why a formal process for routinely identifying and challenging assumptions is so important. Ask yourself:

- Am I building safeguards and checkpoints into protocols to ensure our assumptions are regularly reviewed and challenged?

- Am I inviting fresh eyes onto projects that might see what I've become blind to due to overexposure and reinforcement over time?

TEST ASSUMPTIONS

Open-mindedness in the form of an equal opportunity methodology can help transform human subjectivity into a plus rather than a minus.[22] This requires framing and empirically testing competing subjective judgment, preferably simultaneously. For example, if you are testing a product to find out why consumers choose it for a particular occasion, you must also allow consumers the option to mention that they *don't* choose it for that occasion—that is, supplementing a check-the-box question with a fill-in-the-blank section, or allowing for open-ended interview questions instead of only yes-or-no questions. Human subjectivity can be a useful guide to project set-up and which methodologies you decide to use. However, it also means first identifying what you hope the data will support and then ensuring that the project design and planned analysis allows for disconfirming data to emerge as well.

MUTUAL MIND-READING ATTEMPTS AND UNCONSCIOUS INFLUENCES

We have noted that a questioner's thinking can seep into a question and thus bias responses to it.[23] People make unconscious inferences about what the questioner is seeking and, in many cases, supply the answers they believe the questioner wants. This is not a surprise to readers familiar with survey and laboratory research, or who conduct focus groups. It happens regardless of how a question is delivered (whether in informal conversation, a group discussion, a formal interview, or written survey). Nor are questioners generally aware of their biases.

We've seen how the mere addition of the words "or not" changed answers to the question, Would you recommend this service to a friend or colleague? Here are other examples that show how tweaking a question can radically change results:

- When asked what children most needed to prepare them for life, 61.5 percent of a representative sample chose "To think for themselves" when this alternative was offered on a list. But when no list was presented, only 4.6 percent volunteered an answer that could be assigned to this category.

- When asked how successful they have been in life, 34 percent reported high success when the numeric values of the rating scale ranged from −5 to 5. But when the numeric values ranged from 0 to 10, only 13 percent did.

- When asked how often they experience a variety of physical symptoms, 62 percent of a sample of patients reported symptom frequencies of "more than twice a month" when "twice a month" was the lower bound on the scale (all other options were more frequent). But when "twice a month" was in the highest bound on the scale (all other options were less frequent) only 39 percent chose "twice a month."

Let's explore another example. When a survey question about life satisfaction preceded a question about how satisfied people were in their marriages, a correlation of .32 was obtained between the two questions. When the questions were reversed, the correlation was .62. Now, you might be tempted to conclude that the "real answer" is somewhere in between. But finding a middle ground between two potentially wrong answers will not produce the correct answer. A second experiment was conducted in which respondents were informed in advance that both questions would be asked. Then the questions were posed as before, alternating which one came first. This time, the order of questions didn't matter. In both cases, the correlations were statistically nonsignificant.

As for questioners, sometimes they can be so sure of their mind-reading abilities—and their ability to trace proper, logical effects springing from perceived causes—that they will disregard the answers their respondents give them if they don't accord with their expectations. Our self-confidence in our own reasoning ability is such that if we feel that an answer doesn't quite add up, we'll likely supply and even act on one that we feel does.

Hopefully this doesn't scare you off from asking questions, although it can shake one's confidence to see such large differences emerge from seemingly small changes in how a question is worded. The important takeaway is to be cognizant of the fact that *how* you ask questions matters greatly. Consider asking the same question in different ways to understand more fully what people really think. Even if you believe you've collected the "right" answer, keep probing with more questions in case it actually means something different than you think. Finally, consider creating a space for questions that explore *why* interviewees answered as they did, because more connections may be lurking beneath the surface.

If you're worried that you're not asking the "right" question or receiving the "right" answers, don't lose faith in your research. There are always different ways to phrase a question, and exploring them will get you closer to the right answers than if you don't ask the questions at all. There is no one magic question—but there *are* questions that are more or less appropriate for what you're hoping to find out. Ask yourself:

- Am I asking my questions in more than one way, in order to capture the nuances between different question formations?

- Do I assume that others understand my question in the way that I mean it?

- Am I aware that they might try to answer my question the way they think I want them to answer, and do I guard against these biases?

CONCLUSION

Questions are always present in conversation, but often they are silent or invisible. On the surface, we are simply exchanging thoughts with a discussion partner. Many of those thoughts, however, arise from unverbalized questions that we simply assume are in the other's mind.

KEY QUESTIONS TO ASK MYSELF

1. Am I consistently leveraging the power of questions to drive exploration, uncover unexpected connections, and inform better decision-making, even when the answers are not immediately apparent or easily obtained?

2. Am I actively seeking out questions that illuminate parallels and commonalities across seemingly unrelated domains, embracing the power of analogical thinking to drive innovation?

3. Am I consistently evaluating the quality and value of my questions based on the usefulness and impact of the answers they generate, rather than settling for easily obtainable but less consequential responses?

4. Am I rigorously examining my assumptions and biases when formulating questions and interpreting answers, striving to ensure optimal clarity and comprehension on both sides of the exchange?

5. Am I proactively leveraging questions as a tool to uncover potential errors and prevent costly mistakes, consistently interrogating the quality and validity of my data and assumptions?

6. Am I staying alert to the potential for unconscious biases and mutual mind-reading, and actively working to mitigate them?

7. Am I attuned to the implicit questions underlying my conversations and interactions, recognizing that many of the thoughts exchanged stem from unverbalized queries?

KEY QUESTIONS TO SHARE WITH COLLEAGUES

1. Are we encouraging our teams to ask broadly focused questions that challenge assumptions and yield insights beyond our immediate scope, providing rich context for more targeted inquiries?

2. Are we actively promoting the use of sunrise/reset questions to inspire bold, novel thinking?

3. Are we fostering a culture of serious playfulness and rewarding this habit of mind?

4. Are we consistently challenging teams to ask and answer difficult questions, recognizing that navigating messy problems entails discomfort?

5. Are we employing motivational questions in all of our communications, to stimulate curiosity, engagement, and buy-in among key stakeholders?

6. Are we evaluating the quality of questions based on their decision-making value and helpfulness to our collective goals?

7. Are we instilling a culture of critical thinking and healthy skepticism, consistently questioning and carefully interpreting data to ensure sound decision-making?

8. Are we implementing formal processes for identifying and challenging assumptions to mitigate the risk of faulty decision-making?

FIVE

The Art of Being Curious

CHASING YOUR CURIOSITY

Engaging in serious play encourages managers to identify what they don't know and thus to articulate relevant productive questions. However, without energetic or "hungry" curiosity, finding useful answers is unlikely. This chapter encourages you to reflect on what curiosity feels like. How does it feel when it's satisfied? When someone says that "curiosity killed the cat," an apt reply might be "at least the cat died knowing!" or more optimistically, "but satisfaction revived the cat." Curiosity is much more than an indulgence, at least for some people—but perhaps not as many as we would like to have in our organizations.

In this chapter, we will define curiosity, explore its different types, examine cases that show how valuable it is in the workplace, and see how easy it is to stifle. Finally, we'll make the case for staying curious, even in a world that pushes for quick decisions and surface-level thinking.

Most people, especially those who consider themselves curious, would like to set a high standard for indulging their own and their colleagues' curiosity. However, being a basic need, curiosity is often difficult to assess, improve, and share. The Am I? questions that follow can help with that.

- Am I cultivating a mindset of joyous exploration, embracing curiosity as a catalyst for insights and a driver of personal and organizational growth?

- Am I fostering an environment that encourages curiosity, recognizing its power to uncover valuable insights and drive innovation, even in the face of pressure for quick decisions and surface-level thinking?

- Am I vigilantly guarding against curiosity's foes, which can stifle imagination and creativity and limit our ability to unlock the full potential of our minds?

WARM-UP

Human beings are naturally curious. When we don't understand the cause of an event or a phenomenon, we are driven to find an explanation. Finding one is satisfying, and so is the process of getting there. Indeed, it has been shown that opiate sensors in our brains are activated when we process information that seems to yield an understanding. Unfortunately, the drive often weakens with time.

When most adults see the rather odd-looking image shown in figure 5.1, they stop thinking about it once they decide what it is. What do you see in it? The face of an elderly woman, right? A bit peculiar looking perhaps but still an elderly woman. What else do you see? Quite likely nothing. Now turn this page upside down. What do you see now? Yes, a young woman.

Changing the orientation of the image changes what you see. When you change what you see, entirely new questions and ideas bubble up that might not have emerged. But changing orientation entails time and effort. The question, Are we looking at this the right way? is easily avoided when we have a sense of urgency, a lack of boldness, or when the costs of being wrong are more salient than the benefits of being right. Yet, as figure 5.1 shows, changing our orientation with, say, a novel question, might yield a very different insight.

For another example, what would you think if I asked you to tell me how a business executive is like a pirate? The negative facts relating to piracy and crooked businesspeople will likely come to mind first. But if you are curious enough to consider different perspectives, you can also find qualities in both that are admirable: a focus on the job at hand, knowing when to delegate tasks and how to build loyalty in their organization, being a sound planner, having a map, taking risks, and being alert to unexpected opportunities, among others. Curiosity impels you to keep going and to see a bigger, richer picture.

FIGURE 5.1   What Do You See?

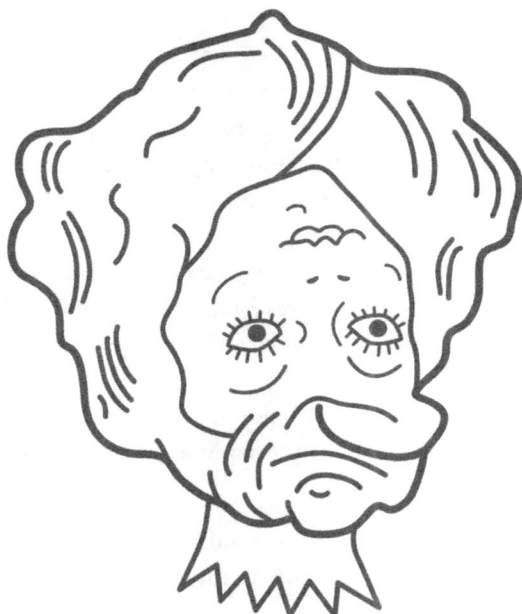

SO WHAT?

Some things are right in front of us, just waiting to be discovered. Seeing them, however, requires a different way of looking. We must always challenge the idea that we have seen all there is to see and remain alert for alternative views that produce different insights. Even when we are satisfied that we understand some-thing, we need to ask ourselves critical questions:

- Am I being curious enough?
- What cues am I missing?
- What change in perspective do I need?
- What am I most uncertain about?
- What disconfirming evidence about a position am I missing or even avoiding?
- Do other people see things that I don't?

WHAT IS CURIOSITY?

Curiosity is our response to our need to know, and as such is a catalyst for insights. As one of the leaders we interviewed put it, "It is the itch we want to scratch." Another described it as "the desire to replace question marks with exclamation points." The psychologist Susan Engel refers to curiosity as having a hungry mind."[1] Your own curiosity led you to pick up this book and persist in reading this far.

Curiosity can be sparked by the suspicion that something we accept as true—for example, a painting is a representation of something that exists in the real world—is not. Curiosity tells us there is more to be found, discovered, or understood.

In an aesthetic context, the puzzle of not knowing can be enjoyable. Yet in many cases curiosity makes us uncomfortable, as its nagging questions don't let us rest. Ask yourself:

- Am I driven to satiate my "hungry mind"—and the minds of my peers—by clearing pathways to search for what's missing, or to uncover new perspectives about known information?

The following business case shows how teams of researchers and managers became curious about unexpected clues they could have easily dismissed as simple anomalies.

CASE STUDY: CROP SEEDS

When you think of farmers, you probably think of fierce, stoic, independent people who are relatively matter-of-fact. Our client, a global agribusiness, wanted us to help them gain a deeper understanding of farmers' feelings about crop seeds, so we initially expected our interviews to yield some technical details about their choices, and maybe their feelings about some brands. We could have let these assumptions narrow our research and keep it within the bounds of these preliminary hypotheses. But our initial interviews sparked our curiosity to the point where we realized we needed to refocus the investigation, from the farmers' choices of seeds to how deeply those choices meshed with their feelings about their lives, legacies, and deepest anxieties. The final crop was important, of course. But the farmers' sense of their identities was even more important, and it was clear the seeds played play a central role in that.

Instead of asking only about seeds, we realized we also needed to know: *"Why* do you farm?" Farmers see their work as a generational saga, in which land and knowledge are passed on. This gives them a sense of purpose and connection. Farming also entails a delicate balance between risk and reward. Deciding which seeds to plant involves not only economic calculations but emotional and ethical considerations. Yield and cost figure in their choices, to be sure, as do the risks of crop failure and market fluctuations. But we learned that seeds are even more deeply connected to farmers' self-esteem. When a crop fails, farmers feel like *they've* failed.

Our curiosity led us to a paradox: While farmers cherish the autonomy and freedom that come with managing their own land, they're acutely aware of their dependence on factors beyond their control such as weather, government policies, and global markets. This fosters a complex relationship with the land and their communities. Had our curiosity not led us to dig deeper, we would have never reaped such valuable insights.

HOW CURIOSITY WORKS

Some say curiosity is the bedrock of human cognition. This especially includes imagination and creativity. We may be curious about something we clearly do not know or perhaps suspect is missing without knowing exactly what it might be, only that it is important. This is *epistemic curiosity*, the desire to fill a knowledge vacuum. Then there are curiosities aroused about the basic assumptions being made by managers, the models they employ, the specific research tools used, and even the assumptions made by people responding to research questions. These instances of curiosity are sometimes labeled *ontological curiosities*. Oftentimes, too, we are curious about the origins of differences among our colleagues when they interpret data differently than we do. Such puzzlement is a kind of *semantic curiosity* that asks, what assumptions are they making that I am not?

Indulging curiosity is certainly essential for all the other actions of an open mind—and for the survival and evolution of our species. Yet for all that, curiosity is not well understood.[2] For example, we often don't know where our knowledge stores are lowest.[3] As a result, we may prematurely declare an avenue of exploration a dead end or write it off as too demanding. We may decide that we already know the answers to matters colleagues are curious about. Sometimes, too, we are reluctant to admit we don't have answers.

Curiosity is an adaptive tool we are endowed with early in life, so when people claim they are born with it, they're not entirely wrong. But like everything else in life, it is shaped by society and culture.[4] The psychologist Cecilia Heyes regards curiosity as a tool that is socially constructed and acquired.[5] It's also a skill, and like tools (and most other skills), it can get rusty if we don't use it.

Interestingly, there is evidence that curiosity is a basic disposition across topics. Of course, we may be more curious about some domains than others. But people with high levels of scientific curiosity typically don't turn this trait off when they are contemplating politics, sports, or art. They are likely to be open to information that defies their opinions about contested issues.[6] For curious, open-minded people, questioning things and questioning themselves are two sides of the same coin. Curiosity widens our comfort zones. Once a comfort zone has been stretched, it never quite returns to its narrower boundaries.

The following thought experiment gives an intuitive feel for how curiosity works. Imagine that your—and everyone else's—level of curiosity about food is suddenly *cut in half*. Assume that you remain just as hungry as usual, but you're simply less interested in exploring new foods.

What do you think the economic and social impact would be? What would happen to food-focused television programs, magazines, newspaper columns, and books? How might food-dependent businesses such as supermarkets, restaurants, wine and liquor stores, catering services, and all their dependent industries be affected? What would the impact be on social and business meetings, on destination locations for social and work events, and even on holiday travel? What would the consequences be for the farmers we just met in the case example—the seeds they buy, the food they cultivate, their self-esteem, the value of their land?

Now, consider what might happen if curiosity levels about food were not halved but *doubled*. Would you dine out substantially more often to sample new and different restaurants and cuisines? Would you begin subscribing to (more) food magazines and collect more cookbooks? Would food advertising have a greater impact on you? What crops might the farmer and his peers consider raising? What industries would suffer if more money was spent on food-related goods and activities? Answers to these questions ought to suggest how essential curiosity is in driving the well-being of just about any economic sector. Ask yourself:

- Am I considering what happens when society's curiosity in certain areas waxes and wanes?
- How can I leverage this strategically to either work in accordance with it or even try to change what people are curious about?

TYPES OF CURIOSITY

There are many other types of curiosity besides the few I mentioned above (epistemic, ontological, and semantic). Here are a few of the most important:

DIVERSIVE AND SPECIFIC CURIOSITY

Two types of curiosity have special relevance to creative problem-solving and decision-making: *diversive curiosity* and *specific curiosity* (also known as *scouting curiosity* and *trapping curiosity*, respectively).[7] Diversive curiosity is an interest in exploring unfamiliar topics and learning something new. Specific curiosity is an interest in seeking information to reduce uncertainty and fill in knowledge gaps.

Diversive curiosity is a generative demand or requirement for imagination and creativity. Without the need to satisfy our curiosity about a knowledge deficit, we are unlikely to engage in divergent thinking about solutions. As we'll see in our chapter on panoramic thinking, diversive curiosity and the broadened vision it brings are essential for providing analogies—the very foundation for creative thinking.

If diversive curiosity has been likened to scouting an area to find interesting things to address in the future, specific curiosity has been likened to trapping: you return to the territory you scouted to capture something interesting for more detailed study. The challenge is that too often we do our scouting in other people's traps and so miss alternative solutions. This happens when we simply mimic what another brand or company is doing. These are circumstances when you need to ask yourself:

- Am I continually questioning the body of knowledge that my peers and I draw from and seeking new information to either add to it or change it?

- Am I keeping my curiosity honed as a sharp "cognitive gadget" that doesn't acquire rust?

CAUSE- AND CONSEQUENCE-RELATED CURIOSITY, AND CURIOUS WONDERING

Cause-related curiosity is when we ask, How is this possible? Where did this come from? *Consequence-related curiosity* is when we ask, What's going to happen next? Consequence-related curiosity drives us to worry about what could happen if we are wrong, or even if we are right. There is another kind of curious wondering that leans further into the unknown to challenge imagination. It involves curiosity about what a perfect though impossible solution to a problem would look like. This kind of aspirational thinking is reported to substantially broaden the range of possible solutions being considered. People who indulge in these types of curious wondering tend to do it for the sheer joy of it, while it also strengthens their ability to manage uncertainty. In a recent study, this type of curiosity was singled out as having the highest correlations with well-being, life satisfaction, and meaning.[8] I may add that joyous exploration is also the most prominent curiosity component of playfulness. The following example demonstrates cause- and consequence-related curiosity in action.

Case Example: Hair Management

A project for a major hair products firm focused initially on men's feelings about graying hair. But early on, we encountered a previously overlooked dynamic that the client felt merited closer scrutiny. Cause-related curiosity led us to think, "Hang on—feelings on gray hair don't just spring out of nowhere. What else is involved here? Maybe we should examine thoughts and feelings about the cause of gray hair—getting older." So we broadened the scope of our interviews to include their feelings about aging overall.

Male participants were still interviewed about how gray hair affects their identity and social interactions. But their repeated use of metaphors related to "transformation" led us to explore how the physical signs of aging were linked to changes in how they saw themselves. We learned that there was a tension between the gains in respect and wisdom associated with gray hair and the loss of youth. The team could have left it at that, but instead became even more curious and decided to push more deeply into the interviewees' language. This produced unexpected but very useful insights into how societal standards influence self-perception and self-esteem, resulting in a new metaphorical theme we called "acceptance."

For some, acceptance meant reconciliation with societal standards that value youth over age. Others embraced their gray hair as a symbol of life experience and maturity. Many men saw hiding their gray as embarrassing and even clownish. Some compared it to wearing face paint at a football game. But they still wanted to *feel* youthful, as indicated by their many references to driving fast sports cars. So how could the hair products company innovate to resonate with this theme of "acceptance" that was so important at this stage? This is where consequence-related curiosity comes in. How could the company incorporate these insights into what was going to happen next with their brand?

We had unlocked a story that embraced both the natural pace of change and the paradox that aging men want to look youthful yet natural. Because graying was gradual, getting rid of it should be, too—an insight that led to new product innovations. This became absolutely clear when the team wondered about the "perfect though impossible solution" to the "problem" of gray hair. Funnily enough, the "instant gray away" wasn't the perfect solution for the interviewed men. Neither was never going gray at all, since the prestige of gray was aspirational—at the desired time. Instead, the "perfect solution" lay somewhere between adjusting the natural pace of graying as well as feeling like the pace of appearance matched the individual's self-image.

DEPTH- AND BREADTH-ORIENTED CURIOSITY

Yet another way of characterizing curiosity is to think of it as either depth- or breadth-oriented. *Depth-oriented curiosity* impels us to immerse ourselves in the minutiae of a specific question; *breadth-oriented curiosity* compels us to widen our scope, engaging in lateral and panoramic thinking. The relative depth and breadth of our curiosity is strongly correlated with our tolerance of uncertainty and our openness to starting all over again, if necessary.

The question this raises is: How comfortable are you with being uncomfortable? And for how long? This, we'll see, relates to whether one views ambiguity as a foe or a friend. A major conclusion from my interviews can be summed up this way: The greater the ability to sustain curiosity before it is satisfied, the greater the willingness to embrace ambiguity and the more likely someone is to be creative. Alternatively, sustained curiosity in ambiguous circumstances encourages creative thinking and outcomes.

Whether or not we're comfortable isn't always in our control.[9] Conditions, including the wishes or directives of other people, sometimes require us to follow paths we wouldn't have otherwise chosen, causing us to feel lost and perhaps less motivated. We will discuss the notion of serendipity in a later chapter, but it's worth noting here that such paths can also lead to favorable encounters we would have missed. This attitude of opportunism was very evident among the executives we studied. No one said it in quite this way, but as a group they described their determination to make the most out of difficult circumstances, especially when those were not of their making.

Being lost while mind wandering has its upsides. Some people find long, meandering brainstorming sessions intolerable. Why are we spending so much time exploring these ideas when we won't use half of them?, they might sigh. We've all been in these circumstances, perhaps even contributed to their occurrence. My personal experience is that efforts to rein in the diversity of ideas can be counterproductive. It leads to the premature dismissal of gateway ideas. These are ideas that can potentiate or empower other ideas that are helpful.

While it's true that some meetings really don't need to be as long as they are, it's also true that "getting lost" can lead you to new information you didn't consider at first—which makes getting lost a worthwhile pursuit, even if doesn't feel like the most business-efficient one. Call it taking the scenic route instead of the highway if you like. The insights you gain don't have to be immediately relevant to the project at hand to have value—the desire to know is healthy in its own right. It provides the seeds for solving future problems.

Studies in the sociology of science see the distinction between conceptual learning and instrumental learning as having more to do with motivation than utility, as conceptual knowledge is often the precursor of instrumental or applied knowledge. The cross pollination of ideas in a brainstorming session may lead to a valuable insight for the next project. So ask yourself:

- Am I applying my curiosity to explore both unfamiliar topics farther afield as well as information that fills my immediate knowledge gaps?
- Do I know when it's strategically helpful to widen or deepen my scope of information-gathering?

Taking the extra time to indulge your curiosity almost always pays for itself.

EMPATHIC CURIOSITY

Empathic curiosity—our interest in others' thinking—is especially important at work. Empathy is not about being right or wrong, but about accessing and understanding alternative perspectives. Learning about someone else's thinking broadens our own. The insights we gain may change our views, or aid in our efforts to modify the view of their holders. Empathic curiosity has room to thrive when each member of a team has a chance to be heard. But there is a catch: being heard and listening to others make you vulnerable to having your thinking challenged and maybe even changed.

The practice of mutual sharing and influencing is one reason group solutions to messy problems are often superior to those of individuals. It's no wonder that human-centric methodologies for solving complex problems like design thinking place such a high value on the power of interdisciplinary teams and cocreation. Mutual, empathic curiosity also characterizes most successful negotiations when self-interests are not quite so aligned.[10]

FOES OF CURIOSITY

Beneficial as it is, curiosity has its foes—mindsets and habits that tend to close rather than open our minds. I've introduced some of them already. Here are a few more:

PROXY THINKING

When we think by proxy, we abandon the exercise of our own minds and rely instead on sources we consider authoritative such as news networks, political leaders, and even machine-driven algorithms, allowing us to conserve our cognitive resources.[11] People that do this reflexively are curious in the way that zombies are curious—hardly at all![12]

Thinking by proxy is especially problematic when people (1) rely on authorities who confirm their own thinking, (2) are indifferent to the reasoning and evidence those authorities use, and (3) take positions that impact a far broader population than just themselves.[13] We can see the steep societal costs when we consider the US's shambolic reaction to the COVID-19 pandemic or the fact that a sizable minority of its population believes the 2020 presidential election was fraudulent.

The resource-conserving instinct isn't always bad, however. Sometimes it's necessary to allocate scarce resources like attention, time, skill, or money. But one danger of accepting others' thinking is that it can lead to uncritical imitation. This can be a problem because a shoe that fits another's foot won't necessarily fit your own, and if you commit to wearing it, you may find yourself with sore feet down the road.

CONFIRMATION BIAS

Confirmation bias is the tendency to collect and evaluate data in ways that unduly support our established positions. Its cousin is unwarranted confidence in specific information brought about by fears of what curiosity might find and an aversion to uncertainty. This is illustrated in figure 5.2. An overreliance on experts may contribute to this, as can the unconscious tendency to treat any information as true.

FIGURE 5.2 Fear of Curiosity.

SOURCE: MARKETOONIST, LLC.

DISMISSAL OF ANOMALIES

Anomalies demand special attention, requiring time, additional information, and sometimes skills we don't have, with the result that we may have to revise deeply rooted theories.[14] Since our attentional resources are limited, it's tempting to dismiss them as random noise. It's a temptation we should resist.

GROUPTHINK

When it comes to curiosity, groupthink is a particularly vicious foe. Whether we consider historical examples like the decision-making processes that led to the disastrous Bay of Pigs Invasion in 1961 or the decision to launch the Challenger despite the cold weather, or business examples like the ill-fated launch of New Coke, or Blockbuster's decision to pass on an opportunity to buy Netflix in 2000, groupthink is built on "rationalized conformity." Charlan Nemeth has noted the importance of disagreement in a world in which majorities bend reality in their favor.[15]

Groupthink gets even more powerful when the issue at hand is complex and involves ambiguity, as people mistake consensus for getting things right and clear. When we indulge our curiosity, we're granting ourselves permission to ask hard questions.

Another tool for overcoming groupthink is structuring brainstorming meetings intentionally so the most influential voices speak last or take on the role of "Socratic Questioners." For example, a project manager may wait to share her own insights until every member of her team has spoken, lest they simply defer to her. When the boss becomes the student asking questions, the team deepens their thinking.

FEAR OF FAILURE

All of the foes of curiosity share a fear of failure. Indulging our curiosity can lead us to pursue red herrings; it's easier by far to go with the flow and not challenge the consensus. We need to constantly ask ourselves, what opportunities are we missing because of our fear of failure? Do we really want to limit our universe of possibilities?

A CASE EXAMPLE OF AVOIDING CURIOSITY

An example involving a global electronics firm illustrates how not being curious for fear it may prove unproductive actually curtails innovation and the ability to respond to evolving customer needs. The firm in question ultimately recognized this as a cause of declining new sales leads along with loss of interest in their offerings at trade shows. This coincided with an increasing rate of employee turnover within their R&D group. With some assistance from a consulting firm, they learned their R&D team seemed generally satisfied with their new idea output. The outside firm provided evidence that their generation of new ideas was actually well below the industry norm and began to explore why that was the case. They eventually found that a culture had developed in which novel ideas that first appeared as dead ends were being prematurely dismissed as unworthy of further pursuit. In effect, the R&D group were asking themselves, Why change something that works so well? Their group leader expressed this as, "Well, we don't change canoes in midstream." Attitudes like this helped create a mindset among team members to the effect that their way of generating ideas had always worked before and they couldn't afford the time and effort to experiment with it. This produced a pattern of making safe decisions about what ideas to pursue further. This reached a point where truly novel ideas were being quickly dismissed as a counterproductive if their worth wasn't immediately evident. Surprise was ruled out before it could arise. Workbench engineers felt subtle penalties for "wasting time" pursuing their curiosity. This inadvertently encouraged ideas that could win easy, quick praise from their team leader. Eventually these patterns brought the R&D staff further and further from what was actually useful to the firm's customers who faced a rapidly changing technology environment.

Processes were set in place for the entire R&D team to have candid discussions about their "safe" operating mindset including their fears of failing and its stifling impact on the pursuit of curiosity. A few of the actions that followed included:

- Allocating more fiscal and especially time resources for pursuing bold ideas. This signaled that bold ideas were expected of everyone.

- To encourage curiosity as a team-based value, they constructed an electronic bulletin board, "Things I'm Entertaining Now," to signal to one another about where their curiosity was currently taking them. In this way, others could be enlisted to collaborate or suggest ideas for pursuing new directions to explore in their journey of curiosity. Bulletin board content soon became the sole topic for a highly anticipated monthly meeting for brainstorming about its contents. Serious play was very evident in these session and clearly stimulated curiosity.

- To counteract perfectionism, an emphasis was placed on the "beauty" of "ugly" starts. R&D engineers were encouraged to be proactive in identifying the blemishes on their ideas and seek constructive improvements. This also provided an atmosphere of mutual support that helped reduce the premature closure of curiosity for fear it might be a dead end.

In time, the team achieved a culture that valued curiosity and included the requisite safety structures so failure was not a paralyzing thought.

TECHNOLOGY AND CURIOSITY

Technology is a new Pandora's box for curiosity. By providing and easing access to so much information, it is a great ally. But on the downside, we can easily get lost in the oceans of data that are available to us as anyone who has gone down a Wikipedia rabbit hole can attest. Alternatively, we become so reliant on technology that we stop thinking critically about the results and solutions it provides.[16]

Think of quick results from internet searches as fast food: it's satisfying, it may even taste good, but it doesn't have many nutrients (and it has a lot of ingredients that aren't good for you). Nurture your curiosity by feeding it healthfully instead. All it requires is that you approach your search results with open-mind actions:

identifying questions and errors, engaging in panoramic thinking, befriending your ignorance, pursuing serious play, embracing ambiguity, nurturing wisdom, and, of course, indulging your curiosity.

CURIOSITY IN THE WORKPLACE

Is there room for curiosity in your workplace? How much latitude do you have to indulge yours? Does your workplace treat curiosity as a resource or an inefficiency? What does it mean to be curious at work? What does a curiosity-friendly work environment feel like, and whom could it serve?

When I posed such questions in our interviews, many responded that their companies considered curiosity fine in moderation. One interviewee who had just begun a new position as the chief marketing officer for an industrial products firm told me he was shocked by the tepid reaction his new colleagues displayed when he asked them what they were most curious about. Another noted that he could "always tell when someone is faking curiosity simply to make you uncomfortable or to show off versus [someone who is] truly inquisitive and feels stumped by something . . . [The latter] are who get my attention and the funding they want."

Curiosity is not a luxury or to be indulged only when you have extra bandwidth, but a necessity. Whether we're asking How come? or What if?, curiosity is our ally. Here are some questions that demonstrate productive workplace curiosity:

- What generated the change in customer behavior?
- Why did the media misunderstand our message?
- What did we miss when we were negotiating the new terms of the contract that resulted in their turning our offer down?
- What if we try to change our sales approach?
- How can we turn this into an opportunity?

Notice that all of these questions are open-ended. If you already have an answer in mind when you're asked such a question and you refuse to budge from it or consider other possibilities, then you're just faking curiosity. You're probably using the discussion to justify your answer, not explore what else it may reveal.

According to LinkedIn data, from 2020 to 2021, engagement for companies' posts about curiosity grew 158 percent across the platform. The same period saw a 90 percent growth in job postings mentioning curiosity, and 87 percent growth in mentions of job skills related to curiosity.[17]

Further encouraging news comes from SAS Institute's Curiosity@Work Report 2021. It highlights the benefits that managers link to curiosity, which include improved performance and job satisfaction, increased flexibility and adaptability, and more inclusive and collaborative work environments.[18] More than 70 percent of the managers it surveyed believe that curiosity is a valuable trait for employees, with almost 60 percent acknowledging that curiosity has real business impact.[19] Ask yourself:

- Am I encouraging a culture of curiosity in my workplace by setting an example with my own behavior?
- Am I providing the fiscal and time-related resources needed to explore ideas and celebrate successful examples that reinforce the understanding that curiosity is not a luxury but is a necessity to do our best work?

CONCLUSION

Unlocking the potential of an open mind requires you to actively train yourself. We suggest you begin your regime by pushing yourself to ask thoughtful questions, introducing yourself to varied people and contexts, and entertaining very different perspectives.

Can there be too much of a good thing? What if we lose ourselves in the curiosity vortex? These are valid concerns, and indeed, training your curiosity also means taming it. By taming it I don't mean suppressing or narrowing it, but rather learning how to use it smartly and make the most of it. Sometimes we do need to leave something in the realm of the (for the moment!) unexplored so we can pursue other avenues more fully. Life is full of trade-offs.

Plenty of room for exploration remains. In closing, I want to challenge you to go beyond the cognitive and emotional framing of curiosity and explore it through all your senses. How does curiosity feel in your body? What does it sound like? How does it smell? What would curiosity look like if you were to picture it in a snapshot? Engaging in a multisensory exploration not only brings in new perspectives; it also invigorates your sense-making skills and your open-mindedness training routines.

KEY QUESTIONS TO ASK MYSELF

1. Am I making a consistent, conscious effort to indulge my curiosity, recognizing that it is a powerful tool for satisfying my unconscious sense-making needs and driving my personal growth?

2. Am I actively nurturing my curiosity through continuous practice, seeking out supportive environments, and understanding that a thriving curiosity is essential for maintaining an open and agile mind?

3. Am I welcoming the unexpected insights that curiosity can bring to my thinking and decision-making processes and embracing the discomfort of the unknown?

4. Am I regularly engaging in joyous exploration, allowing myself to wander intellectually and embrace the unknown to build my resilience in the face of uncertainty?

5. Am I vigilantly guarding against the temptation of proxy thinking, recognizing that while it may conserve cognitive resources in the short term, it ultimately leads to closed-mindedness and stunted growth?

6. Am I consistently demonstrating the courage to question my assumptions and the willingness to be vulnerable when my ideas conflict with others?

7. Am I actively training my curiosity to enhance its utility rather than suppressing or narrowing it, and using critical thinking and error sensing to guide my exploration?

8. Am I embracing a multisensory approach to curiosity, leveraging all my senses to open up new perspectives and continually refine my sense-making skills?

KEY QUESTIONS TO SHARE WITH COLLEAGUES

1. Are we consistently demonstrating and celebrating the value of curiosity in our workplace, recognizing its power to drive critical thinking, creativity, innovation, and organizational success?

2. Do we recognize that authenticity is essential for fostering an open-minded and productive work environment?

3. Are we actively challenging the notion that curiosity impedes quick decision-making and replacing it with the idea that suppressing curiosity leads to suboptimal outcomes?

4. Are we actively encouraging both diverse and specific curiosity in our problem-solving efforts, recognizing the unique value each brings to the creative process?

5. Are we consistently practicing empathic curiosity, demonstrating a sincere interest in our colleagues' perspectives and using this to inform and refine our own thinking?

6. Are we actively guarding against groupthink in our teams and implementing strategies to ensure all voices are heard and valued?

SIX

Panoramic Thinking

TRANSITIONING FROM HEDGEHOG TO FOX

Being authentically curious requires having the daring to pursue it even in unfamiliar territory. A hungry mind, after all, needs to know where the best restaurants are. This chapter tells you what it means to think like a fox or a hedgehog—and more importantly, when to switch back and forth between them. You'll learn why inviting a Formula One race-car pit stop team to a hospital emergency room was such a good idea, and I'll suggest who to ask for help when you're afraid you "don't know what you don't know" (spoiler: they may be further afield than you think). We'll understand the jobs that panoramic thinking can do and the challenges we face when pursuing it. Finally, we'll examine the connection between panoramic thinking and metaphor—and how to use them to your advantage.

Three particular questions will be helpful as you reflect on the ideas in this chapter. These questions will encourage you to be more strategic, proactive, and inventive as you travel beyond customary boundaries in seeking information.

- Am I strategically alternating between broad exploration and deep focus in my thinking to maximize insights?
- Do I proactively seek out surprising sources of expertise, even from very different fields, when confronting difficult problems?

- Am I leveraging the power of metaphor and analogy to reframe challenges, simplify complexity, and inspire creative solutions?

WARM-UP

A fragment of an ancient Greek text says, "A fox knows many things, but a hedgehog knows one big thing." The philosopher Isaiah Berlin explored the implications of this statement in a famous essay about how people see and learn about the world.[1]

For our purposes, hedgehogs tend to deepen their knowledge of just their "one big thing." This can be very limiting. The fox, on the other hand, eagerly seeks out all sorts of information, but lacks depth on any one topic. The two approaches are complementary, but they are seldom used together. When they are, it's called panoramic thinking.

A good metaphor for a fox-hedgehog partnership can be found in homebuilding. The general contractor is foxlike in that he or she knows about many things—electrical work, plumbing, finished carpentry, and so on. But the general contractor does not specialize in any one of them. To ensure that they are done properly, the contractor will call in an electrician, a plumber, a carpenter, etc. Those tradespeople are the hedgehogs. Together, they form a team that gets the job done.

EXERCISE

Think about the following questions:

- Is one creature, fox or hedgehog, more descriptive than the other of how you and your colleagues seek information? If so, which one?
- How often do you actively arrange for a mix of information-seeking styles?

As you reflect on these questions, remember that your team isn't just composed of humans. Which creatures do your information and AI systems resemble? Think about your notes, your databases, your libraries, in whatever form they take. Even consider the search engines you rely on. How would you describe the knowledge-seeking behavior of these "creatures"?

SO WHAT?

I don't like to pigeonhole people, and I don't believe you should do it to yourself. There are undoubtedly some occasions when your curiosity favors broad scanning and others when it is narrowly focused. Both produce insights. But even more insights arise when you employ a thoughtfully balanced approach.

An illustration of this comes from my client work. As part of the strategic planning for the launch of a new brand of bottled water, I was invited to assemble a panel of outside experts. I was encouraged to go broad, so I included a theologian, an anthropologist, a historian of science, and an ethnomusicologist, among other specialists. Their insights had a major impact on the marketing team's thinking about packaging, naming, and positioning. When it came time to develop promotional content, we decided to explore the cultural dimensions of sensory experiences. To that end, we brought in an expert on that topic for specific guidance. The exposure to many disciplines and their messages set the stage for our deepest dive yet.

Most leaders I've studied tend toward the foxlike, though they appreciate the value of the hedgehog's approach. Importantly, they know when to switch from one to the other, which is increasingly necessary in our digital and AI-impacted world.[2] Their rules for switching approaches are more or less as follows:[3]

1. In the early stages of problem-solving, they ask themselves and their colleagues questions like:
   - Are we thinking broadly enough?
   - Where else should we look for guidance?
   - Where is our knowledge incomplete?

2. After a solution is selected, they ask:
   - Are we focused enough?
   - Where do we need to drill down further?
   - What might we be missing that could impact our outcome?
   - Where can we find it? (This question may send them back to question 1.)

The questions take different forms in different circumstances but involve the same two tasks. First, a judgment is made about when and how to shift from a broad scanning mindset to a focused one. Then, a judgment is made about the best strategy for focusing in on an unfamiliar discipline.

WHAT IS PANORAMIC THINKING?

We live in a time of abundance, especially of information. Never in history has so much knowledge accumulated so quickly. The knowledge explosion is both a cause and a consequence of burgeoning specialization. Specialties tend to exist in silos, and while silos have much to teach each other, they seldom do. To change that you need leaders who are able to venture beyond their intellectual comfort zones. Doing so requires curiosity, daring, and most importantly, *analogical thinking,* the ability to see similarities in differences. Douglas Hofstadter and Emmanuel Sander called analogies "the fuel and fire of thinking,"[4] noting that they "spring up inside our minds numerous times every second. We swim nonstop in an ocean of small, medium-sized, and large analogies, ranging from mundane trivialities to brilliant insights."[5]

I describe this type of thinking as "panoramic" to suggest the many contexts in which similarities in differences can be found. The vistas are wide and extend in all directions! I like to think of panoramic thinking as wide peripheral vision. But you have to be willing to explore what catches your mind's eye.

How often do you hunt for ideas in unfamiliar disciplines? When did you last challenge yourself or your colleagues to do that? Less open-minded managers tend to answer these questions with some version of "I know I should but I don't." Why is that? Why don't they indulge their curiosity?

Time and other resource constraints are real, of course. But challenging problems have minds of their own and don't really care about your constraints. Moreover, advances in information systems and AI are rendering justifications involving limited resources less and less tenable.

THINKING ACROSS DISCIPLINES

There are many ways to insert your curiosity into other disciplines.[6] Frédéric Darbellay describes four levels of collaboration and integration of ideas.[7] They range from disciplinarity being the lowest level to transdisciplinarity being the highest level.

Disciplinarity refers to work within a specific field (e.g., marketing, finance, sociology, botany) or one of its subspecialties (e.g., business-to-business marketing, operations research, the sociology of science, art therapy, etc.). Disciplinary specialists are like sole proprietors who stay within their fields or subfields. Their work, however, has great value, not only within the discipline but potentially for other fields as well.

Multidisciplinarity occurs when the viewpoint of one discipline or field informs those of others. Think of it as an alliance. For example, my doctoral thesis in the sociology of science allied ideas from sociology with communication practices in theoretical high-energy physics.[8] One outcome was the design of a better global communications system for physicists.

Interdisciplinarity is more of a partnership with shared goals. To use another personal example, for several years I worked as a marketing expert in partnership with the National Institute of Mental Health. Our shared goal was to use marketing concepts to get advanced research into the hands of frontline practitioners faster.

Transdisciplinarity is like a merger. Consumer psychology, for instance, is an independent field formed by the joining of marketing and one or more areas in behavioral science.[9] The goal of the merger is to see deeper into the mind of the market. As with business mergers, certain unfamiliar thoughts are likely to come "onboard," requiring an acculturation or transition process to accommodate them. This entails a reexamination of existing ideas that may have to be changed or jettisoned. Some new ideas that seem relevant at first may simply not work out.

Let me take a moment in the midst of all this multidisciplinarity to stress that while open-minded executives are panoramic thinkers, they remain attentive to research and best practices in their home fields. When facing a difficult problem, a good first step is to inventory your "first responder" knowledge— the ideas and practices of your primary field. Sometimes that's as far as you'll need to venture for answers. But given the complexities and interdependencies of our fast-changing world, it is increasingly likely you'll need to search more broadly.

In doing so, it's important to remember that panoramic thinking is a dispositional or mindset tool, not a goal.[10] You're exploring other fields to find insights or ideas you otherwise wouldn't encounter, which—you hope—will help you address your problem. After finding those insights and ideas, they will need to be adapted.[11]

EXAMPLES OF PANORAMIC THINKING

When significant changes occur, you'll likely need to look beyond your home discipline's knowledge repository for answers to the new questions that arise. When recreational cannabis became legal in certain states, for example, there was very little in the way of systematic market research to help cannabis entrepreneurs. Some of them tackled the problem by seeking out research on ways healthcare companies promote products and practices subject to public misinformation and misuse.

Ask yourself:

- Am I forging alliances across disciplines that will add nuance and inspiration to the topic at hand, and am I contributing to other's projects as well as asking for inspiration for my own?
- Relatedly, do I make myself available as a cross-discipline resource?

BIOMIMICRY

One of the most interesting examples of panoramic thinking is the inspiration that architects and design engineers draw from biology.[12] This practice has many other labels. One term, "biospiration," hints at its value in generating novel insights. Research involving sharks, woodpeckers, mollusks, owls, and burdock plants have led to improvements in vehicle backup cameras, construction equipment, air filtration systems, fuel efficiency, and better ways of securing objects in zero gravity.[13]

Engineers tasked with designing safer construction tools first asked, "Where does shock absorption occur in nature? What mechanisms are involved? Who studies them?" Casting their nets wide, they found that woodpeckers' crania absorb tremendous shocks. When it was time to drill down, they asked, "How do we imitate nature's mechanisms for human use? Is there a specific biologist we can hire to guide us?"

FINDING SIMILAR PROCESSES IN DIFFERENT ENVIRONMENTS

It isn't just nature that inspires breakthrough metaphorical thinking. Great Ormond Hospital in London was desperate to find a better way to transfer patients from intensive care units to operating rooms, a chaotic, high-stress process in which too many life-threatening mistakes were being made. They began as foxes, asking, "Where might we learn about choreographing a team's actions to avoid disaster?" The answer they came up with was a Formula One pit stop, where up to twenty people collaborate to change four tires and fill a tank of gas in a matter of seconds. The Great Ormond team observed a Ferrari pit crew in action, and then invited its members to observe their processes at the hospital and make suggestions for improvements. The result? A whopping 66 percent reduction in errors.[14]

USING CONSTRAINTS TO ENCOURAGE CREATIVITY

Sometimes we feel constrained by the lack of experience others have in a novel area or when experts in those field are unavailable to guide our search and use of ideas they offer. That thinking can sometimes be a mistake and needlessly deprive you of insights. Consider an example of thinking further afield that was recently shared with me. It involved a research team trying to think like poets despite their never having attempted to write poetry.

The team did know that poets have to rely on structure and constraint, which can actually inspire their creativity. The sonnet, for example, requires a rigid rhyme scheme and number of syllables and emphases per line. Haikus are similarly dictated by rules on syllables and subject matter. And yet these strict forms have birthed some of the most inventive and poignant expressions of language in human history. A poet must be creative indeed to fit the object of their study into such tight rules, since it leads them to think about which rules they *can* break to achieve their goal. Conventional word order and grammar become flexible, and the poet must think about what other tools can be used to convey meaning compactly, such as using metaphors, alliteration, or repetition to underline certain thoughts—instead of writing "this idea is important!" in bold letters with lots of arrows (like we might do in a presentation).

Using this analogy the research team practiced thinking like a poet while brainstorming about how to revive a struggling restaurant chain. (None of the participants, I was assured, knew any more about poetry than what I've noted above.) Taking inspiration from the constraint of sonnet rules faced by poets, the team gave themselves artificial constraints that led to new ways of thinking. By setting rigid rules, they allowed themselves permission to be flexible in other areas. These included the following decisions or actions:

They agreed to disregard the obvious solution to their problem. Instead of jumping on the first plausible way forward, they decided to come up with as many alternative solutions as possible. An obvious solution would be to take cost-cutting measures like closing some locations and letting some staff go. However, they tabled this idea in lieu of other ideas like perspective-taking: What emotional benefits brought customers to their restaurants? How could they better cater to those emotional needs, instead of only considering the physical service of offering food? How could they learn which emotional needs were core to the brand, and which ones were open for adjustment? These questions let them explore where cost-cutting was and wasn't an option when it came to what was vital to their brand.

They also took time to think purely visually. Each team member drew on paper what the restaurant chain meant to them personally, and what they each believed the brand stood for. This helped illuminate what about the brand the team agreed on and where they differed and what was cohesive about the brand and what was variable. For instance, the restaurant's iconic light fixtures were in most drawings, as well as the fact that the restaurant was popular among large groups dining out together. At the same time, there was little overlap in the foods shown as being served. This exercise offered the team insight into what was well-loved and memorable about their brand, the kinds of gatherings they catered to, and the lack of any signature menu choice.

They took their ideas outside their team for feedback. Upon concluding their think like a poet exercise, each team member was tasked with gathering ideas from one other person *outside* their team. This included their sharing the pictures they drew just before finishing their discussion. It didn't matter who—it could be a conversation with a customer, with a colleague from an unrelated business, or a family member. One team member even interviewed his child to understand the seven-year-old's favorite memories at the restaurant. The team then reconvened with the additional ideas they collected thus refreshing their entire pool of thinking.

These "rules" weren't meant to lead directly to the answer. Rather, they were designed to encourage jumpstarting creativity by looking in unexpected places for original ideas. In this case, the decision to think like a poet broke the cycles of revisiting the same ideas over and over and helped them escape their well-worn ruts.

THE CHALLENGES OF PANORAMIC THINKING

Peering into unfamiliar domains can be demanding, as it requires us to revisit our intuitions, imagination, reasoning, and past uses of knowledge.[15] I can recall my early struggles as I began my study of neuroscience. Many of the disputes about brain structures, functions, and processes that I was reading about were still unresolved. It didn't help that participants in these disputes sometimes used different terms for the same things. Readers who have tried to learn a foreign language may recall their initial feelings of being lost and overwhelmed.

Two challenges in particular need to be addressed:

Inertia. When faced with a messy problem, it's much easier to hope that it will somehow sort itself out than confront it head on. Unfortunately, it almost never does. One consequence of the tendency to avoid tackling messy problems is that a staggering 40 percent of CEOs do not believe their companies will be economically viable by the end of this decade.[16] Would they have less reason for pessimism if they demanded more panoramic thinking in their companies, starting with themselves? The answer is very likely yes.

It's worth noting that most general research is in the public domain.[17] Accessing it requires little financial expenditure—*but you must go out and look for it!* This brings us to the next challenge.

Hypocognition. It's no wonder that we often feel flooded by information. The sheer glut of it contributes to the problem of not knowing where to look or what to look for. When we're not even aware of the concepts or ideas we're lacking, we're experiencing hypocognition.[18] The firm that asked for expert input from unfamiliar disciplines while preparing their bottled water launch was inoculating itself against hypocognition. Its marketers understood they were hedgehogs in need of a fox. It should be added, that the "fox" in this particular instance (me) felt that he also learned a great deal from the hedgehog/managers. Whether you are a generalist in need of a specialist, a specialist in need of a generalist, or somewhere in between - intentionally choosing a point of view (or style of thinking) that is different from yours will help you and your thought partners exercise open-minded behavior. Another way to think about this is whether your circumstances call for a variable focal length lens or a fixed lens. Most cameras have variable lenses, but habit confines us to just one setting. Important questions to ask yourself include these:

- Am I able to wade through the inertia that accompanies messy problems and the task of connecting disparate fields?

- What resources do I have to manage the potential flood of less relevant information?

- How do I prioritize action and make decisions based on what's relevant?

THREE KEY JOBS OF PANORAMIC THINKING

Panoramic thinking performs many jobs, when allowed to do so. Three deserve special mention.

JOB 1: FUEL CURIOSITY

Panoramic thinking is both a cause and a consequence of curiosity. It exposes us to intriguing ideas and the satisfactions that come from learning. Encountering alternative viewpoints also stimulates serious playfulness by encouraging experimentation. An example of that is what happened when an upscale supermarket chain hired architects specializing in fitness centers to redesign its delicatessen areas. Another example I've encountered involved having store managers and architects imagine themselves as shopping carts. What did the supermarket look like from the shopping cart's point of view? How would a cart redesign it? Explorations like these bring intuition, imagination, and careful reasoning to the table.

JOB 2: GENERATE WARM-UP IDEAS

Ideas that come from unfamiliar disciplines don't always prove practical. But even impractical ideas serve a purpose. In the words of an electronics manufacturer we interviewed, "They provide a kind of warm-up, like the batter loosening up in the on-deck circle." Another executive we interviewed talked about "stretching tolerance zones"; still another noted that such warm-ups are tools "for reminding colleagues of their creative potential."

JOB 3: ENCOURAGE US TO CROSS CATEGORIES, ANALOGIZE, AND CREATE METAPHORS

When we think panoramically, we venture into unfamiliar settings to look for ideas and insights that can help us solve problems in our home territory.[19] Note the metaphors I just used: "home territory" for our particular area of expertise; "unfamiliar settings" for other areas. Bahare Heywood, the first chief risk officer at the global law firm Clifford Chance, uses analogies to describe his role: "You are basically a firefighter. You're a diplomat. You're an investigator. You're an agony aunt."[20] Each of these comparisons brings a very long list of qualities to mind.

The ability to categorize was one of the first cognitive functions we humans developed. It is how we distinguish friends from foes, cars from aircraft, and a hand from a foot. We use that same ability when we find and use analogies to create metaphors. Categorization, analogy, and metaphor are deeply intertwined; all of them require us to change our viewing lenses, opening up an almost infinite world of concepts.[21] Once we notice their relevance, they are hard to ignore, and can transform our understanding.[22]

Aristotle celebrated the use of metaphors in his *Poetics*: "The greatest thing by far is to be a master of metaphor . . . It is a sign of genius, since a good metaphor implies an intuitive perception of the similarity in dissimilar things."

Poets and novelists aren't the only ones who use metaphors. You do too—every day, in every arena of your life. One linguist suggests we use an average of six metaphors per minute of speech.[23] As a quick test of this, try having a meaningful conversation with someone in which neither of you use metaphors.[24] You'll quickly grasp the point of the exercise. Many metaphors are drawn from your bodily experience. Recall the metaphor of a handshake I used in chapter 1 to represent a mind.[25]

Metaphor can open up new ways of looking at things, revealing hitherto unconsidered attributes and similarities. But there is a downside: metaphor can also trigger our unconscious biases. Consider the metaphor of the fox and the hedgehog. It refers to information-seeking, but other qualities associated with those animals likely also came to mind. The word *fox* suggests slyness, stealth, and trickery. The word *hedgehog* has associations with shyness or sensitivity—perhaps you thought of the hedgehog's dilemma, the philosopher Arthur Schopenhauer's observation that hedgehogs try to huddle together when they are cold but can't because of their sharp quills. (Yes, hedgehogs have a type of quill, though their sharpness is debated.) Schopenhauer wasn't talking about real hedgehog behavior, of course, but the emotional risks of intimacy. Unintended associations like those can lead you far astray.

Implicit association tests indicate that the unrelated meanings contained in metaphors influence our unconscious attitudes.[26] Sometimes strategists deliberately use the biases that metaphors activate. For example, using warlike metaphors to describe crime statistics can produce harsh, punitive public policy responses, while presenting the same statistics using metaphors relating to public health results in more prevention-oriented responses.[27]

RULES FOR USING METAPHORS

So how can we use metaphors honestly and responsibly? The following rules come from my experiences, those of my Olson Zaltman colleagues, and our global partners working on thousands of metaphor-based research studies. Each is supported by an extensive literature on metaphor use and its impacts across many disciplines and applied settings.[28]

RULE 1: FULLY EXPLORE YOUR METAPHORS

This rule can be hard to follow because so much of our metaphor use is unconscious. Active self-listening can help with that. Once you are aware of the metaphors you're using, your next task is to make sure you've considered all they have to offer. Some hidden meanings you may want to avoid, others you may want to stress.

Consider the example of the retailer IKEA and how it took advantage of an overlooked aspect of the metaphor of a maze. IKEA's customers complained constantly about the chaotic layout of its stores. They often used the metaphor of a maze to describe the experience of getting lost and not finding the things they were searching for.

But management knew that metaphors have hidden meanings, so before shifting to a store design with straight rows and long shelves, they thought deeply about the meaning of a maze. In doing so, they discovered another aspect of mazes: they can be fun and feel like an adventure. Now IKEA stores have even less offramps than they used to. You wind your way through a twisty path and see everything the store has to offer. Customers find the shopping experience immersive and entertaining, and the incidence of unplanned purchases has increased.[29]

Two metaphors that marketers use to describe strategies are "market-driving" and "market-driven."[30] The metaphor in "market driving" is the idea that the company is the force that decides which way the market will move, just as the driver of a car decides which way the car will move. Companies that aim to be market driving develop their product ideas internally and then try to convince consumers that what they are offering will satisfy their needs. Conversely, "market driven" implies that the company is the vehicle and the market is in the driver's seat. The firm creates offerings around the market's stated desires, adjusting their resources and vision accordingly.

If a company adopts a market-driving strategy and its results are beginning to flag, it may be tempted to jump to the other strategy. But as with IKEA's maze metaphor, there may be advantages to the market-driving model that have yet to be discovered.[31] Marketing managers must interrogate themselves about what they may be missing. The interrogation might look something like this:

1. What other firms are driving the market? What is their impact? Can we collaborate with them? Who within our firm controls market-driving decisions? Who else ought to be involved? Who is currently excluded?

2. What drives the market? Are those resources owned by research and development? Marketing? Government agencies? Current or future sources of competition?

3. What delivers the resources? Is the delivery happening in an optimal manner?

4. What potholes and detours should be anticipated in market-driving strategies? How did they get there? Are they legislated? Competitively determined? Who is responsible for anticipating them?

5. When the road seems wide and smooth, is there danger of it quickly becoming snarled with traffic? Competition from new entrants might create blindside accidents in the absence of sound competitor intelligence. Is there risk of pollution in the form of customer confusion?

You might be thinking, "This is about out-of-the-box thinking." It does involve broadening your viewpoint—but not necessarily by changing boxes. I'll lay my cards on the table here: We are always thinking inside a box as figure 6.1 suggests. The question to ask is, What box am I in? You might be surprised by the lengthy pauses that precede attempts to answer that question.

But I want to stress that adhering to Rule 1 means taking full advantage of whatever box one is in before hopping into a new one. Panoramic thinking doesn't have to mean flighty thinking. It's okay to spend time with a certain metaphor (e.g., If I'm *driving* the market, what does the road look like?) to see what

FIGURE 6.1 You Are Always in a Box.

SOURCE: MARKETOONIST, LLC.

it has to offer, before imagining your scenario through a different lens or committing to another business strategy. Test-driving metaphors is a form of serious playfulness. Ask yourself:

- Am I thinking analogically often enough to see similarities in differences, fuel my curiosity, and generate ideas?

- Do I know when to broaden or narrow my attention depending on what the situation calls for?

- Am I aware of possible hidden and perhaps not so hidden cultural meanings attached to a specific metaphor?

RULE 2: BLEND CONCEPTS

Like a painter combining yellow and blue to make green, we often achieve mental breakthroughs by merging different metaphors to create a new idea or understanding. Johannes Gutenberg was familiar with vintners' use of presses to squeeze juice from grapes. Also, he and his father were goldsmiths so he understood the mechanics of die-stamping coins. The two unrelated fields came together in his mind as the moveable printing press, which arranges metal letters in frames that are then covered with ink and pressed onto paper.[32] The result changed history.

A more recent example of the fruitful blending of metaphors happened at Frito-Lay. Company marketers were looking for a way to reposition Cheetos to include adults without losing the core equity it had built up over sixty years as a beloved kids' snack. They commissioned a ZMET study to search for ideas. One of the people we interviewed brought in a Ray-Ban advertisement that showed Catholic schoolgirls climbing out of a schoolhouse window to play hooky. A few of her comments to the interviewer included in response to the image in the ad included "These are three Catholic schoolgirls escaping . . . and have a blast"; "Whenever I eat Cheetos I feel like a kid again. You are getting your hands dirty— it's almost like going out and playing in the mud"; and "You feel free. Ever since you were a kid they have been telling you 'don't do this,' 'don't do that.' With Cheetos I can suck on my fingers because I like the flavor. It's being mischievous." Eating Cheetos was this respondent's way of asserting her independence and extending, in the words of another interviewee, "an upraised middle finger to all the rule makers who dictate how a proper and mature person should behave."

Our key insight was that Cheetos gives adults a moment of escape from their adult responsibilities. The orange residue the snack leaves on their fingers is a badge of cheeky, harmless mischievousness. Teasing out the metaphor, market-ers created the Orange Underground marketing campaign. Its results were phe-nomenal: Cheetos sales increased 11.3 percent, nearly double the original target; Google searches for "Cheetos" increased tenfold year-over-year in the first year of the campaign, and the campaign won an Advertising Research Foundation Grand Ogilvy Award for excellence in advertising research. So, ask yourself:

- Am I testing my messaging for both intended and unintended meanings?
- Am I looking for new messaging opportunities in the unexpected thinking our testing uncovers?

RULE 3: USE METAPHOR TO SIMPLIFY

Metaphors can allow you to get a handle on complexity. The number of stars seen on a clear night takes your breath away. But you can orient yourself by spotting some familiar constellations—the Big Dipper and Orion, for example. Constel-lations are man-made concepts. The eight stars that make up the Big Dipper are not associated in any way, except that their arrangement in the sky resembles a dipper.

Metaphors can also help us learn how to use something. The metaphor of a desktop helped millions learn how to use home computers in the 1980s. The first computer to popularize it was the Apple Macintosh, which used visuals (file fold-ers, documents, a trash can) rather than command codes to guide people in tasks like copying, saving, and deleting documents. Keep this in mind when you have to share something entirely new with your audience, your team, or consumers. What intuitive metaphors can scaffold their understanding?

Ask yourself:

- Am I researching my metaphors to understand what extra meanings are packaged into the ones I want to use?
- Will those hurt or help my objective?
- Am I using those metaphors effectively and responsibly, understanding their power to shape thinking, perhaps in unintended ways?

RULE 4: IMAGINE THE BIGGER PICTURE

The metaphors we use often share things in common. In ZMET, we call those common denominators *deep metaphors.* They represent a kind of archetype emerging from a set of other metaphors. Identifying them helps us squeeze more insights from other metaphors.[33] The deep metaphors in the Cheetos repositioning include avoiding *control*, escape from a *container,* and *transformation.* Think about the following deep metaphors and how recognizing them can lead to marketing insights:

To understand how deep metaphors can help with problem solving, think back to the IKEA example. By seeing the maze metaphor as a representation of the deep metaphor of container, the company was able to shift away from the negative associations with mazes (anxiety, being lost) and emphasize the positive ones (fun, adventure). Instead of wanting to *escape from* the store, they found benefits by *remaining within it* longer. This also would have been true if the managers recognized traveling through a maze as an example of the deep metaphor of a journey: once you remember that it's not the destination but the journey itself that's important, you are ready to make something positive of the maze metaphor.

CONCLUSION

Metaphors, both those that show up in everyday speech and perhaps more robust metaphors that guide whole business strategies, are examples of panoramic thinking. When we liken one thing to another, we're inviting others to also use this connection as a mental shortcut to conceptualize and grasp new information.

Fresh perspectives also emerge from serious play that stretches the edges of metaphorical scenarios. For example, if your CEO says your company is "struggling to stay afloat," maybe spend some time exploring what that metaphor means in your context. Does your company want a life raft, or will the company try to swim to dry land? What would the life raft look like—a loan? Merging with another company? What's on dry land—stabilized sales? Bringing in consultants? Maybe your CEO will be annoyed at first, but the exercise can help you explore your options, surface potential risks, and assess how much energy you're willing to exert to "stay afloat." By drawing inspiration from metaphor inspired scenarios, you're engaging in panoramic thinking. Ask yourself:

- Am I open to having concepts I encounter in different landscapes challenge and change my perceptions of my own field?

Panoramic thinking also encourages us to seek unlikely allies across disciplines. Your elusive "expert"—the perfect fit to advise your problem—may not be the person who claims to know everything about problems like yours. It could be someone with little or no perspective on your field. A very different view can expose your hidden assumptions and shake you loose from them with very constructive results.

Panoramic thinking is proactive—go and talk to people across disciplines, instead of just imagining what they might think! What can a preschool teacher tell you about indoctrinating handwashing habits in a commercial kitchen? What can a board game designer teach you about workplace motivation? What opinion might a Broadway stage lighting technician offer about the design of a jewelry store?

Now, think panoramically for yourself. Who might have unexpectedly helpful perspectives for a project you're working on? Or think how your open mind might benefit another discipline: Where could *your* experiences help other fields? What panel of unlikely allies would *you* like to sit on?

KEY QUESTIONS TO ASK MYSELF

1. Am I intentionally combining deep dives and wide exploration to uncover high-impact insights?

2. Am I curious enough to venture outside my intellectual comfort zone?

3. Do I have the courage to pursue unexpected connections across seemingly unrelated domains?

4. Do I actively resist inertia and hypocognition, pushing myself to engage with messy problems and uncover blind spots?

5. Do I apply ideas from other fields to gain perspectives on my own domain?

6. Am I thoughtfully examining the metaphors I use, leveraging them for insights to clarify, inspire, and expand my thinking?

KEY QUESTIONS TO SHARE WITH COLLEAGUES

1. Are we adapting our thinking style to match the problem-solving needs of each situation?

2. Are we actively breaking down silos and nurturing a culture of interdisciplinary collaboration and insight sharing?

3. Are we fully leveraging our domain expertise and current strategies before exploring alternatives?

4. Are we using panoramic thinking to spark our curiosity, broaden our idea generation, and stimulate creative metaphors to enrich our strategic conversations?

5. Are we fostering a safe environment in which to explore unconventional ideas?

SEVEN

Don't Be Afraid of the Dark

USING THE "VOYAGER OUTLOOK" TO EMBRACE AMBIGUITY

Each of the previous chapters have addressed in various ways the absence of clarity involving the nature of a problem or its solution. That is, we engage in serious play to achieve greater comfort in situations lacking clarity, especially coming to terms with what we don't know and the hard questions we need to ask. We also spoke about the role of a hungry mind or curiosity in daring to engage in panoramic thinking in search of problem solutions. Inevitably, even when we are successful in those actions, there will still remain important residual ambiguities. This chapter explores ambiguity further, especially when it must be accepted as a fixture in our decision-making. We will learn more about ambiguity and understand our "gut reactions" when we experience it. Confronting, never mind embracing, ambiguity is uncomfortable, but practicing the "voyager outlook" helps us make the most of it. Not wishing ambiguity away or not seeking immediate clarity deepens our understanding of what we do and don't know, allowing innovation to emerge from the gray areas in between. Embracing ambiguity enables us to find hidden insights within it, including the very meaning of what ambiguity itself tells us. The following questions facilitate this constructive approach to it.

- Am I recognizing my gut reactions to ambiguity?

- Am I willing to confront and even embrace ambiguity despite the discomfort?

- Am I practicing a "voyager outlook" to make the most of ambiguous situations?

- Am I resisting the urge to wish ambiguity away or seek immediate clarity prematurely?

- Am I allowing innovation to emerge from the gray areas of ambiguity?

WARM-UP

At any given moment, part of what we experience is determined by external stimuli. But the way we experience and interpret those stimuli is determined in part by our past experiences. People with different past experiences will interpret the same stimuli differently. But sometimes the information we receive is hard to understand.

Have a look at figure 7.1. What do you see?

If you are like most people, you see a meaningless mixture of black and white splotches. You might feel challenged to make sense of them, to solve the puzzle, as it were. But if the image still doesn't make sense to you after you've stared at it for a while, you will begin to feel uncomfortable. Stare at it a bit longer and your discomfort will likely turn to irritation or frustration. No one wants to stay stumped forever! The novelty of a fresh challenge can wear off very quickly, even when you don't have much at stake.

When I learned the truth about figure 7.1 I was reminded of an art lecture I once attended, at which the speaker told a story about an Impressionist painter—I can't remember which one—whose newest painting was too confusing for prospective buyers. They just couldn't make sense of it. But when a local farmer visited the artist's studio and saw it, he recognized its subject immediately. "Oh," he exclaimed, "You've painted the waterfall at the edge of my field!" Unlike the artist's hoped-for customers, the farmer had intimate prior knowledge of the scene. To him, the painting was crystal clear.

Now, let's put you in the shoes of that farmer. Look at figure 7.2. You should be able to decipher it easily: it's a bearded man. Now, return to figure 7.1. What do you see? A bearded man, right? In fact, if you return to figure 7.1 tomorrow, next month, next year, and quite likely beyond that, you will immediately see the same bearded figure. You will no longer be capable of seeing only meaningless splotches. Looking at figure 7.2 was a learning experience. You have acquired knowledge that will stay with you for a long time.

FIGURE 7.1   What Do You See?

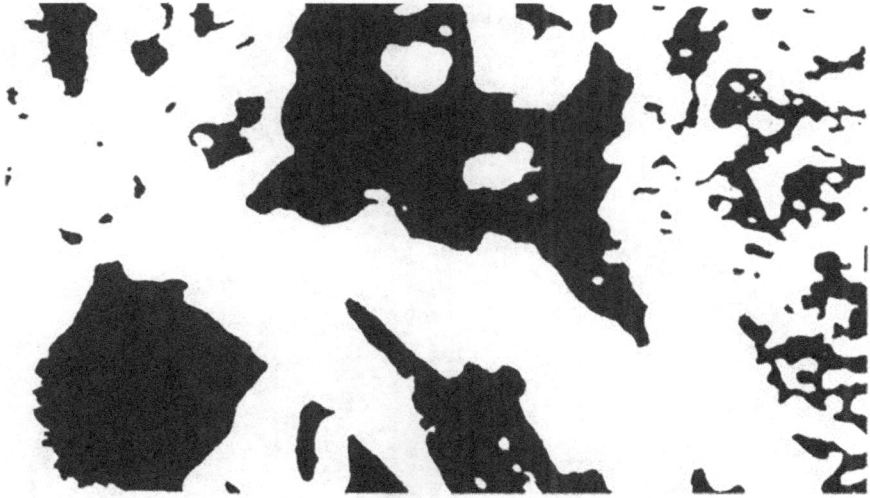

SOURCE: T. ALBRIGHT, "ON THE PERCEPTION OF PROBABLE THINGS," *NEURON*, APRIL 26, 2012, HTTPS://DOI.ORG/10.1016/J.NEURON.2012.04.001.

FIGURE 7.2   Now What Do You See?

SOURCE: T. ALBRIGHT, "ON THE PERCEPTION OF PROBABLE THINGS,"
NEURON, APRIL 26, 2012, DOI:10.1016/J.NEURON.2012.04.001.

SO WHAT?

While this exercise involves vision, the same lesson applies to our other senses. Our past experiences make it possible for us to create meaning from information available to us in our current context. Think of it as an active collaboration between your senses and your memory. Other names for this are conceptual blending and cocreation.

Knowing that present context and past learning interact when we interpret new stimuli, the next time you get into an argument with someone about the meaning of an ambiguous political, artistic, or advertising message, you can now do something new: you can pause and ask, What is it in our respective current or past situations and experiences that might account for our differing interpretations? The ambiguity of a situation or problem is as rooted in our different personal histories as it is in its objective "facts."[1]

DEFINING AMBIGUITY

Ambiguity can be defined as the absence of clarity, which is the hallmark of hard-to-solve problems.[2] When knowledge of past experiences fails to clarify an ambiguous situation, human minds respond by exercising their imaginations. As we imagine or envision what may be missing, we begin to "connect the dots," a creative exercise, and have an insight or moment of clarity. This is a compelling reason to view ambiguity as an opportunity, something to embrace with innovative thinking.[3]

Oftentimes consumer data is ambiguous. For example, the brand team for a popular candy bar needed to streamline its advertising messaging due to budget restrictions. However, a survey the team had commissioned to help identify its new focus had proved unhelpful. It revealed that many more segments than anticipated existed with respect to consumer purchase motivations. Ordinarily this might have led to a larger budget to reach more varied segments. The survey research wasn't wrong—further exploration just wasn't in the budget. However, an in-depth study involving one-on-one interviews revealed that a single theme, that of "resource," was shared among most segments. Each participant described the candy bar as a "tool" that enabled very different experiences. The focus on "resource" enabled cocreation among consumers. They were reminded that the candy bar was a personal resource although they varied greatly in the ways it served as a resource. The single concept of resource was very effective although in very different ways with different segments.

For another business example of how ambiguity can be turned into an opportunity, let me tell you a brief story about a client, a global brand that provided a vital repair service to consumers. The service was affordable, convenient, and risk-free—all attributes that were admirable, to be sure, but didn't sufficiently differentiate it from its competitors. The problem, we discovered, was that they were too focused on their transactions with consumers.

As the client saw it, the consumer could rely on the brand to fix their broken devices. End of story. But as we saw it, they were missing the most important part of the story. It wasn't the transaction between the client and the customer. Instead, it was the relationship the customer had with their broken device. That insight was just as hidden to them as the bearded man was in the first picture in the warm-up.

The device was something the customer relied on and used every day. What's more, it reflected the customer's self-image and status. When it was broken, the customer didn't just experience it as an inconvenience, but as a kind of personal lapse—how could I have allowed this to happen to this thing that I care about? By fixing it quickly and efficiently—and even more importantly, by investing the same care in the device that the customer does—our client could restore the customer's relationship with it. Their customer needed to know that the company understood the deeply meaningful role of the product in their lives. It was captured by one of the metaphors that came up in research which involved bringing an ill child into an emergency room.

Unlike the picture in our warm-up, which had one solution, many ambiguous situations can be interpreted in more than one way. Working toward a solution is much like solving a riddle. Try to solve this one:

A man is at home. Another man on his way to the same home. The man at home is wearing a mask. What is happening here?

When I challenge groups with this puzzle, some people respond immediately, confidently, and wrongly, suggesting the presence of an availability bias, which describes a readiness to act on whatever scant information they have at hand. But most people answer much more tentatively, offering their suggested solutions in the form of questions: Is it a robbery? A costume party? Is the man at home a handyman spraying something? Do the two men know each other? Almost everyone expresses surprise when I tell them that what is happening is a baseball game. The man at home is a catcher, and the man on his way home is the base runner.

Most Americans are familiar with baseball. The riddle, however, is challenging because it lacks context. Imagination can provide that. In this example, however, it requires perseverance in visualizing alternative contexts. As one noted researcher points out, "There is never a truth without a context with which it interacts: there is a context for everything in the real world."[4] Managers need to keep in mind that nothing happens alone. Imagination is required perhaps more so than reason to identify what else is going on. That certainly describes the thinking of interviewees confronting ambiguous situations. We may not have enough data or enough remembered information to clearly define the problem and identify its causes and/or its consequences. This engenders confusion, which in turn can cause stress, further interfering with problem-solving.[5] Worse, those feelings can be contagious in group settings.[6]

The discomfort some people feel with ambiguity can lead them to rely on conveniently available information even when it won't really solve the problem. This, sometimes called the "law of the instrument," is illustrated in figure 7.3. Here the arbitrary criterion is to use what is readily available even when it requires redefining the problem.

If the speech patterns—the voice "signature"—of someone proposing a solution seem sufficiently confident, others may take that as proof of their credibility.[7] Be-

FIGURE 7.3 The Law of the Instrument.

cause this typically happens below awareness, the possibility of being biased might not even occur to them. In a research study I conducted for a former federal agency about consumer fraud among the elderly, my team and I encountered countless examples in the form, "the [con artist] seemed/sounded/looked so sincere/honest/kind."

When we are trying to make sense of an ambiguous situation, there are certain things to keep in mind that should give us confidence in our judgments.[8] First, accurate claims tend to outnumber inaccurate ones in our everyday lives. Our bias to accept incoming information (i.e., to judge claims to be true) does not always steer us wrong. Second, subjective feelings can convey useful information about the world. In many cases, we really can infer the truth from them. And finally, people believe statements that match information they retrieve from memory and reject those that don't. Those unconscious memories are often accurate. Subjective feelings are often—and wrongly—depreciated when it comes to problem-solving.

FEELINGS AND AMBIGUITY

How do you feel when confronted with ambiguity? If you were to describe your attitude with a visual image (or a sound, a fragrance, a feeling, or any other sensory metaphor), what would you choose? Take a moment to think about this. Now think about what your chosen metaphor says about you:

1. Does it suggest you view ambiguity as a necessary evil? Something to be avoided if possible and endured for as little time as necessary?

2. Does it suggest an attitude of grudging tolerance, that can be borne so long as it doesn't consume too many resources?

3. Does it suggest you see ambiguity as something to embrace with patience as an opportunity to invent and discover?

The first two attitudes encourage conventional thinking. The third allows for more exploration. For this reason, I call it a "voyager outlook." People with voyager outlooks trust their feelings and are willing to engage in analogical thinking. They do not automatically reject what their training has taught them to think, but suspect that there are other approaches too, and are eager to explore them.

As noted in the warm-up, when we first confront an ambiguous situation we may enjoy the challenge, but those feelings seldom last. One of my interviewees described this with an image of a chameleon whose colors changed with the team's mood. Another shared a photo of a shar-pei dog whose signature look involves a great many irregular, enveloping folds of skin. She explained her reason for sharing it:

> I love this picture of this dog . . . It is just looking straight into the camera with an unblinking gaze. It makes me think you have to deal with reality, you have to face things even when they are vague or cloudy . . . You can't really hide from confusion or expect every moment to be a moment of great pleasure. Dealing with uncertainty . . . leaves wrinkles, battle scars. [*Can you elaborate?*] Yeah, not everything is smooth. It is not all smooth sailing, right? And there are shadows, there are a lot of shadows in this picture. [*Shadows?*] Yeah, there are shadow moments, dark moments, especially at the start, when everything about the problem I described earlier is confusing. You have moments of self-doubt and misgiving about being tasked to solve it when you don't even think you know what the real problem is. That's a huge wrinkle.

Later on, the interviewee noted:

> I think there is a great place for humor [in dealing with ambiguous situations], and I think humor is not only a survival mechanism, it's . . . an essential for getting anything done. [It is] an operational tool. If you can get humor into an unclear situation—and I don't think you can do it necessarily consciously—but if it is there, oh gosh, everything kind of slides into place and, I don't know, also it is more fun to work that way. I tend to fall asleep at things that are deadly serious. I don't think you should be silly, either, but I think there is a big place for humor.

All that said, the nagging sense that you've been asking the wrong questions or looking for answers in the wrong places can test even the most robust sense of humor.

Feelings are especially informative when there is a noticeable change in them. One interviewee spoke of noticing a change in the CEO's mood: "Normally, he is upbeat, so when he comes across otherwise, we all know the problem being discussed has serious consequences the rest of us don't see. Few things get us wondering as much as that does."

Another interviewee described how a feeling alerted him to a problem with a supposed solution: "I felt it in my gut, this voice saying, 'Don't let this happen!' I knew it was late in the game to nix [the solution], but in the end, I couldn't bring myself to support it." The interviewee's body telegraphed a response before it arrived in his conscious mind. This is not surprising. One of the strengths of unconscious thinking is its capacity to process many bits of information at the same time; it tends to be better at pattern recognition than our conscious minds, and faster.[9]

This does not mean that gut feelings are always trustworthy—on the contrary, we have seen that they can reflect unexamined biases. Research suggests that when we are under enough pressure, we can go so far as to generate false memories to expedite our decision-making.[10] Solutions that come from our unconscious minds must be interrogated thoroughly. But often we don't even know that that's where they're coming from.

FLAIL-SAFE, OR TEAM EFFORTS OF DISCOVERY AND INVENTION?

Invention and discovery are a problem-solver's best friends, but when faced with ambiguous situations, people too often fall back on what one executive calls "flail-safe" measures—behaviors designed to hide the fact that you're "flailing around in search of a way out of the problem." Avoidance is a similarly unhelpful way of dealing with difficult situations. One executive we interviewed represented the not-dealing-with-it attitude with a picture of a slumbering mouse in a maze. When the interviewer asked, "What might the Z's [over the sleeping mouse] represent?" the reply was, "The easy way out." When the interviewer asked the executive to elaborate, he answered that his company's department heads simply do "some unimaginative version of what other firms do, even when [those firms'] outcomes are a mixed bag."

Our chapter warm-up and the riddle were ambiguous situations with single solutions. As we've seen, in real life such problems are usually addressed by discovery-oriented means—asking questions and testing them against objective and remembered data. To make sure you're asking the right questions and connecting the dots in the right way, you may commission research or seek out colleagues, consultants, or other experts familiar with the problem at hand.

But most ambiguous situations and problems do not contain one sole correct solution. You may be familiar with the Rubin Vase in which either a vase or a face in profile is seen. Nearly everyone sees both but only in alternating sequences. Both are present but not visible at the same time.[11] Recent experiences will likely determine which version you see first and even how readily you can "leave" that view and suddenly see the other one.

Problem-solving benefits from a strong dose of imaginative adaptation, which is what we do when panoramic and analogic thinking leads us to find a similar problem in another field that has been satisfactorily resolved.

One interviewee drew a picture of a two-headed sheep to illustrate what she labeled "the kindness of 'and' "—that is, making use of both discovery and invention. Another executive made the same point in a different way. He used a picture of a blindfolded child standing beneath a pinata at a party, holding a stick in his hand. The piñata was the problem, he said, the blindfold represented feeling lost, and the stick was curiosity. Questioned further, he said that a swirling motion with the stick helped the child discover the pinata's location. It then took him a little while to figure out—to invent—a motion (apparently a violent jabbing motion) that could break it open. Ask yourself:

- Am I aware of my emotions and even my body's reactions when faced with an ambiguous situation, noticing when I am inclined to avoid ambiguity and take "flail-safe" measures, or when I embrace it as an opportunity to invent and discover?

CASE STUDY: WHEN HELPFUL ANSWERS AREN'T FORTHCOMING

What happens when a research project template doesn't yield the answers to the questions you're asking? To design a project studying women's health, our market research team used a previously successful healthcare study as a template, since the objectives and questions to answer were similar. We wanted to discover what the patient's disease meant to them—their emotional landscapes—so we could craft a compelling message.

But while the project design worked well in the first study, the second study was not yielding clear insights. After participant interviews and analysis, our team was still in the dark about this patient segment's identity and motivations. The team was feeling frustrated and even a little desperate. If the participants couldn't tell us who the patient was, then who could? It was uncomfortable to look at a body of data and not see clear patterns.

So the team started again from scratch. It took courage to forge into new, unknown territory, especially on a deadline, but it was clear that doing more of what we knew how to do, like scheduling more interviews, wouldn't help us. We had to use our imaginations to discover a new way forward. Instead of seeking answers that fit the fill-in-the-blank style of the template (i.e., "Her disease means _____ to her; therefore, she feels _____ and fears _____ so we should talk to her in _____ manner"), we revisited the premise.

Thinking more broadly, we discovered that the blank we were drawing was a powerful insight in and of itself. The participants, who all suffered from the disease in question, couldn't tell us about themselves because their identities were overwhelmed by the immense, specific kind of pain they felt as a result of their disease, a dynamic we hadn't encountered in the first study. We pivoted to address this new insight.

The story became, "In order to understand who this patient is, we need to know her pain." The product message was about validation and acknowledgment—"the world may prefer to deny your pain, but we understand it." The message was dark, but it matched what the patient was looking for in communications about her disease and treatment options. The treatment wasn't asking her to fight, but offering her a chance for some peace.

Discovering that the lack of data was an insight was like looking at a random collection of splotches and suddenly realizing a face was hidden within them. All the information was there, but we had to accept the ambiguity to redraw the outline in a new and unexpected way.

A DIAGNOSTIC QUESTION

A question I often ask executives when the topic involves ambiguity is a variation of the following:

Which of these two statements most closely describes your experience in your job?

A: I love being right.

B: I hate being wrong.

Yes, you are likely to experience both feelings. But take a moment and chose the one that is uppermost in your mind, no matter how close by the other option is.

Option B is chosen somewhat more often than A. A frequent explanation is that the subtle and not so subtle penalties for being wrong are more potent than the rewards for being right. Being fired is a lot worse than receiving a bonus is good.

As one newly appointed executive put it to us, when describing his frustration with his new reports: "Their fear of being wrong is evident in the questions they ask. They prefer safe questions [which] they can answer confidently"—and which lead to unimaginative actions. Simply put, there are many more ways of being wrong in ambiguous situations than of being right, especially when exercising imagination. Rein in imagination and you rein in the chances of being wrong.

But breakthrough innovations arise from breakthrough sense-making, which requires seeing ambiguity as a friend and embracing it. The settings where that is likeliest to happen are those where the rewards for being right offset the penalties for being wrong. In commenting on the notion of risk aversion, one executive notes that she isn't terribly concerned with her colleagues being risk-averse or risk-seeking as a general trait. Rather, her concerns are with what issues they are risk-seeking or risk-averse about and how they spill over on one another. In elaborating on this, if they are risk averse with respect to career issues, sooner or later in her judgment, they will be risk-averse in the decisions they make. Their decisions and related actions in their area of responsibility will tend to maintain the status quo. In her words, "This contributes to a lack of innovation in their thinking and eventually in our service offerings and other client retention efforts."

WHAT AMBIGUITY OFFERS US

Most of the research on ambiguity focuses on our tolerance or lack of tolerance for it. That suggests it is like a chronic condition, something unpleasant that decision-makers would prefer to avoid but must learn to live with. But early in the chapter I suggested that ambiguity deserves more than just tolerance and should be embraced. Why? A classic article from the world of computer design suggests these answers:

- Because ambiguous information impels people to ask difficult questions like, Is my assessment of cause and effect valid?
- Because ambiguity about the context in which a problem arises may raise questions about the methodologies and tools you are using, impelling you to acquire new ones.
- Because relational ambiguity prods you to call on other perspectives, resulting in the recruitment and creation of the right teams.
- Because addressing informational, situational, and relational ambiguity encourages the sharing of valuable ideas.[12]

When we welcome ambiguity, we make our minds more receptive to three important friends of constructive thought and open-mindedness: engagement, imagination, and creativity.

Engagement. Many of the managers, artists, and others I've interviewed describe their encounters with ambiguity as stimulating, even fun, at least initially. It gives them energy and makes them feel involved.

FIGURE 7.4 The Implied Presence of Missing Information

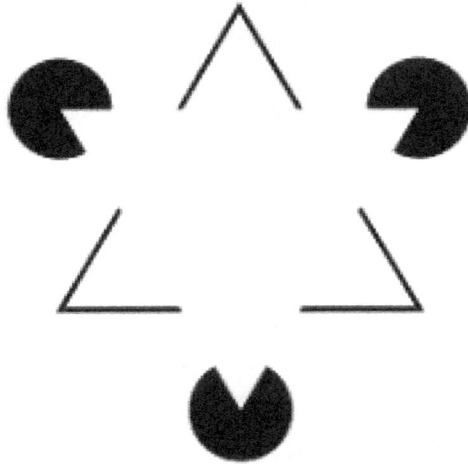

Imagination.[13] I've emphasized the importance of imagination throughout this book. Imagination allows us to see what's missing. Look at figure 7.4, in which two triangles are suggested based on available cues.

In the business world, imagination allows us to use our prior knowledge about competitors or customers to make educated guesses about their future actions. White spaces in the market become like the implied triangles in this image. We may not be able to interrogate what's not there, but we can certainly learn more about it by interrogating what we see around it. Imagine if figure 7.4 had only one of those circle-ish shapes and two of those chevrons. Would we still be able to see the hidden triangles? Possibly not. But by gathering more evidence, the implied shapes would become clearer. In business, this could mean combining market research and competitor analysis to form a more detailed picture.

Creativity. If imagination is the highway we use to find solutions, creativity is the off-ramp that brings us closer still to our destination. Creativity is pragmatic—it allows us to combine our discoveries in novel ways to resolve specific problems, building on the insights that imagination led us to. Ask yourself:

- Am I using ambiguity as a signal that it's time to change my behavior, to call on other perspectives, and to welcome more creative approaches when we feel stuck?

WISHING AMBIGUITY AWAY

The interviewees who spoke enthusiastically about embracing ambiguity also spoke about why so many of their colleagues and bosses prefer to wish it away. If there's no ambiguity, there's no need to spend scarce resources getting comfortable with it, and no risk of incurring the mental anguish it can cause. Sometimes they go into overdrive and create meaning where none exists, prematurely shutting down the search for more legitimate—albeit more challenging—answers. Rumors, conspiracy theories, and fake news are all ways of avoiding ambiguity. Inventing them requires mental gymnastics, and when those mental gymnastics are repeated too often, they become automatic biases. A few are noted below as reminders of our discussion of the foes of curiosity.

Groupthink. Groupthink and its mind guards have been mentioned in earlier chapters. Once a group reaches a consensus about a problem, there is great reluctance to reopen the discussion, even when new information suggests it may be necessary. Mind guards resist premortems, the predictive equivalents of postmortems. You'll recall from chapter 3 that where a postmortem examines reasons for failure after the fact, a premortem investigates potential reasons for failure before they occur, by identifying and challenging the most relevant underlying assumptions.

Risky shift. A special danger of groupthink is the risky shift: people are more apt to make high-risk decisions when working with groups than when acting alone, because they know that the blame for failure will be shared. This results in a false-confidence bias, which is another reason to engage in a premortem.

Confirmation bias and dismissal of anomalies. Two foes of curiosity, confirmation bias and the tendency to ignore anomalies, are also foes of ambiguity. Our tendency to collect and interpret data in ways that confirm prior beliefs make it less likely that anomalies will be recognized.

AMBIGUITY AND DECISION-MAKING: INTUITIONS AND LEAPS OF FAITH

Complete, clear information is generally absent when making complex decisions. Moreover, the answers to some important questions may be intrinsically unknowable. In those situations, ambiguity is as hard to avoid as shadows on a sunny day. Consumer perceptions, new product development, projections about the potential of new-to-the-world goods and services, planning and strategy decisions, the use of competitor intelligence systems, and the selection and implementation of research methods are all vexed by ambiguity.[14] So how are we to make decisions? My interviewees revealed that it frequently requires a leap of faith. One nicely summed up the consensus of what that leap is: "Having confidence that somewhere in your thinking there is rational reasoning for every important intuition. That confidence lets you find your way to action." It reveals a very considerable confidence in the wisdom of unconscious thinking. Another praised intuitive leaps of faith: "Intuitions have a batting average [that is] every bit as good as formal reasoning."

When pressed to describe what they meant by intuition, most interviewees seemed to agree that it is a feeling held with conviction that is difficult to justify. But just because intuitions are difficult to justify doesn't mean they are exempt from challenges. Indeed, they should be challenged as vigorously as their well-reasoned cousins, not because they are wrong—which is always a possibility, of course—but because explaining and justifying them can clarify them in ways that can improve outcomes.[15]

Using an image of a rock climber scaling a treacherous outcropping, one interviewee described how tenaciously people can cling to their intuitions:

> [The climber] knows he's in a difficult position with no clear solution. Yes, he has a harness, but he wants to come up with his own way out of the fix he's in. The harness represents a conventional way out. But he wants to find his own solution, his own path, something unique to him that he can be proud of, not the conventional prescriptions . . . That's like me. I let my own sense of a solution, my intuition, surface and then see if it is enough or I can improve on it . . . If [my ideas] don't work, there is always the harness.

This interviewee also shared a favorite quote, often attributed to William James: "If you have intuitions at all, they come from a deeper level of your nature than the loquacious level which rationalism inhabits." When the interviewer asked how reliable the interviewee's intuitions were, the interviewee acknowledged the importance of challenging them:

> No, they don't always work. When they don't, it is usually because I felt pressured and was too quick to use them when what I should have done is slowed down, gone through the tedium of reviewing what others have done, or consulted experts. Mostly this happens when I underestimate the complexity of a complex problem or see [the complexity] yet feel pressure. I've learned . . . I need to put my intuitions out there, describe them for what they are, and encourage challenges to them. This was a tough lesson to learn. This is a difficult environment to learn it in.

Whether or not a team member's intuition-based idea or solution is accepted depends on several factors. One is that member's credibility, their history of being right. Another is whether the member's intuitions are in line with those of the rest of the team. When someone else's intuitions remind us of our own, we more readily accept them as true. Conversely, if we have never experienced or felt what is being described, we are likely to reject it.

People are endowed with a strong drive to find meaning. That, after all, is what a mind is for. Its presence of that drive is evident when we speak of "meaningful experiences, meaningful gifts, meaningful sex, and meaningful expenses, all presumably in contrast to their meaningless counterparts."[16] Meaning-making is central to defining complex problems, and to finding and/or creating solutions to them.

Making sense of problems that arise in volatile, uncertain, complex, or vague situations demands intensive use of our cognitive capacities, which consume a great deal of energy. But as I've noted previously, our brains are designed to conserve energy.[17] We prefer to have someone else give us the answer, so we hire consultants or look for best practices to imitate. Or we redefine a problem as one we can answer more readily.

As noted earlier in this chapter and elsewhere in the book, one of the most important questions you can ask when facing ambiguity is, What is missing? Detecting critical gaps in our knowledge is the first step to filling them. Meaningful thought is needed to conceptualize alternatives and bring them to reality.

Counterfactuals are also useful. Let's say we are facing a familiar situation that we handled badly in the past. We now have information that was previously missing—we know one thing that didn't work. So we can ask, What else might I try that would produce a better outcome?

Testing alternative actions in controlled, experimental situations may yield missing information. I strongly recommend, for example, using your imagination to invent a hypothetical research study and then asking, What if the results looked like this? What would we do in response?, and then repeating the process with different outcomes. Providing simulated findings to hypothetical questions fine-tunes our thinking and stimulates the imagination. It sparks debate within teams, eliciting previously dormant knowledge. In this manner, you can prepare yourself for welcome and unwelcome surprises.

PANORAMIC THINKING CAN REDUCE AMBIGUITY

The need for panoramic thinking is not limited to the immediate decision-maker. It is sometimes required of other stakeholders such as customers. Consider the challenge of designing appealing exterior and interior features of future vehicle models. There is a long elapsed time from stated customer preferences through to product launch. This delay does not tolerate errors. And errors are quite likely as the design team for a major vehicle manufacturer consistently discovered. Learning about appealing vehicle designs fell victim to the "I'll know it when I see it" paradox. Customers could easily describe various desired design features only to ignore many of them when they appeared much later in time. In other words, their current expressed preferences were poor predictors of what they would later find attractive. The design teams needed a better way of tapping into customer "thinking that had long legs," as one designer put it. They needed to obtain design preferences that were fundamental and stable enough to predict behavior a few years into the future.

The solution was to rely on a customer's natural ability to think analogically. Accordingly, representative customers were not asked about automotive vehicles. In fact, we instructed them not to use images involving vehicles. Instead, they were asked to find several images or pictures of other things whose designs held great appeal for them. For instance, they brought to their ZMET interviews pictures of kitchen cutlery, dishware, household appliances, their favorite places for vacation, works of art they admired, references to music in a few instances, architectural features of varied buildings, furniture, items of clothing and footwear, and so on.

By deliberately having representative customers think in non-vehicle terms, the research team was able to identify the "stylistic unity" for each interviewee. This referred to the common design features found across multiple contexts. Design features relevant to diverse other settings had a high chance of being relevant to vehicles. Moreover, as the features were present in very different settings provided confidence that they were deeply held and thus enduring over time. Furthermore, and importantly, certain design features constituting each customer's stylistic unity were shared by many customers to produce a consensus map. That map became the design architecture for designers to consider when creating interiors and exteriors for future vehicles. And later testing of these designs validated the results.

This example also illustrates the willingness of the design teams to confront their lack of clarity about customer preferences and go beyond their customary ways of understanding customers. This can itself be a major exercise in panoramic thinking. It was facilitated by having members of the design team engaging in the same ZMET interview and image collection assignment used separately with consumers. This brought them outside their comfort zone regarding behavioral research while also increasing their confidence in the data they would later be using.

CONCLUSION

The desire for clarity can be so great that it results in a narrow, unrealistic definition of the problem, one that nicely fits a convenient solution. Major problems, however, are often endowed with unavoidable ambiguity. For that reason, it requires courage to embrace ambiguity. This act is the center piece of Nobel Laureate Wisława Szymborska's essay, "I Don't Know," mentioned in chapter 1. "I don't know" is a source of inspiration, not something to hide from. As one executive noted, he had to "learn how to be comfortable with the uncomfortable!" He continued, "The more we embraced ambiguity, the more power we found within it." Embracing ambiguity is the source of many Am I? and Are we? questions occurring in earlier chapters involving other open-minded actions. Ask yourself:

- Am I approaching ambiguity with courage, humility, and patience?
- Am I willing to get comfortable with uncomfortable situations?
- Am I willing to adapt our processes when our "tried and true" routines let us down or don't quite get us where we want to be?

For some people, the most terrifying thing is to admit "I don't know" or "I'm not really sure." This invites questions and judgments by others: "Well, why aren't you sure?" "How soon can you be sure?" "What about an estimate?" "If you're not sure about that, are you sure about anything else?"

If you possibly can, gently shift those questions to something more productive that acknowledges the opportunities your uncertainty creates for discovery. This is what the vehicle design team did. "Can you help me look for what we're missing here?" "Can we try a new approach?" "Since our first method didn't give us what we needed, why don't we try a new method instead of trying the first way again?" "How can we adapt so we have room for this ambiguity?" "Who else can we ask for a new perspective?" "If we don't know what we need to know, how can we bridge the gap to get there?"

Protocol works well in stable environments . . . until those environments change (and they inevitably do!). When that happens, open-minded thinkers re-address the protocol and find new and better ways of doing things.

KEY QUESTIONS TO ASK MYSELF

1. Am I willing to engage with ambiguity, recognizing that it can open up space for engagement, imagination and creativity?

2. Am I resisting the temptation of "flail-safe" measures and convenient options, instead adopting discovery and invention-oriented attitudes?

3. Am I creatively adapting approaches from diverse fields to navigate ambiguous situations effectively?

4. Am I embracing a "voyager outlook," patiently exploring without demanding immediate clarity? Do I heed the information value of my feelings while examining them carefully before relying on them?

5. Am I vigilant against falling into denial, recognizing its dangers to sound decision-making?

6. Am I on guard against confirmation bias and ignoring anomalies?

KEY QUESTIONS TO SHARE WITH COLLEAGUES

1. Are we as a team acknowledging ambiguity as a potential ally that spurs us to assess our judgments, problem-solving approaches, and team composition?

2. Are we consistently asking ourselves "What's missing?" to pinpoint knowledge gaps as a first step to gaining real clarity?

3. Are we considering how each team member's background may shape their unique perspective in order to build mutual understanding?

4. Are we vigilant against groupthink, employing premortems to challenge consensus that could breed false confidence?

5. Are we resisting research that merely confirms what we already believe or points to familiar solutions?

6. Are we giving due weight to team members' intuitions based on their track records, rather than dismissing or blindly accepting them?

EIGHT

Being Smart Isn't Enough

HAVING AN OPEN MIND MATTERS MORE

This chapter focuses on *being* wise, or practical wisdom, because wisdom over there on a shelf is not of much use.[1] An ambitious study of the concept across twelve countries and five continents and involving nineteen characteristics of wise people found two positively related underlying dimensions of wise behaviors: *reflective orientation* and *socio-emotional awareness*.[2] Both qualities and their active expression are the underlying hallmarks of the wise-acting executive interviewees who helped inform this book. Their open-minded actions and apparent inner-directed questions that help power them are indeed wise.

Inevitably, we'll also look at foolishness—and how foolishness can lead to wisdom if we listen to it. We'll parse the difference between linear causal thinking and systems thinking and dispel a couple of damaging myths about fixed intelligence. Finally, I'll share my own definition of wisdom. You might be surprised to find out that you're familiar with it already! But first let's take note of a few Am I? questions to focus your attention.

- Am I open to learning from my own and others' foolishness?
- Am I thinking in terms of complex systems rather than simplistic linear cause-and-effect?

- Am I questioning assumptions about innate, fixed intelligence?

- Am I behaving adaptively to demonstrate true wisdom?

WHAT EXACTLY IS WISDOM?

Because the term is so familiar, we assume we understand its meaning and that others agree with us. But we shouldn't. Wisdom is what I call a "superconcept"—meaning it is used in many ways in many contexts.[3] One source identifies nearly thirty definitions for wisdom, not one of which is generally accepted.[4] If you write down your own definition of wisdom and then ask another person to do the same, the odds are good they'll be quite different.

Though wisdom has been widely discussed in the literatures of religion and philosophy, it has only been a topic of formal study in the social sciences for a little more than forty years.[5] For that matter, there's very little in the way of sound research about wisdom's opposites, either—foolishness and stupidity.[6]

A few descriptions or explanations of wisdom from the field of psychology illustrate some of the concept's many nuances. Wisdom:

- Is gained by resolving daily crises.[7]

- Is "uniquely human, a form of advanced cognitive and emotional development that is experience driven. It can be learned; it increases with age and can be measured."[8]

- Builds on knowledge, cognitive skills, and personality characteristics and requires an understanding of the cultural context.[9]

- Is demonstrated by the ability to form a sound judgment when there are competing interests.[10]

- Is orchestrated when intelligence, creativity, openness to experience, psychological-mindedness, and general life experiences combine.[11]

- Is characterized by excellence of judgment and advice; knowledge with extraordinary scope, depth, and balance; the perfect synergy of mind and character; and balancing the good or well-being of one's self and that of others.[12]

- Has neurological foundations.[13]

Most discussions of wisdom emphasize having substantial knowledge and the ability to process it rapidly, often described as intelligence. (These features, incidentally, are often used to describe artificial intelligence. They do not, however, constitute wisdom, much less artificial wisdom, whatever that might be.) You'll recall from chapter 1 that scores on intelligence tests have risen in the last century during many pressing social and economic problems that ought to benefit from intelligence but have become crises. These crises are both local and global.[14] Given that intelligence is such a frequently mentioned component of wisdom, let's look at it more closely. In particular, let's consider a damaging notion about intelligence: that it is innate and fixed.

THE MYTH OF FIXED INTELLIGENCE

Perhaps at some point in your education you were labeled as bright and talented. Or perhaps you were labeled as slow. It's amazing how those labels can cling, despite abundant stories of so-called slow learners reaching great heights, or gifted people who never, in the eyes of the world, live up to their potential. It appears to be hard to dislodge the notion that people are born with a limited number of intelligence tokens, and while we can buff and polish them, we're not getting more. But that is not true: intelligence can be developed.[15]

The psychologist Robert Sternberg urges caution regarding the notion of innate intelligence that can be measured by standardized tests:

One of the most serious falsehoods permeating our society is the belief that standardized tests of intelligence and related attributes—IQ tests, SATs, ACTs, GREs, most standardized achievement tests, and the like—are good and somehow highly meaningful and comprehensive measures of intelligence and what emanates from it . . . *Intelligence is not about problem solving on a contrived standardized test; it is about problem solving in the real world.*[16]

Joseph E. LeDoux, a leading expert on emotions, goes so far as to say, "There is no measurable entity in a person that constitutes their intelligence."[17]

The notion that intelligence is fixed encourages other mistaken ideas relevant to problem-solving:

- That performance is a measure of intelligence and personal worth.
- That effort is only for those who lack competence.
- That learning new things is risky; it is better to stick with something you already do well.

There is evidence—not uncontested—that praising someone's accomplishment by emphasizing their intelligence ("Wow! You're so smart to have come up with this solution!") significantly dampens their motivation to solve subsequent problems, and hence their success, while praising someone's efforts ("Wow! You really worked hard to create this excellent solution!") has a positive effect on their subsequent problem-solving. The theory is that in the former case, the performer doesn't see the achievement as within their control—it's down to something innate. The takeaway from the second is that their hard work paid off, motivating further efforts.[18] There is quite a bit of discussion about effective motivation and praising techniques in K–12 classrooms, but the subject is germane in nonacademic environments as well. While we all carry what we've learned from our formative years into adult life, we continue to learn and mold our behavior to our environments. Learning (not just of information, but also of habits and behaviors that are both helpful and unhelpful) is never static.

These ideas may unsettle those of us who are accustomed to being praised for our innate talent or ability. Now, to be on the safe side, I'd prefer leaders to be well endowed with innate intelligence (if it exists). But what I'd prefer even more—what I'd require, if I could—is that *they have the good sense and ability to behave adaptively*. Those are the traits that enable us to deal wisely with difficult problems in a shifting, changing world.[19] Those are the traits we seek in our colleagues, when we work together to solve problems.

Consider this quip from the late Charlie Munger, former vice chairman of Berkshire Hathaway: "It is remarkable how much long-term advantage people like us have gotten by trying to be consistently not stupid instead of trying to be very intelligent." Being wise always takes place over time. It isn't about making the most perfect or flashy decision every single time but about making enough good decisions to steer your ship along an intentional course.

COMPLEX PROBLEMS AND COMPLEX THINKING

While simple problems are clear-cut and discrete, difficult ones are often amorphous, complex, and connected to other equally difficult problems. Fortunately, the mind is also complex, with many interconnected parts and abilities. Decision-makers are wise, then, to the extent that they employ the six actions of an open mind in concert, adapting the mix to respond to changing needs and problems. If we've been building an open mind toolbox, then being wise is knowing what situation calls for a wrench and which for a hammer. And also whether that hammer needs to be applied with force or just a quick tap.

One of my interviewees was disappointed by the narrow mindsets she'd encountered among the staff she had inherited in her new position. She described their curiosity as "stunted." In her words, "A big opportunity for [a new service] was staring them in the face, and they blew right past it. It never occurred to them to ask [two questions]. Had they, it would have been plain as day. I hit the roof." During a postmortem, she discovered they had fallen prey to the convenient-light syndrome: "[They were using] an embarrassingly narrow beam of light to find opportunities in a roiling market," she said.

The ability to shift from a linear, causal thinking process to a multidirectional, systems way of thinking is one sign of wisdom, as the two approaches are very different.[20] Whereas linear thinking is narrowly focused and operationalized, systems thinking is open-ended and unpredictable. It allows for both pleasant and unpleasant surprises and as a result can be more demanding. Linear thinking often involves a highly defined set of workers and organizations with clear responsibilities, whereas systems thinking involves a more fluid set of actors sometimes performing unexpected tasks. Similarly, linear thinking usually occurs in highly prescribed work contexts where opportunities and constraints governing innovation are clearly laid out. Thinking in systems mode often entails a much broader set of constraints and opportunities to innovate. It encourages thinking about exemptions to normal work-related constraints. This includes what I call having "switching rules." These are permitted (or readily forgiven) deviations from formal procedures and informal expectations. They allow for more speedy decisions about changing goals midstream and deciding when to terminate a project.

It's difficult to shift between linear and systems thinking. This is partly because we are taught to think in linear ways starting at a young age. Additionally, managers are often unwilling to allocate the time and energy that systems thinking requires and may lack the courage to think independently, preferring to think by proxy.[21]

The systems thinking approach is generally a wiser posture in today's world. Why? Because the world is one big system that is changing faster than ever. Linear thinking will only match a situation for a narrow window before it ceases to be relevant.

NURTURING WISDOM

The six actions of an open mind that we've explored throughout this book all help your garden of wisdom to flourish. If you cultivate serious playfulness, befriend your ignorance, indulge your curiosity, ask the right questions, use panoramic thinking, and embrace ambiguity, you're well set up for wise decision-making.

But I want to highlight a few practical activities that can also help.

SET A "DING ALARM"

The preeminent cognitive scientist and philosopher Daniel C. Dennett urged frequent use of what he called a "ding alarm," a mental warning bell set to ring whenever anyone—including you—tries to induce agreement by mere assertion. In Dennett's words, "Whenever you [encounter] the word 'surely,' a little bell should ring—'ding!'—and you should pause to scrutinize what follows, since this is typically the weakest spot in the [source's] case . . . Try it, and you'll soon see how often this word papers over a big crack [in their thinking]."[22] Dennett was inspired in this by Richard Feynman, a Nobel Prize–winning physicist who once defined science as "organized skepticism in the reliability of expert opinion."

My question for you is this: How often, in reading or conversation, do you encounter words and phrases like "surely," "it goes without saying," "it is generally understood," "clearly," or "let's just assume"? Such expressions attempt to hurry past possible counterarguments or questions. In fact, things may *not* be necessarily sure, they *do* need saying, a general understanding may be incorrect, or an analysis or conclusion may not be clear at all. Simply assuming something may be dangerous, even.

Your ding alarm should also be set to go off whenever you feel unclear about or unfamiliar with what someone else believes you know. There is a good chance others share your lack of clarity or familiarity. If you phrase your question tactfully—Could you remind us how we actually know that?, Can you clarify why those assumptions apply to us?, I'm missing the connection you are making between X and Y. Could you fill that in?—most presenters will welcome the opportunity to explain themselves further. If, on the other hand, they are presuming more than they should, your calling them out might avert a serious mistake.

EMBRACE IMPROVISATION

The ability to improvise—to solve problems and create solutions on the fly rather than as a part of carefully laid out plans, and to do this drawing on materials at hand—is important, especially when open-minded actions identify new areas of not knowing that require changing the questions asked and redirecting panoramic thinking.[23] Improvisation happens when your conscious thinking subtly interrogates your unconscious thinking, and your unconscious, in turn, playfully yet constructively answers with its own interrogation of your explicit thinking and actions.

Improvision is not just for "Houston, we have a problem" level emergencies. Engaging in serious playfulness using the tools that have been introduced throughout this book—asking so-what and what-if questions, playing the role of Wizards and Clairvoyants, or imagining a conversation between a problem and a solution—can enrich and improve responses even to garden-variety difficulties. It can be deployed at multiple decision waypoints.

If imagination is recognizing what is absent from a business strategy or action plan, creativity is the active tinkering that brings it into being. Working together consciously and unconsciously, imagination and active creativity produce improvisation. This is how open minds acquire and translate market knowledge into a successful business strategy and how a deep understanding of customers becomes a successful new product or service.

There is some mystique involved in improvisation, of course. We can't plumb all of the thinking executives use as they improvise. What is unmistakable, however, is that they constantly engage in it, just as the artists and musicians I interviewed do. That is why I view most of the executives I've interviewed as artists whose tools are the six actions of an open mind.

ACKNOWLEDGE THE LEGITIMACY OF DIFFERENCES OF OPINION

Many of our interviewees described situations in which open-minded, dedicated participants in a problem-solving session reach different, even conflicting, conclusions.[24] I call this "the hard problem of difference." Stated formally, this happens when colleagues acting wisely—that is, employing the actions of an open mind—arrive at different and even conflicting conclusions that complicate collective decision-making.

How does this happen? Recall two ideas introduced at the start of this book. First, everyone is unique in important ways, even if we also share many qualities. Second, our unique qualities are a source of comparative advantage, not just for ourselves, but for our colleagues, workplace, and community, who benefit when we hone our abilities. When everyone hones their special skills, different people will surface different ideas. Sometimes this is no problem—people appreciate the differing perspectives and incorporate them into a decision. Agreement is more likely to emerge than conflict when the differing parties are able to describe the paths they followed.

But sometimes the differing ideas result in sincere disagreements, or as some interviewees put it, "good-faith conflicts." Sharp differences seem more likely to arise and persist when they are rooted in or justified by the very same data. Judea Pearl and Daniel Mackenzie observed that data is profoundly dumb; it is people and their ways of making causal inferences that create meaning.[25] One interviewee expressed these sincere disagreements with an image of two bighorn rams locking horns.

While both parties can have legitimate claims, only one will prevail. She described particular colleagues as "equally bull-headed . . . Just watching these guys argue gave the rest of us headaches." Further into the discussion, she observed that conflicts are more likely when a problem is urgent, resources are scarce, and egos oversized. In her experience, the disagreement was ultimately resolved by the highest-ranking person in the room.

That said, those disagreements serve a purpose. The cognitive psychologist Donald Hoffman argues that evolution favors answers that are useful as opposed to right.[26] If your hunter-gatherer band includes a wide range of perspectives, you will likely find more of the things that you need. Having diversity within a team of decision-makers helps broaden the range of potential actions, thereby increasing the likelihood of finding a useful solution.

WISDOM IN ACTION: WORKING THROUGH DIFFERENCE

Differences of opinion are legitimate and arise even when people are working in good faith toward the same goal. Acknowledging that fact and embracing creative improvisation can open up a path forward.

I worked with a client in the pharma industry and its advertising agency as they planned a major product launch. As we moved toward the final creative brief for advertising and communications, I brought key decision-makers together for a collage-making exercise. The task I gave them was to create an image that represented the most important ideas they wanted the campaign to communicate, drawing on all the key visuals and phrases, motivations, and emotions that they believed were most vital to the campaign's message. The result? The hard problem of difference. Despite being informed by the same data and using the same terms, the client's and the advertising agency's collages represented completely different ideas.

Fortunately, the relationship between the client and agency was strong. Both sides wanted the campaign to succeed and felt free to speak their minds.[27] It also helped that the exercise involved only a small group of people.[28] What ensued was another day and a half of collage making. Over the course of it, both sides reconfigured their previously preferred cues to be better aligned with each other's. The clarity they gained made it possible to create a more powerful creative brief and tell a richer brand story. For example, the two groups had disagreed about the role the medication could play in achieving a more balanced lifestyle. One group interpreted "balance" in terms of dietary practices, because the medication would allow "forbidden" foods back into a diet. The other felt "balance" meant the peace of mind that came from knowing that the medication lessened the risk of debilitating illness. As they reexamined the data and explored one another's understandings, they came up with a new message: living life fully. This allowed different market segments to view balance through their preferred viewing lens.

FERTILE FOOLISHNESS

Throughout this book we've observed the importance of humility. When addressing the hard problem of difference, you have to allow for the possibility that someone else's idea might be better in some important way than yours. The absence of humility puts a special spin on ignorance, resulting in its most pernicious variant: foolishness.

Foolishness is very common. How often do you observe seemingly knowledgeable, sensible, thoughtful people making foolish decisions? Take a moment to reflect on this and provide your answer. Now for an important follow-up question: Did you include yourself in your sample? If not, why not?

Can you really be wise without having been foolish? How much of what wise people know is learned from their own foolish mistakes? Probably a lot. Foolishness isn't a state we want to stay in, but we can learn a lot from our own foolish actions and mistakes and those of others.

Consider this observation from Bruce Charlton, the editor in chief of the medical journal *Medical Hypotheses*: "The most intelligent people have personalities which over-use abstract analysis [and] are predisposed to have silly ideas and to behave maladaptively when it comes to solving social problems."[29] The very title of a book by Robert J. Sternberg, a leading expert on wisdom and critical thinking, reminds us of the prevalence of foolishness among those we consider wise: *Why Smart People Can Be So Stupid.*[30]

Indeed, the wise leaders my teams have interviewed and whose thinking is so prominent in this book are no strangers to foolishness. They, their colleagues, and, I suspect, most readers are very much like me: we all have an insider's view on foolishness. The fact that my interviewees were quite comfortable discussing their own foolishness is an indication of their confidence in their ability to learn from mistakes—and their resulting wisdom. Although their interviews were strictly confidential, I suspect they were motivated to share their foolish experiences because they knew they would be helpful to others.

Here are just a few examples of their admissions:

> I was told in no uncertain terms I'd look foolish approving it, but I knew I was right.

> I wasn't gonna make the same stupid mistake twice. That [embarrassment] still haunts us.

I have to admit: with hindsight, I was pretty stupid.

The blankets [included in a collage] refer to how everyone is always look-ing for cover to avoid looking dumb. You can guess why I chose an image with lots of blankets. They get a lot of use here.

[I don't want to include any] picture at all. Ideally, I'd be invisible. No one would know how badly I screwed up.

We used several methods to gain further insights into how foolishness made interviewees feel. Sometimes they were prompted to describe their emotions in terms of their senses. For instance, when asked what color might express feeling embarrassed, one participant replied, "Dark red. A glowing dark red to show my chagrin." Another said, "Green, the color of being seasick. That's exactly how I felt when it was pointed out what I had overlooked." In a few instances, circus clowns were referenced as exemplars of foolishness. There is no way of knowing for sure that feelings about being foolish are experienced more intensely than those associated with being wise. However, the research team conducting the interviews concluded that feelings of foolishness registered more vividly with in-terviewees. These emotions can be powerful (sometimes blunt!) teachers as we gain experience and stretch our wisdom muscles.

Fortunately, just as feelings can be direct causes of open- and closed-mindedness, they can also serve as traffic lights, prompting us to abandon an old state of mind and shift to a new one. We can go from being close-minded to open-minded . . . or the reverse.[31] As the neuroscientist and primatologist Robert Sapolsky points out, which direction we move in depends a lot on "context, con-text, and context."[32]

BEING ADAPTIVE AND PRAGMATIC ENCOURAGES BEING WISE

In the opening of this chapter, I noted the many different definitions of wisdom, but I didn't share mine. If asked, I would say that having and using the ability to behave adaptively is what constitutes being wise. And what leads to that adaptive behavior? The very actions we have covered in this book:

- Being playful yet serious to help gain different perspectives,

- Befriending our ignorance or identifying what we don't know,

- Approaching our lack of knowledge with deep curiosity,

- Being comfortable with the ensuing ambiguities,

- Asking the right questions for clarity, and
- Thinking panoramically, exploring other fields for answers.

These six actions matter in every part of our lives.[33] Importantly, each requires the following: (1) timely reflection, (2) careful self-assessment, and (3) adjusting our thinking and behaviors as necessary. When those three conditions are met, the odds of arriving at the right decision and implementing it in the right way, at the right time, and for the right stakeholders greatly improve.

Sometimes we can be sorely tempted to leave it to others to sort out messy problems, whether at work, in our private lives, or as citizens. But we court trouble if we leave that vital work entirely to others. Would-be and real tyrants do sometimes emerge, especially when otherwise well-intentioned people lack humility, courage, and discipline.[34] We always hope, of course, that decision-makers are wise. Hoping, however, is not a sound strategy. We need the courage to express our convictions and the diplomacy to do it in constructive ways.[35] That too is part of wise thinking and behaving.

CONCLUSION

Even absent a consensus definition of wisdom, few can deny that we live in times that demand a lot of it. Fortunately, I believe the know-how we need is within our reach. I believe this because I've had the good fortune to be exposed to talented mentors, colleagues, managers, and students throughout my career. Those experiences have assured me that people can learn to act wisely. Hopefully this outlook makes us all feel optimistic! Wisdom is not an innate talent available only to some. Everyone can achieve it with intentional practice.

In this chapter, I noted that being wise involves multidirectional systems thinking using the six actions of an open mind. Being wise means being actively attuned to and responsive to the emergent effects that come from doing so. Some of those effects may suggest opportunities while others may signal danger. Being wise means inviting your explicit and tacit knowledge and thinking to come together for some serious playfulness and then using judicious improvisation to navigate your way through them. Stated differently, it means identifying your established habits of mind and entertaining new ones.

Different minds that engage diligently in the same open-mind actions may reach conflicting understandings of a problem and its fix. Acting wisely in this circumstance requires the team (1) to listen to one another with empathy and (2) to challenge their collective imaginations through improvisation or serious play.

Note that my definition of wisdom does not stress the importance of high levels of knowledge and/or intelligence. Those qualities are nice icings on the cake, but they cannot replace good character. And, as one set of researchers point out, "the educational system has traditionally valued intelligence and academic skills, but these do not necessarily translate to increasing wisdom" in the form of wise behavior.[36] Wise behavior includes self-reflection, emotional regulation, and prosocial actions. These, of course, are expressed in various Am I? and Are we? questions whose answers demand humility, courage, and discipline.

KEY QUESTIONS TO ASK MYSELF

1. Am I acknowledging my own subjectivity and genuinely considering different perspectives, even when they conflict with my own?

2. Am I humble enough to own and learn from my foolish mistakes as part of the path to wisdom?

3. Am I focused on continuously learning and developing my intelligence rather than seeing it as innate and static?

4. Am I adjusting my thinking and behavior to navigate complex, changing situations?

5. Am I balancing creativity and discipline to improvise wise solutions as new challenges arise?

6. Am I consistently putting in the hard work to gain wisdom through intentional learning and reflection?

KEY QUESTIONS TO SHARE WITH COLLEAGUES

1. Are we attentive to the emotions and social dynamics that influence how open- or closed-minded we are?

2. Do we praise effort rather than innate talent in order to sustain motivation and effective problem-solving?

3. Are we fostering an environment in which we can courageously yet diplomatically share our views?

4. Are we devoting time to reflect upon—do an audit of—the learnings available in our collective experiences?

5. Are we supporting each other's practice of the six actions of an open mind?

NINE

Fluid Thinking, a Reprise

**LEVERAGING THE POWER OF BEING
CONSCIOUSLY UNCONSCIOUS**

There's a final skill I'd like to introduce you to before you close this book, which brings together many of the ideas discussed earlier in these pages. The skill involves the use of a practical process—a theory-in-use—that most interviewees appear to embrace.[1] I've often reminded you that context matters a great deal and yours is no exception. So, the following theory-in-use is suggestive, and I encourage you to engage its features in the spirit of serious playfulness. As important as the ideas are, they are to be employed *your way*. That means being selective and creative—which is the same wise behavior I've been urging here all along.

Most leaders we interviewed and whose thinking informs this book are not narrow, linear thinkers. On the contrary. They are nimble and adaptive. They know when to pause and rethink, and when to follow constructive detours. Their decision-making process is much like a graceful, complex, and challenging dance that unfolds via multiple variations of the six actions of an open mind. I call this dance *fluid thinking*. I define it as "the more or less coherent flowing together of open-mind actions and traits to produce insight and problem solutions." The insights that arise are earned, not given. They are the product of wise actions emerging from a reflective orientation and socio-emotional awareness. These, in turn, require humility, courage, and discipline.

AN INNER VOICE

From time to time I've referenced an inner voice, a kind, wise conscience that prompts you with strategic and tactical Am I? and Are we? questions. Everyone has an inner voice, but not everyone listens to it. We are reminded of this whenever we hear the voice of hindsight singing, "woulda, coulda, shoulda."

Figure 9.1 represents the salient features of fluid thinking and its waypoints such as memory and intuition. One or more open-mind actions like befriending ignorance, panoramic thinking, and so on are likely to be engaged at each waypoint. Your inner voice plays an important role in orchestrating this process. It guides your involvement at each waypoint and your decision to revisit earlier waypoints. In other words, the entire process is a complex, adaptive system.

FIGURE 9.1   An Open Mind in Action.

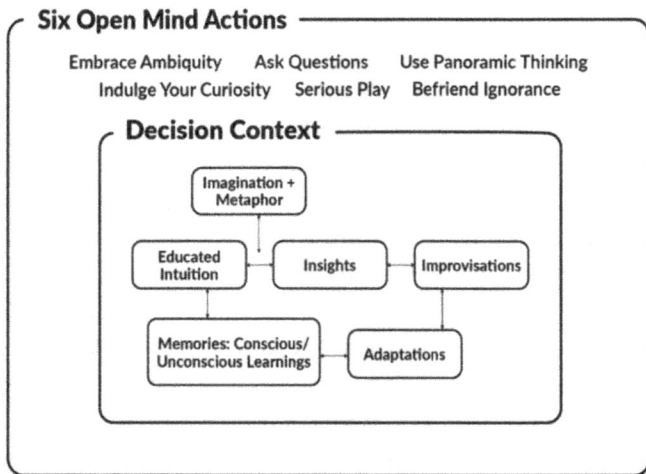

DESIGNED BY BROOKE DANIELS.

OVERVIEW OF THE DECISION CONTEXT

The six open-mind actions drive your use of your conscious and unconscious knowledge stored in your internal and external sources of memory. (And yes, even relying on AI involves your unconscious use of someone else's assumptions.) The knowledge produced provides judgments or intuitions, which are augmented by imagination to yield insights. Analogical thinking and the use of metaphor are especially prominent here. Insights stimulate improvisation in the form of planned or actual behaviors. These behaviors provide constructive feedback, which may lead to changing or adapting initial actions. Feedback may be either instantaneous, as we rapidly contemplate our plans, or delayed, as we wait for results after putting a plan into action. In either case, feedback provides learning that updates or alters prior knowledge. These updates become stored memories available for future use.

What makes this system adaptive is that each waypoint can receive direct feedback from any other waypoint. Moreover, each waypoint is an adaptive system in and of itself making creative use of the system of the six actions. Think of your mind as a kind of dance hall, in which the conscious and the unconscious operations involved in the various actions meet up and introduce themselves through overt and covert signals to the conscious and unconscious operations of each waypoint. The architecture for this becomes our mental models or theory-in-use.

Recall the image of the trapeze artists from chapter 2, which captured their natural, fluid, and seemingly effortless movements. We know their coordination is a product of extensive trial-and-error learning, not to mention focus, discipline, and courage. While they have enough confidence in their prowess to take to the air, they are humble enough to take nothing for granted.[2] As they hone their skills, their inner voices constantly ask and answer questions of themselves and partners. Similarly, our interviewees constantly interrogated themselves as they passed through the waypoints in figure 9.1. Their questions are variations of these:

- Am I engaging in serious playfulness to ensure novel thinking?
- Am I friendly enough with my ignorance to be able to address it?
- Are the questions I ask bold enough?
- Am I allowing my curiosity to bring me to unfamiliar domains?
- Am I willing to learn the languages spoken by other disciplines?
- Am I viewing ambiguities as sources of opportunity?

As we've seen throughout the book, these questions can be formulated in different ways. For example:

- Am I relying on unexamined assumptions?
- Am I seeking diverse perspectives or am I locked into just one?
- Am I being bold enough to seek disconfirming evidence?
- Am I seeking meaningful alternatives or just relying on what's familiar?
- Am I considering alternative ways of framing a problem?
- Am I listening to dissent?

Conscious Am I? questions help bring hidden or tacit knowledge into view, which is a good thing, because such knowledge may be incorrect, and if it remains hidden, it can't be tested or corrected. It may be correct, too, in which case surfacing it makes greater leverage of it possible.

I hope that your encounters with Am I? questions have helped you identify which habits of mind come easily to you and which need targeted practice. This is an important step maintaining educability.[3] Even though these questions can be answered yes or no ("Yes, I *am* listening to dissent. No, I *am not* engaging in serious playfulness"), I hope they prompt more nuanced reflection. The devil, it is said, is always in the details.

Am I? questions help you decide what to do next. For example, you may learn that you need to widen your sources of information and advice. Or perhaps you believe that you're not engaging in serious playfulness but notice that you enjoy using your imagination to approach rock climbing or some other sport as a challenging puzzle. Consider how to apply the habits of an open mind to the rest of your life, including whatever projects you are immersed in. It might also help to write out or verbalize your answers to Am I? questions. Over time it will become easier to visualize the actions you need to take.

Surfacing inner voices requires patient pursuit. One of the executives we interviewed brought a picture of a dark alleyway with trash bins to her interview. "You need to ask a lot of questions," she told us. "What's in [the trash bins]? Anything useful? Harmful? Things like that." The interviewer invited her to elaborate. Her response: "Well, you grope around for light switches. I mean, you gotta be confident . . . they're there somewhere. Just keep at it. Remind everyone you've solved worse problems before. There's a good answer in that alley. You'll see it if you keep at it."

Now let's consider each waypoint a little more closely and take note of some of the Am I? questions our interviewees pose to themselves when they arrive at them.

MEMORIES

The extent to which memory influences our present and future cannot be over-stated. When we think of memory, we usually think about particular past experiences encoded in people's brains. But memories also reside in organizations, artificial intelligence and other information systems, and social norms and practices. Moreover, in the case of human memory they may change dramatically as they are brought to awareness.[4] As a result, writes the neuroscientist Charan Ranganath, they are neither false nor true—they "are constructed in the moment, reflecting both fragments of what actually transpired in the past and the biases, motivations, and cues that we have around us in the present."[5] This is one of the ways in which they provide us with analogies.

Although memory has its own box in figure 9.1, it is involved in every way-point and every action. As the cognitive scientist Andy Clark observes, our expectations are rooted in our past histories.[6] Memory allows us to anticipate the future and, in so doing, to shape it. It directly fuels our intuitions, contributing to our insights and helping us construct and evaluate actions. Most of these tasks occur below the threshold of our awareness. Am I? questions involving memory can help us view our answers more clearly with conscious reflection.

EDUCATED INTUITION

We remember our experiences for a reason: they inform our actions and help bring about sound outcomes. This implicit knowledge is powerful yet hard to verbalize and codify. It is powerful because it is attached to the *feeling* of know-ing. This lends confidence to what we know (justifiably or not) and what we can confidently imagine about what we don't know. As Christopher Engel and Wolf Singer report, "Calculating the best response is cognitively way too taxing. This, however, is true only for the consciously controlled handling of information. The automatic system handles huge amounts of information in almost no time. Only the end result is propelled back to consciousness as an intuition."[7]

Robin M. Hogarth in his authoritative work on the topic defines intuition as "thoughts that are reached with little apparent effort, and typically without con-scious awareness."[8] It is a domain or work-specific form of *practical intelligence* having little to with standardized notions of intelligence. The specific actions discussed throughout this book are examples of the thoughtful attention required to improve both intuition and conscious reasoning.[9] Furthermore, Hogarth also argues as I have throughout the book that imagination and creativity are also required: "The quality of intuition," he notes, "depends, not just on gaining exposure to appropriate experiences, but also on the mechanisms that people use for learning from experience. . . . Instead of just learning automatically from what we see, we also need to learn from what we do not see."[10]

Intuitions, then, are strong impressions of our current situation that are based on memories. More precisely, they are modifications to the lessons we have encoded from prior experiences. For this reason they are properly considered one of the four main pathways to knowledge.

We engage our intuitions, for example, when we draw inferences about the most probable cause or an event or anticipate the outcome of an action.[11] Formal or explicit knowledge provides the reasoning we offer when challenged to explain our actions. As we'll see below, improvisation occurs when we act on an intuition. The feedback we receive may impact whether and how we use or adapt that intuition in the future.

INTUITIVE THINKING QUESTIONS

- Am I trusting my gut instincts while remaining open to new information that might challenge them?
- Am I creating space for reflection and self-awareness?
- Am I relying on appropriate "truth" tests?

IMAGINATION AND METAPHOR

Intuition often requires a midwife to assist in its delivery of insights. This duty falls to imagination. Imagination makes insights visible so they can be consciously assessed, improved, and converted into actions. As we've discussed in earlier chapters this is accomplished via analogical thinking and especially metaphors. Such thinking juxtaposes different things in ways that surface unexpected similarities.[12] Not all insights arising from imagination are practical, but if they are they can be very successful.[13]

IMAGINATIVE AND METAPHORICAL THINKING QUESTIONS

- Am I exploring multiple metaphors and analogies to expand my understanding?
- Am I using imagination exercises to break free from habitual thought patterns and generate fresh ideas?

- Am I befriending what I don't know and inviting it to help chart my forward path?

INSIGHTS

Because insights are also addressed in appendix 1, I'll not say too much about them here, except to note that they are not always productive or sound. However, they also arrive with a feeling of conviction which emboldens us to use them. More importantly, there is evidence that solutions arising from insights are correct more often than those produced by formal analysis.[14] A possible explanation for that is that unconscious processes are more robust and complete than conscious analytic solutions made under pressure and subject to situational biases.

INSIGHT QUESTIONS

- Am I actively seeking out diverse experiences and knowledge to broaden my pool of potential insights?
- Am I sharing my insights with others and inviting their feedback and collaboration?

IMPROVISATION

When we improvise, we apply available insights, cognitions, feelings, and social resources in new ways.[15] Remember, our minds can neither record nor replay our experiences the way a video camera does. Instead, its draws on them in ways that often produce novelty. This can create the illusion that an idea came out of nowhere, which is far from the case. It is likely a product of *conceptual blending* (sometimes called cocreation). This involves a recombination of familiar (and sometimes unfamiliar) conscious and unconscious thoughts and memories to make something new. For example, we combine "fire" with "wall" to produce "firewall"—a whole new idea—or with "cracker" to produce "firecracker."

I noted earlier improvisation is frequent and usually unconscious. For example, we improvise as we:

- turn market knowledge into business strategy,
- recall and reconstruct memories,
- imagine a scene in a novel,
- hear music in response to sound,
- see art instead of colors,

- engage in cocreation or conceptual blending especially in response to advertising,
- draw inferences and form intuitions, and
- predict the outcomes of potential actions.

Improvisation may involve a series of rapid-fire rehearsals or mental simulations in the theaters of our imaginations.[16] Expressions such as "It was a split-second decision," "It just felt right," and "I don't know why, but I knew to do it" are indicators of such rehearsals involved in intuition.[17] Typically, those rehearsals provide corrective feedback. This feedback can be so fast that, as we say, it "unfolds as we think it."[18]

In short, improvised actions are experiments, which, as we repeat them, either reaffirm the validity of our action or suggest changes, which brings us to the final waypoint, adaptation.

IMPROVISATION QUESTIONS

- Am I embracing spontaneity and adaptability in the face of changing circumstances?
- Am I cultivating a mindset of experimentation and learning from both my successes and failures?
- Am I fostering a culture that values and encourages improvisation and creative problem-solving?
- Am I my own best devil's advocate?
- Am I playful while serious and serious while playful?

ADAPTATIONS

The executives we interviewed frequently recalled mistakes they made because they applied a past lesson too rigidly, failing to pause and ask whether the problem at hand required modification of that lesson.

Adjusting a past action to a current problem is not only rational but essential. This is why figure 9.1 uses double headed arrows to indicate feedback among the elements of fluid thinking. As noted above, feedback can happen so rapidly that we may not be aware of it. It can also be protracted and unpleasant—what interviewees called "learning the hard way." I encourage premortems, which help catch missteps before they materialize, precisely to avoid that unpleasantness. Corrective actions create new learnings that update our stored knowledge or memories and prune away prior biases, making better intuitions possible in the future.[19]

ADAPTATION QUESTIONS

- Am I treating actions as learning experiments?
- Am I updating or correcting my beliefs?
- Am I valuing long-term progress over short-term appearance?

A FINAL OBSERVATION

It was both gratifying and inspiring to learn from our interviewees, who gave generously of their time to explore their decision-making with such candor. Their confidentiality was assured, of course. But I believe they were as open as they were because they wanted to learn more about themselves. For all of these leaders, decision-making is precisely that: an act created or manufactured within a complex, adaptive system. This contrasts with the off-the-shelf actions typical of routine decision-making.

All minds emerge from the same forces introduced in chapter 1. But how those forces are experienced is idiosyncratic. Even when a strong consensus emerges within a team, its members quite likely got there via different paths. Much like those trapeze artists in chapter 2, their movements are graceful and complementary. What the audience doesn't see is the effort that went into their performance.

The practices that make up the dance of decision-making aren't always pretty. They may have an unruly quality to them, befitting the unruly nature of the problems being addressed. The results, however, are often beautiful, and the process generates an energy that is highly addictive, which explains why virtually all of our interviewees loved their work.

Aha! Spas

CREATING PERSONAL SPACE FOR SERIOUS PLAY

Coauthored with
SANAYA SHIKARI
Senior Insight Associate, Olson Zaltman

Insights, often called "aha! moments," are sudden, typically fresh conscious real-izations or comprehensions of ideas.[1] We've covered a lot about the mental pro-cesses that promote them, but have said very little about the physical settings that support thinking—an issue that has perhaps even more salience in our new era of remote work. It also relates to an aspect of the mind—the role of physical environments in its operations—that has received little attention so far in this book.[2] Physical settings play a major role in the operations of the mind. However, like the impact of body, brain, and sociocultural forces—this impact is largely unconscious. As a shorthand for physical settings influencing our professional lives, we call these physical environments "Aha! Spas."

Typically, Aha! Spas require very little if anything in terms of fiscal resources. At the same time, facilitating their use has major payoffs in terms of problem-solving, job satisfaction, and overall feelings of well-being. For some people an Aha! Spa is an imagined space—a mental "room" one retreats to for reflection. For others, it is an actual location, such as a hammock or a path in a wooded area. Often being in an Aha! Spa (whether imagined or real) involves a physical activity—hiking, for instance, or playing a musical instrument. It may even be a special conference room or convenient offsite location.

A few questions to consider as you read this appendix include:

- Do I and my colleagues have appropriate tools available during brainstorming sessions?
- Have I anticipated possible conflicts in terms of my staff's preferred physical settings?
- Are there specific elements of our corporate culture that should be present and others excluded from ideation sessions?
- Are we staying focused on the policy objectives we want to satisfy or are we getting distracted by peripheral elements of our thinking?
- What physical cues or reminders of policy objectives ought to be present in ideation sessions?
- Have we programmed constructive pauses?
- Are we supplying the right material aids for each person? For instance, an executive from Hallmark Cards, Inc. described the firm's attentiveness to the personal preferences for writing and drawing implements in its Aha! Spas.
- Are we ensuring that outside intrusions have been isolated?

FIGURE A.1   Related Dimensions of an Aha! Spa.

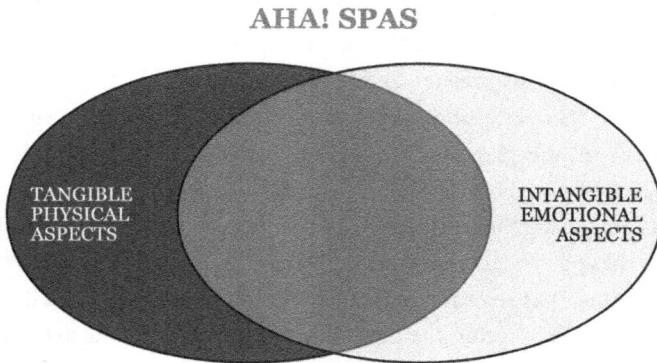

AHA! SPAS

TANGIBLE PHYSICAL ASPECTS

INTANGIBLE EMOTIONAL ASPECTS

DESIGNED BY SANAYA SHIKARI.

A SAFE PLACE FOR OPEN-MINDED EXPLORATION

Wherever or whatever your Aha! Spa is, it is a place where you can freely and safely play and explore.[3] No single setting will appeal to all people or be good for all tasks all the time. Some people prefer early-morning brainstorming sessions; others prefer meeting in high-ceilinged conference rooms, which are thought to support abstract thinking, while standard rooms are preferred for detailed planning tasks.[4] That said, it's not possible to accommodate every individual preference.

It's important to note that the distinction between personal and collaborative Aha! Spas is somewhat arbitrary.[5] The workplace physical environment affects the creation of both. What's important is that all the participants feel they have some degree of control over it.

When you are ready to create your ideal space for insight generation and evaluation, put in a call to your inner architect. You're already acquainted; it's the part of you that designs your vacations and other indulgences. Many of us keep this part of ourselves so tightly locked up that we forget it exists, so give it a get-out-of-jail-free card. Encourage it to play, because, in the words of Stuart Brown, "If we leave the emotion of play out of science, it's like throwing a dinner party and serving pictures of food."[6]

Certain architectural features have been linked to concentration and the ability to complete certain tasks. Ceiling height has been mentioned. Others include types and sources of light, color choices, and types and styles of chair. Scent can also influence insight generation: a surprising number of employees at a major information technology firm independently mentioned the fragrance of one or another citrus fruit as conducive to having insights.

Familiarity is another important design element. Just as an unfamiliar object in your bedroom would be unsettling, unfamiliar or new stimuli in the cocoon space of an Aha! Spa can distract individuals who are on the cusp of generating new insights. Familiar environments enhance object and spatial memory in younger and older adults alike, and memory is important in evaluation, decision-making, and the ability to recall knowledge.[7] A study conducted by Olson Zaltman to uncover thoughts and feelings about home revealed that comfortable personal spaces provided "mini rejuvenations" that kept individuals energized. One participant remarked, "I think [in most offices] you never feel like you're in your own surroundings. So with this new office that I'm putting in, *I can put whatever colors that I want, and it's just me. It's not anyone else. It's not anyone else's influence*" (emphasis added).

This, it is argued, is why so many people enjoy working at home, and are so insistent on personalizing their workspace if they work in an office.[8] Cold, impersonal environments that drive us to continuous productivity curb our ability to be vulnerable, creative, and open-minded. While it may be impossible to find a permanent escape from results-driven expectations, it is essential to find times and places to reflect.

Design alterations that support meaningful interactions and trust between teams can be made.[9] If workspaces are too far apart, that can hinder or even prevent in-person interactions. Vertical distances require even more of a mental effort to traverse than horizontal distances; offices that are more than one floor apart experience almost no communication between them.

Some companies seek to encourage interactions by putting people in big common spaces. But when large groups work together as undifferentiated masses, people feel unimportant and worry about being watched. Breaking large groups up into smaller groups with their own spaces gives people a greater sense of control and makes them more willing to share ideas.[10]

At the Conscious Cities conference in 2018, Kate Jeffery, a behavioral neuroscientist at University College London, explained how places with rotational symmetry that look the same from all directions (like the Lotus Temple in Delhi or Piccadilly Circus in London) leave people confused and disoriented in relation to the outside world, while bilateral symmetry allows people to navigate easily and feel more at ease to communicate and socialize. Another preference that is evolutionarily hardwired into us is for spaces from which we can see without being seen.

We asked forty-seven thought leaders from diverse settings to describe their preferred, insight-friendly settings via the following question: If you could design your ideal setting for developing insights about an important professional challenge, what would it be like?

Forty-three responded. The special role of nature and the outdoors was a dominant feature in most of their answers. This artist's response was echoed by a number of executives and scientists:

> Open minds can be cultivated by being in open places . . . Having the experience of physical and visual openness inclines us to think differently . . . Expansive views expand thinking.

Others were naturally attuned to the notion of serious playfulness:

> My ideal arrangement for developing insights involves an *"experimentation playground."* . . . I strongly believe there is beauty in the 'messy middle,' and that's where creativity and innovation reside.

The notion that companies are differently prepared or inclined to engage in serious playfulness came up in another leader's comments:

> [I am bemused by] how much we value imagination when it comes to early childhood vs. our undervaluing it when it comes to "serious" business contexts, although people are asked to be more and more innovation driven. So, we are left with the puzzling challenge: be creative/innovative but also be right all the time.

Another senior executive described the alterations he'd made to his office space.

> We redesigned the space to foster creativity and reflect creativity, which was, of course, the business we were in. There was *something almost childlike about the space*—bright colors, novel materials (e.g., grass walls), games/other diversions, multimedia, erasable walls, and getaway spaces with fun names [such as] the "treehouses," where you could "escape." There were open spaces and private spaces, and easy access to beverages and snacks.

Still another respondent, a leader in the field of finance, reflected on the benefits he gained from walking.

> Aristotle was so enamored with walking that he named his philosophy school the *Peripatetic School,* which translates to "given to walking about" . . . I notice a meaningful improvement in the overall quality of my thinking, especially creative thinking, while walking.

Another spoke about the benefits of empathic listening:

> A helpful colleague will serve as a sounding board for my ideas, will offer their own ideas without fear of being wrong, will respect my ideas even if they are off target, and will consider angles for approaching ideas that are different than mine.

Still another spoke of his need for a devil's advocate:

> I have always found it useful to have a naysayer—someone who will tell you what they think is wrong with your ideas. I'm not saying these are ultimately joint decisions, but I am saying that *teamwork is my way of thinking through insights and strategies.*

Many respondents spoke about achieving comfort with ambiguity in a variety of situations. A respondent spoke about dreams:

I have gained many incredible and helpful insights through paying attention to my dreams, how they change, themes and patterns, etc. Talking to a friend who is a Jungian analyst and generously shares her time with me helps, too.

And yet another stressed the importance of quiet listening—to herself:

I think for my style of learning, it is really important to talk about things. The old Karl Weick saying, "I don't know what I think until I hear what I say," seems to be true for me. It is not as if I don't know what I think at all. It is that I struggle with extracting it as clearly unless I say it out loud to another person. Then things really crystalize for me.

SUMMARY

Personal and personalized work environments have a major impact on learning in organizations as they do elsewhere. It is not a surprise that many executives stress the importance of Aha! Spa settings in their being open-minded and subsequently in their success. Aha! Spas provide a safe haven for self-candor, the exercise of imagination, and mental simulations of creative problem solutions among other benefits. In group Aha! Spas there develops a greater appreciation of others' points of view and the satisfaction of knowing your own position is heard. These and other benefits of attending to Aha! Spas personalized to one's own and/or group needs encourage being open-minded and ultimately to lead personal and team well-being.

KEY QUESTIONS TO ASK MYSELF

1. Am I being attentive to the impact on my thinking of both intangible and tangible features of my work setting?

2. Am I aware of how those features facilitate or inhibit my thought processes?

3. Am I proactive enough in leveraging them both to encourage deep, open-minded thinking?

4. Am I being as imaginative and creative as the workplace, time of day, and somatic stimuli allow?

5. Am I tuned in to the possible outsized impact on me of seemingly trivial elements of my work environment?

KEY QUESTIONS TO SHARE WITH COLLEAGUES

1. Are we allowing for the diverse creative needs of each member of the team?

2. Are we allowing individuals to control and express their creative needs and adapt to their physical environments appropriately?

3. Are we allowing collaborative Aha! Spas to inadvertently censure their collective decision-making?

4. Are we generating trust and a sense of safety so that diverse ideas and thoughts can weave together smoothly?

5. Are we clear and in agreement about the reasons for establishing a common Aha! Spa?

6. Are we tolerant of colleagues who opt for a more private Aha! Spa space?

The Zaltman Metaphor Elicitation Technique (ZMET)

A TOOL FOR SURFACING UNCONSCIOUS THOUGHTS AND FEELINGS

Coauthored with
JAMES FORR
Head of Insights, Olson Zaltman

BACKGROUND

An accepted premise in psychology (and other sciences related to the study of human thought and experience) is the value of "analogical reasoning," with analysis of metaphors as its primary tool.[1] Analyzing metaphors helps us understand the mind's unconscious and conscious operations. Furthermore, conscious metaphors are a primary avenue used by clinicians to identify mental activity occurring below our awareness. The analysis of metaphors, by a trained investigator, is like a can opener allowing access to unconscious thinking processes.[2] Metaphors are a way to consciously probe unconscious thoughts and feelings. Colleagues at Olson Zaltman have accumulated more than twenty-five years of experience doing this with customers and with managers regarding topics important to both groups. This book reports on an extensive use of metaphor elicitation techniques with executives and other leaders in the form of ZMET (Zaltman Metaphor Elicitation Technique), a patented tool owned by Olson Zaltman. Because of this tool's important role in informing *Dare to Think Differently*, it merits some description here.

Specifically, we outline of most of the steps used by highly skilled interviewers and identify a few of the research foundations for each one. Interviews are one-on-one, sometimes taking up to two hours. The focus is on the disciplinary foundations of technique rather than on the training required for collection and analysis of the resulting insights. These multidisciplinary foundations and their complementarity are what make the method so robust in its applications. It is important to note one caution. Interviews are designed to surface thoughts and feelings that lie below awareness. For this reason, interviewers must also be prepared for situations when interviewees gain unexpected and even unwanted insights about themselves.

BEFORE THE INTERVIEW

Study participants are recruited approximately one week in advance of their interview and are asked to collect a set of images (usually between five and seven images) that represent their thoughts and feelings about the focal topic. This assignment is called the ZMET Question.

Respondents come to the interview well prepared, having reflected deeply on the topic and carefully considered the selection of their images. They are also reminded that the images should be reflections of their feelings rather than literal in nature. (For example, in a ZMET study about how consumers feel while dining at a chain of pizza restaurants, respondents would be advised to avoid collecting images of pizza or ads for the brand.)

Participants report taking different approaches to the assignment. Some have described setting aside snippets of time over multiple days to collect their images. Others may not gather their images until the night before. However, because participants are recruited days in advance, the assignment has time to marinate in their minds, so to speak, meaning that even a hastily assembled collection of images will be informed by both conscious and unconscious mental processing.[3]

STORYTELLING

In the Storytelling step, participants describe each image they collect and discuss how the pictures relate to the ZMET Question. Interviewers take respondents through the images, one at a time, seeking to understand the unconscious meaning and emotionality behind each picture. Because thought is image-based, these visual images, which are metaphorical in nature, enable participants to better articulate the nuances of their thoughts than using words alone.[4]

Interviewers deploy multiple techniques in the Storytelling step as they develop an understanding of participants' thinking. One such technique is laddering, in which the goal is to establish the connections among product attributes, their functional outcomes, psychological and social outcomes, and emotional end benefits.[5] Common laddering probes include: Why is that important to you?; What does that give you?; What happens next?; and How does that make you feel? The psychological, social, and emotional experiences often function at least somewhat unconsciously. For example, laddering revealed that many respondents choose a particular candy bar because it makes them feel like a kid again, which in turn offers a moment of escape from a world that can be harsh and unrelenting. Although these thoughts likely are not top of mind when these consumers are purchasing or consuming the candy bar, they are feelings that nevertheless quietly influence the purchase decision.

Another technique is to explore various aspects of a spoken metaphor.[6] In a study about the experience of choosing a college, a high school senior nearing the end of the application process stated, "I can see the light at the end of the tunnel." The interviewer responded with a series of questions designed to help the participant think carefully about—and explain—the unconscious feelings that prompted her to use that metaphor:

Q: In your mind's eye, what does the tunnel look like?

A: It is a long, dark tunnel. I can see the end now, but for a long time it was just darkness.

Q: Why do you describe it that way?

A: Because I felt a lot of pressure from my parents to get into a good school, and that was stressful enough. But then how do you pick? You're weighing all these factors—cost, location, social life, the quality of the school. How do you even make that decision? It seemed like a hopeless task almost.

Q: Take me inside the tunnel. What else is in there?

A: Well, I am. I am almost out, but I am still there. But then the floor of the tunnel is almost like a treadmill at times. You think you are moving forward, but then you're not. And the walls are actually flowering, you just can't see the flowers.

Q: Why?

A: The flowers symbolize the fact that high school is actually a great time of life and you should be enjoying that time, but sometimes you are so focused on tests and grades and college applications that you ignore the fun stuff and the things that really matter, like your friends and your family and your after-school activities. It's like your mind is somewhere else much of the time, just worrying. I wish I could stress out a lot less and just enjoy the moment because I'll never have this chance again.

Interviewers also ask participants to relate specific real-life stories about the topic.[7] Humans remember experiences in stories and communicate in stories, so a simple probe like, "Tell me about a time that happened" can unleash a torrent of thoughts and feelings. Moreover, stories help bring emotions and unconscious feelings closer to the surface for respondents, open up additional lines of inquiry for the interviewer, and crystallize abstract concepts in the minds of clients who are internalizing and acting upon the research.[8]

MISSED IMAGES

Participants may struggle to find the perfect image for certain ideas. Furthermore, during the course of the Storytelling discussion new concepts come to mind that the participant had not previously considered. In other words, they may have learned something unexpected about themselves. Therefore, at the conclusion of the Storytelling step, participants are asked if there were any images that they couldn't find or any new ideas that emerged that they would like to capture in an image. Typically, the answer is no. However, if new images come to mind, the participant may describe what these images look like in their imagination or may, with the help of the interviewer, create the image spontaneously using an AI image generator. The interviewer then asks questions about the new image, using the laddering and metaphor elaboration probes that were part of the Storytelling step.

CONSTRUCT ELICITATION

Categorization is a fundamental way humans understand their experiences.[9] The Kelly Repertory Grid is a categorization technique that has been used for decades on children as young as preschool age to more deeply understand how they see their lives.[10] In its original form, the Repertory Grid asks children to compare and contrast three different people (for example, father, mother, and best friend) by asking how any two of those people are similar to each other and yet different from the third, across any important dimension of the child's choosing.

In a ZMET interview, interviewers select three of the participant's images, usually but not always at random. The participant is then asked to describe how any two of them are similar to each other, yet different from the third, in terms of what they represent regarding the primary topic. This is an especially helpful step when several images seem to represent similar feelings or ideas. It often turns out that seemingly repetitive images prompt very different thoughts.

For example, in a study about how parents approach their child's chronic medical condition, one mother's images included a person atop a mountain, Wonder Woman, and someone flexing her muscles in a gym. At a broad level, all of these images were about confidence. However, using the modified Repertory Grïd technique, the interviewer enabled the participant to reveal that the latter two images were mostly about the present day and her feelings of control over the day-to-day aspects of her son's condition. The mountain image was more aspi- rational about the future, and how she is optimistic that she will be able to look back at her son's childhood and feel that she has been a successful parent who has given her child the skills necessary to manage his condition and become a happy, thriving adult.

METAPHOR ELABORATION

In an approach borrowed from art therapy and other clinical practices in psy- chology, the interviewer selects one or two of the participant's images and asks them to imagine zooming out on the picture. They are then asked to describe what in their mind's eye would enter the image, either in the expanded frame or in the foreground or background of the original image, that would better illus- trate the image's relationship to the research topic.[11] The participant typically is asked to modify the image in other ways, as well. Those probes can include the addition of other symbolic characters to the image, imagining the image as part of a before-and-after sequence, or pretending that the image could become ani- mated, such as in a movie or cartoon.

In a US study for a company that offers tax preparation services, a participant selected an image of a lighthouse perched on a rocky cliffside amidst turbulent waters. When asked to expand the frame, the respondent described seeing a boat in the distance approaching the rocky outcropping while being buffeted by the waves, which symbolized the anxiety he feels as tax season approaches. When asked where he would be in the image, he described himself as the captain of the ship struggling with a faulty navigation system. This reflected his feelings of inadequacy when doing his own taxes. When asked to animate the image, he imagined the tax preparation software he recently began using as a character that races up the stairs of the lighthouse and turns on the light, thus preventing him from crashing into the rocks, which is how he metaphorically conceptualizes the potential outcome of making a costly mistake on his taxes. These types of probes are intended to disrupt participants' thinking and help them explore the more unconscious aspects of their experience.

SENSORY METAPHORS

Here, respondents are asked to use senses other than sight to further elaborate on their thoughts and feelings. This is one aspect of what is known as embodied cognition, which relates to how sensorial experiences, spatial orientation, and physical movement affect and reflect perceptions.[12] For instance, humans encode their memories using all of their senses.[13] If you recall the last time you went to a beach, you likely call to mind the smell of the ocean air, the feeling of sand between your toes, and sounds of the wave crashing, among other sensorial experiences. Even if the ZMET interview focuses on a topic that does not inherently contain compelling sensory cues, participants can use sensory cues from other situations to metaphorically explain the emotions and feeling they associate with the research topic. (For example, the smell of chocolate chip cookies might reflect the comfort and security a consumer feels when dealing with a trusted auto insurance provider.) The specific sensory experiences are usually idiosyncratic, but the explanations for why those experiences were chosen can reveal deep commonalities across the study sample.

In interviews with executives about the impact of AI on their organizations, one person captured her feeling with the taste of her favorite wine, which was extremely complex with a multitude of flavor notes. The metaphor symbolized her many conflicted feelings about AI, but an overall sense that the technology would bring benefits to her business and society as a whole.

VIGNETTE

Some therapists use psychodrama to help patients "act out" relevant experiences in their lives and see problems from fresh angles.[14] In a modified version of that approach, respondents create a story with several predetermined characters that reflects their feelings about the topic. By conceptualizing various aspects of their experience as characters with a physical form who can experience feelings and interact, the participant is able to elaborate on the dynamics of the system of relationships that unconsciously underlies their perceptions of the topic. The imagined dramatization of this scenario also makes possible expressions of embodied cognition.[15]

In ZMET research into Americans' perceptions of poverty conducted for the Gates Foundation, participants were asked to create a vignette that included three characters: you, poverty, and society. Here is how a young woman who had been struggling with student loan debt responded:

> I am just going through my day, living a normal life. Poverty is a storm, any kind of severe weather. And society is like a weather forecaster. It is nighttime and the storms are coming. I am listening to the forecaster, who is telling me, "Be prepared. Keep paying attention. The storms are coming to your area." Then a tornado siren goes off, and they tell you that you have to get to the basement and get whatever protection you need.
>
> Poverty is a storm because it is destructive. It can create a lot of anxiety, and there is some predictability to it, but not all the time. If you have been born to a family without a lot of money, then you are probably going to struggle with poverty at some point. But even if that isn't the case, there are things that can just happen. You could have a lot of money and suddenly lose it. Or you can get over your head in student loan debt to a degree you hadn't anticipated. Sometimes it just doesn't matter. You can do everything right and still get into that situation.
>
> Society is like a forecaster because a forecaster tells you things but can't really help you directly. You hear all kinds of things in the news and from your friends about how to stay out of financial trouble, and that is valuable, but if something bad happens, you're still on your own. People can give you advice but no one is going to take care of you but you.
>
> The mood of this story is panicked and terrified. Whenever I had to start paying back my student loans, they sent an estimate of what monthly payments would be. When I first got that I was like, "There's no way I'm going to be able to pay this every month."

DIGITAL IMAGE

The interview concludes with participants working with a graphic artist to create a summary composite image of the pictures they selected. It is dynamic since the participant has the freedom to alter images, morph them together, and juxtapose them in ways that lend visual meaning to the resulting composite. The graphic artist essentially serves as the "hands" in the process, while the participant is the "mind" behind its creation.

It is not uncommon for participants to react with some alarm as this step is introduced, with many telling interviewers something to the effect of, "I don't know if I can do this. I am not creative." However, the step typically proves both satisfying and productive. Indeed, recent research suggests that creativity comes in many forms, is often contextual in nature, and is a universal human trait.[16] Many participants take great pride in their digital images and prize the copies they receive.

Below is a digital image created by a global sustainability executive to summarize her thoughts and feelings about the climate for sustainable innovation inside her company, followed by her description, which captures how sustainable practices can help transform the world.

The first image of that darkness and the tunnel reflects the uncertainty of the current world we live in. Because what I am seeing now is quite uncertain and I am usually on the pessimistic side.

The planet images gives you some perspective on the scale of the issue we have. It is not an easy issue. From the vantage point of space, you can see the significance of this problem.

The seeds are the efforts that people like me try to do on the ground. One

FIGURE A.2 An Executive's Visual Summary of Sustainable Innovation

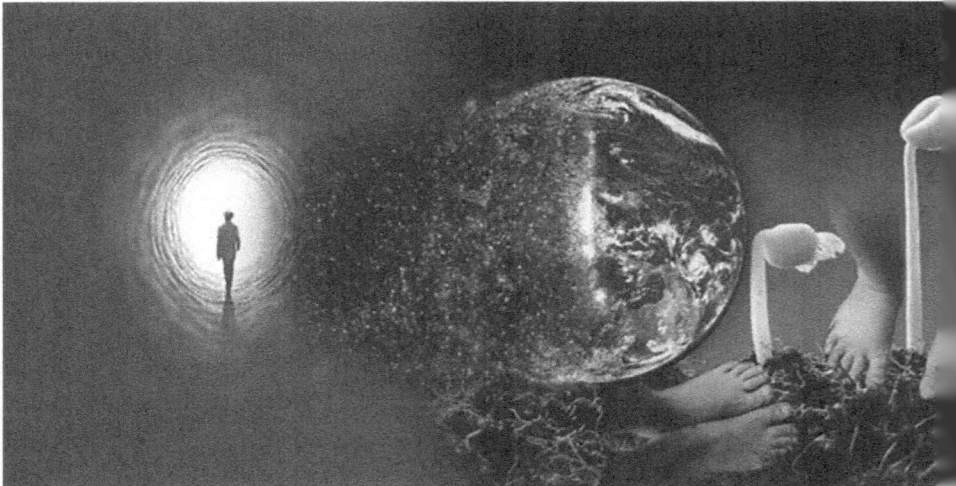

of the most important things that, not just corporations and institutions, but also individuals need to understand is the relationship between humanity and Mother Earth. This is symbolized by the feet on the ground.

The image of the hands and the fist bump shows the different levels of collaboration and partnerships humans can form if we take this issue seriously. This is important because of the future generations, who are represented by the paper dolls. Their future hinges on what we do now on these partnerships. They will be facing even more uncertainty, but we will try to make it better for them. They will be more connected to nature. So, it is just the beginning.

Literary scholar Jonathan Gottschall has written,

Why do stories cluster around a few big themes, and why do they hew so closely to problem structure? Why are stories *this* way instead of all the other ways they could be? I think that problem structure reveals a major function of storytelling. It suggests that the human mind was shaped *for story*, so that it could be shaped *by* story.[17]

ZMET, thus, consists of a series of interconnected stories. Participants tell their own stories through the various steps in the methodology, which helps analysts understand how a product, service, or experience affects and fits into people's bi-

ographies and self-perceptions. Analysts, in turn, tell stories to clients and sponsors of the research in order to summarize the key insights. And subsequently, those clients tell their own stories about the research, sometimes internally within their organizations and sometimes back to consumers in the form of advertising communication intended to appeal to the emotions and one's sense of personal identity.

NOTES

Preface

1. Michael J. Mazarr, Tim Sweijs, and Daniel Tapia, *The Sources of Renewed National Dynamism* (The Rand Corporation, 2024), 3.

2. Mazarr, Sweijs, and Tapia, *The Sources of Renewed National Dynamism,* 28.

3. For an excellent discussion of educability and critique of standardized intelligence measures by a leading computer scientist see Leslie Valient, *The Importance of Being Educable: A New Theory of Human Intelligence* (Princeton University Press, 2024).

Chapter 1

1. Marcelo Gleiser Frank and Evan Thompson, *The Blind Spot: Why Science Cannot Ignore Human Experience* (MIT Press, 2024). The first published article about ZMET made the same argument that Frank and his colleague make today. See Gerald Zaltman, "Rethinking Market Research: Putting People Back In," *Journal of Marketing Research* 34, no. 4 (1997): 424–37.

2. For a recent review of theories-in-use see Valerie A. Zeithaml, Bernard J. Jaworski, Ajay K. Kohli, Kapil R. Tuli, Wolfgang Ulaga, and Gerald Zaltman, "A Theories-in-Use Approach to Building Marketing Theory," *Journal of Marketing* 84, no. 1 (2020): 32–51. For a discussion of the role of metaphor in theories-in-use, see Adam R. E. Beaty and P. J. Silvia, "Metaphorically Speaking: Cognitive Abilities and the Production of Figurative Language," *Memory and Cognition* 41, no. 2 (2013): 255–67. One of the earliest uses of the term can be found in Chris Argyris and Donald Schon, *Theory in Practice: Increasing Professional Effectiveness* (Jossey Bass, 1992).

3. David E. Melnikoff and John A. Bargh, "The Mythical Number Two," *Trends in Cognitive Sciences* 22, no. 4 (2018): 280.

4. John A. Bargh and Ran R. Hassin "Human Unconscious Processes in Situ: The Kind of Awareness That Really Matters," in *The Cognitive Unconscious: The First Half Century*, ed. Arthur S. Reber and Rhianon Allen (Oxford University Press, 2022), 202. They refer to Daniel Kahneman, *Thinking Fast and Slow* (Farrar, Straus and Giroux, 2011), 29.

5. Readers are strongly encouraged to read Iain McGilchrist's account of the operations of left and right hemispheres of the brain. Both spheres do the same basic things but in very different ways. A "healthy" functioning mind requires collaborations between both with somewhat more leadership assumed by the right hemisphere. Problems arise when the left hemisphere tries to dominate the right hemisphere. Iain McGilchrist, *The Matter with Things: Our Brains Our Delusions and the Unmaking of the World* (Perspectiva Press, 2019).

6. Bargh, "The Cognitive Unconscious in Everyday Life," in Reber and Allen, *The Cognitive Unconscious*, 91.

7. Vinod Venkatraman and John Wittenbraker, *Disrupting Dual Systems: A Dynamic Decision-Making Framework for Human Behavior* (The Marketing Science Institute, 2020), 24.

8. Roy F. Baumeister and William von Hippel, "Meaning and Evolution: Why Nature Selected Human Minds to Use Meaning, *Evolutionary Studies in Imaginative Culture* 4, no. 1 (2021): 1–44.

9. Donald D. Hoffman, *The Case Against Reality: How Evolution Hid the Truth from Our Eyes* (Penguin Books, 2019).

10. Andy Clark, *The Experience Machine: How Our Minds Predict and Shape Reality* (Pantheon Books, 2023). He notes in the conclusion of his book, "Human minds are not elusive, ghostly inner things. They are seething, swirling oceans of prediction, continuously orchestrated by brain, body and world" (216).

11. See especially Annie Murphy Paul, *The Extended Mind: The Power of Outside the Brain* (Mariner, 2021).

12. See Roy F. Baumeister and Mark J. Landau, "Finding the Meaning of Meaning: Emerging Insights on Four Grand Questions," *Review of General Psychology* 22 (2018): 1–10.

13. See especially Matthew Cobb, *The Idea of the Brain: The Past and Future of Neuroscience* (Basic Books, 2020).

14. Thomas Nagel, "What Is It Like to Be a Bat?" *The Philosophical Review* 83, no. 4 (1974): 435–50. Ed Yong elaborates on this. He notes in order to understand another creature, "We need to know almost everything about that animal . . . about all of its senses, its nervous system and the rest of its body, its needs and its environment, its evolutionary past and it ecological present." Ed Yong, *An Immense World* (Random House, 2022), 334.

15. For more commentary on this issue, see Daniel C. Dennett, *Intuition Pumps and Other Tools for Thinking* (W. W. Norton Co., 2022).

16. Steven Sloman and Philip Fernbach, *The Knowledge Illusion: Why We Never Think Alone* (Riverhead Books, 2017) 103, 105, emphasis mine.

17. Harry Collins, "The Unexplicated and Its Consequences," in Reber and Allen, *The Cognitive Unconscious*, 289. For more insight about the impact of social structure and culture on specific brain structures and functions, see Tomoyuki Furuyashiki and Scott J. Russo, "Editorial: Neuroscience of Resilience for Mental Health," *Neuroscience Research* 211 (2025), https://doi.org/10.1016/j.neures.2024.11.006; and for more on the importance of body's contributions to mind see Mark Johnson, *The Body in the Mind: The Bodily Basis of Meaning, Imagination, and Reason* (University of Chicago Press, 1987).

18. Michael Platt, *The Leader's Brain: Enhance Your Leadership Build Stronger Teams Make Better Decisions and Inspire Greater Innovation with Neuroscience* (Wharton School Press, 2020).

19. Simon B. Wang and Jamie L. Hanson, "Childhood Socioeconomic Position Relates to Adult Decision-Making: Evidence from a Large Cross-Cultural Investigation," *PLOS One*, November 12, 2024, https://doi.org/10.1371/journal.pone.0310972.

20. McGilchrist, *The Matter with Things* 223.

21. Gerald Zaltman, "Marketing's Forthcoming Age of Imagination," *Academy of Marketing Science* 6, no. 3/4 (2016): 99–115.

22. Garrett M. Graff, *When the Sea Came Alive: An Oral History* (Simon and Schuster, 2024).

23. A very helpful discussion about how we appraise our thinking while engaged in decision making is provided by John Dunlosky and Janet Metcalfe, *Metacognition* (Sage, 2009).

24. Runtial Long and Yaohand Long, "The Influence of Critical Thinking on Creativity: A Moderated Mediation Analysis," *Social Behavior and Personality: An International Journal* 51, no. 12 (2023): 1–9.

25. We'll assume neither "mind" being interviewed is aware this phrase is often attributed to Albert Einstein.

26. World Economic Forum, *Global Risks Report 2024,* 19th ed. (World Economic Forum, 2024), 92, 4.

27. World Economic Forum, *Global Risks Report 2024.*

28. Gerald Zaltman and Lindsay Zaltman, *Marketing Metaphoria: What Deep Metaphors Reveal About the Minds of Consumers* (Harvard Business Press, 2006).

29. Chaim Oren, personal communication, 2024.

30. Chaim Oren, personal communication, 2024.

31. Robert J. Sternberg, "Why Real-World Problems Go Unresolved and What We Can Do About It: Inferences from a Limited-Resource Model of Successful Intelligence," *Journal of Intelligence* 6, no. 44 (2018): 1–9. On this important and provocative topic, see Matthieu Raoelison, Valerie A. Thompson, and Wim De Neys, "The Smart Intuitor: Cognitive Capacity Predicts Intuitive Rather Than Deliberate Thinking," *Cognition* 204 (2020), https://doi.org/10.1016/j.cognition.2020.104381.

32. See for example, Arie W. Kruglanski and Gerd Gigerenzer, "Intuitive and Deliberate Judgments Are Based on Common Principles," *Psychological Review* 118 (2011): 97–109; and Long and Long, "The Influence of Critical Thinking on Creativity."

33. An excellent description of how cultivating positive emotions may be associated with an open mind and help overcome negative emotions is found in Barbara L. Fredrick-

son, "Cultivating Positive Emotions to Optimize Health and Well-Being," *Prevention and Treatment* 3, no. 1 (2000): 1–25.

34. L. A. Maruskin, T. M. Thrash, and A. J. Elliot, "The Chills as a Psychological Construct: Content Universe, Factor Structure, Affective Composition, Elicitors, Trait Antecedents, and Consequences," *Journal of Personality and Social Psychology* 103, no. 1 (2012): 135–57; D. R. Schurtz et al., "Exploring the Social Aspects of Goose Bumps and Their Role in Awe and Envy," *Motivation and Emotion* 36, no. 2 (2012): 205–17.

35. Dacher Keltner, *Awe: The New Science of Everyday Wonder and How It Can Transform Your Life* (Penguin Press, 2023). See also Dacher Keltner and Jonathan Haidt, "Approaching Awe: A Moral, Spiritual, and Aesthetic Emotion," *Cognition and Emotion* 17, no. 2 (2003): 297–314. Other excellent resources are E. T. Bonner and H. L. Friedman, "A Conceptual Clarification of the Experience of Awe: An Interpretative Phenomenological Analysis," *The Humanistic Psychologist* 39, no. 3 (2011): 222–35, and Steve Paulson et al., "Beyond Oneself: The Ethics and Psychology of Awe," *Annals of the New York Academy of Sciences* 1501, no. 1 (2021): 30–47.

36. See E. D. Ihm et al., "Awe as a Meaning-Making Emotion: On the Evolution of Awe and the Origin of Religions," in *The Evolution of Religion Religiosity and Theology: A Multilevel and Multidisciplinary Approach*, ed. Jay R. Feierman and Luis Oviedo, 138–53 (Oxford University Press, 2020).

37. An excellent discussion of the role of awe in stimulating curiosity about science can be found in Piercarlo Valdesolo, Andrew Shtulman, and Andrew S. Baron, "Science Is Awe-Some: The Emotional Antecedents of Science Learning," *Emotion Review* 9, no. 3 (2017), 215–21. See also Paulson et al., "Beyond Oneself" and Marcelo Gleiser, "Science and Awe," *Annals of the New York Academy of Sciences* 1501, no. 1 (2021): 78–80.

38. Examples from higher education can be found in: Yue Peng, "Enhancing Cross-Cultural Well-Being: A Mixed Methods Study on Critical Thinking, Cultural Intelligence, and Eudaimonic Well-Being in Arts Students' Cultural Identity Development," *Frontiers in Psychology*, November 12, 2024, https://www.frontiersin.org/journals/psychol ogy/articles/10.3389/fpsyg.2024.1425929/full; Claude Gratton, "Critical Thinking and Emotional Well-Being," *Inquiry: Critical Thinking Across Disciplines* 20, no. 3 (2001): 39–51; Jose Carlos Vazquez et al., "Critical Thinking and Student Well-Being: An Approach in University Students," *Societies* 13, no. 11 (2023): 1–14; and Yilin Sun and Xiaoshu Xu, *The Development of Personal Learning Environments in Higher Education* (Routledge, 2024). Examples from the field of medicine are articles in a November 16 special issue of *Neuroscience Research* including Tomoyuki Furuyashiki and Scott J. Russo, "Editorial: Neuroscience of Resilience for Mental Health," *Neuroscience Research* 211 (2025), https://doi.org /10.1016/j.neures.2024.11.006; Ma Guadalupe Carillo-Montes, "The Importance of Scientific Training in the Clinical Pathologist," *Revista médica del Instituto Mexicano del Seguro Social* 62 (suppl 1) (2024), https://pubmed.ncbi.nlm.nih.gov/39590883/; and Lee Sy and Chang Cy "Nursing Management of the Critical Thinking and Care Quality of ICU Nurses," *Journal of Nursing Management* 30, no. 7 (2022): 2889–96.

39. Wided Batat, "Introducing Holixec Education: A Human-Centric Approach to Learner Workplace Readiness via the MECCDAL Method," *Journal of Macromarketing* (August 2024).

40. This observation among our interviewees has substantial backing in other domains. For a review of the impact of open-mindedness on feelings of creative competence see, Long and Long, "The Influence of Critical Thinking on Creativity."

41. A recent survey among senior university leaders found their number one most consequential issue affecting their mission and financial stability involved the escalating student mental health and well-being crisis. Tony Donatelli, "Five Things University Leaders are Prioritizing This Year," EAB, January 11, 2024, https://eab.com/resources/blog/strategy-blog/five-things-university-leaders-are-prioritizing/. According to an expert in corporate wellness, this crisis in education is a leading indicator of similar crises in commercial private sector firms (Chaim Oren, 2024, personal communication). Given the strong empirical evidence in higher education that teaching critical thinking leads to student well-being, it is likely that encouraging open mind practices in business settings can have similar beneficial effects.

42. Collins, "The Unexplicated and Its Consequences." See also, Angus Fletcher and Mike Benveniste, *Narrative Creativity: An Introduction to How and Why* (Cambridge University Press, 2025).

43. See Mihnea C. Moldoveanu and Das Narayandas, *The Future of Executive Development* (Stanford University Press, 2021) for more on the short supply of open-mind actions in executive training.

44. Shirley Larkin, "Introduction," in *Metacognition and Education: Future Trends*, ed. Shirley Larkin (Routledge, 2024), 1.

45. A sample of presentation titles: "Knowing About Knowing: An Illusion of Human Competence Can Hinder Appropriate Reliance on AI Systems," "'Should I Follow the Human, or Follow the Robot?'—Robots in Power Can Have More Influence Than Humans on Decision-Making," and "Co-Writing with Opinionated Language Models Affects Users' Views." Nearly all such papers arrive at socially quite worrisome conclusions about the abilities and the inclinations of executives to exercise critical skills.

46. Valdemar Danry et al., "Don't Just Tell Me, Ask Me: AI Systems That Intelligently Frame Explanations as Questions Improve Human Logical Discernment Accuracy over Causal AI Explanations," in *Proceedings of the 2023 CHI Conference on Human Factors in Computing Systems* ed. Albrecht Schmidt et al. (Association for Computing Machinery, 2023) 1–13.

47. Danry et al., "Don't Just Tell Me, Ask Me," 1–13, italics added.

48. Charles Young, personal communication June 10, 2024.

49. An excellent introduction to elements of artificial intelligence, especially the emerging machine-learning and deep-learning processes, presented with a tempered outlook that is at once exciting and yet cautious can be found in Francois Chollet, *Deep Learning with Python* (Manning, 2021). For those unfamiliar with AI, chapters 1 and 14 are recommended. See also Maryam Alavi, Dorothy E. Leidner, and Reza Mousavi, "Knowledge Management Perspective of Generative Artificial Intelligence," *Journal of the Association for Information Systems* 25, no. 1 (2024): 1–12.

50. Trent N. Cash and Daniel M. Oppenheimer, "Generative Chatbots Ain't Experts: Exploring Cognitive and Metacognitive Limitations That Hinder Expertise in Generative Chatbots," *Journal of Applied Research in Memory and Cognition* 13, no. 4 (2024): 490.

51. Moldoveanu and Narayandas, *The Future of Executive Development*. The skills they

refer to fall into three critical-thinking categories: self-control, self-command, and self-regulation.

52. One example can be found in Suzanne Vranica, "Sorry, Madmen: The Ad Revolution Is Here, *Wall Street Journal,* December 14, 2024, p. B1.

53. Quoted in Joseph L. Badaracco, *Your True Moral Compass: Defining Reality Responsibility and Practicality in Your Leadership Moments* (Springer, 2023), 51. Original quote is from the podcast, Peter Attia Drive, April 22, 2023, #51 rebroadcast.

54. Robert M. Sapolsky, *Behave: The Biology of Humans at Our Best and Worst* (Penguin Books, 2017), 5.

55. Cash and Oppenheimer, "Generative Chatbots AIn't Experts," 490.

56. See for, example, Nicholas Humphrey, *Sentience: The Invention of Consciousness* (MIT Press, 2021); and Douglas R. Hofstadter, *I Am a Strange Loop* (Basic Books, 2007). Both authors refer to the self as a phenomenon, experience, or "strange loop" that *emerges from diverse forces* and is not rooted in any one such as the brain.

57. Mark Solms, *The Hidden Spring: A Journey to the Source of Consciousness* (W. W. Norton, 2021), 148–77.

58. See for example, Daniel M. Wegner and Kurt Gray, *The Mind Club: Who Thinks, What Feels, and Why It Matters* (Penguin Books, 2016).

59. Solms, *The Hidden Spring* 148–77.

60. An excellent account of how these probing questions contribute to metacognitive performance and improved decision making can be found in: Stephen M. Fleming, "Metacognition and Confidence: A Review and Synthesis," *Annual Review of Psychology* 75 (2024): 241–68, https://doi.org/10.1146/annurev-psych-022423-032425.

61. Karl Friston, "The Free-Energy Principle: A Unified Brain Theory," *Nature Reviews: Neuroscience* 11, no. 2 (February 2010): 128. See also, Thomas Parr, Giovanni Pezzulo, and Karl J. Friston, *Active Inference: The Free Energy Principle in Mind Brain and Behavior* (MIT Press, 2022). Notably, Friston focuses on the brain's operations whereas I believe the system in which his free-energy principle operates on the larger scale of mind.

62. For more evidence see Francois Quesque et al., "Learning from Illusions: From Perception Studies to Perspective-Taking Interventions," *Neuroscience Research* 195 (2023), https://doi.org/10.1016/j.neures.2023.05.003; E. Pronin and M. B. Kugler, "Valuing Thoughts, Ignoring Behavior: The Introspection Illusion as a Source of the Bias Blind Spot," *Journal of Experimental Psychology* 43, no. 4 (2007): 565–78. This same point is repeatedly stressed in Peter M. Senge, *The Fifth Discipline: The Art and Practice of the Learning Organization* (Random House, 2006).

63. Several sources documenting this effect are provided throughout this book. A few to note now include: Alfonso Montuori, "Integrative Trandisciplinarity: Explorations and Experiments in Creative Scholarship," *Transdisciplinary Journal of Engineering and Science* 13 (2022): 111–28; Manuel London et al., "Developing Self-Awareness: Learning Processes for Self-and Interpersonal Growth," *Annual Review of Organizational Psychology and Organizational Behavior* 10, no. 1 (2022): 261–88; Senge, *The Fifth Discipline.*

64. Italics added. Wisława Szymborska, "The Poet and the World," Nobel Prize Lecture, December 7, 1996, https://www.nobelprize.org/prizes/literature/1996/szymborska/lecture/.

Chapter 2

1. See, for example, Irina M. Verenikina and Helen M. Hasan (2020), "The Importance of Play in Organisation," 2020, University of Wollongong, https://ro.uow.edu.au/hbs papers/1770; Rebecca Rylance-Graham, "The Lived Experience of Play and How It Relates to Psychological Wellbeing," *Nursing Research and Practice*, April 3, 2024, https://doi.org /10.1155/2024/7871499; and Liana Fourie et al., "A Play-at-Work Intervention: What Are the Benefits?," *South African Journal of Economic and Management Sciences* 23, no. 1, https://doi.org/10.1155/2024/7871499.

2. Jonathan Gottschall, *The Storytelling Animal: How Stories Make Us Human* (Houghton Mifflin Harcourt, 2012); Charan Ranganath, *Why We Remember: Unlocking Memory's Power to Hold on to What Matters* (Doubleday, 2024).

3. Donald D. Hoffman, *Visual Intelligence: How We Create What We See* (W. W. Norton, 1998); Roger N. Shepard, *Mind Sights: Original Visual Illusions Ambiguities and Other Anomalies with a Commentary on the Play of Mind in Perception and Art* (Macmillan Learning, 1990).

4. See for instance, P. G. Bates and P. Martin, *Play Playfulness Creativity and Innovation* (Cambridge University Press, 2013); C. Liu et al., *Neuroscience and Learning Through Play: A Review of the Evidence* (The Lego Foundation, 2024).

5. Ashley Montagu, *Growing Young*, 2nd ed. (Praeger, 1988).

6. Stuart Brown, *Play: How It Shapes the Brain Opens the Imagination and Invigorates the Soul* (Penguin Books, 2024), 24.

7. Joao Vieira da Cunha, Ken N. Kamoche, and Miguel Pina a Cunha, "Once Again: What, When, How, and Why: A Prospectus for Research in Organizational Improvisation," in *Organizational Improvisation*, ed. Ken N. Kamoche, Miguel Pina E. Cunha, and Joao Viera Da Cunha, 296–308 (Routledge, 2002).

8. Peter Godfrey-Smith, *Other Minds: The Octopus the Sea and the Deep Origins of Consciousness* (Farrar, Straus and Giroux, 2016). Octopuses are among nature's most intelligent creatures. The analogy can be extended to encompass other elements of the role of neural clusters or images and how they pass information.

9. See Gerald Zaltman, *Engaging Your Inner Wizard and Clairvoyant in Workable Wondering* [working paper] (Olson Zaltman Associates, 2020).

10. Maya Zhe Wang and Benjamin Y. Hayden, "Latent Learning, Cognitive Maps, and Curiosity," *Current Opinion in Behavioral Sciences* 38, no. 4 (2021): 1–7.

11. "History Timeline: Post-it Notes," post-it.com, https://www.post-it.com/3M/en_ US/post-it/contact-us/about-us/. Accessed January 11, 2022.

12. Readers are encouraged to read Anne Frank's *The Diary of a Young Girl*. Also see, Gwen Gordon, "Well Played: The Origins and Future of Playfulness," *American Journal of Play* 6, no. 2 (2014): 234–66.

13. See, for example, Susan Cain, *Bittersweet: How Sorrow and Longing Make us Whole* (Crown, 2022).

14. For more on ubuntu, see Mark Mathabane, *The Lessons of Ubuntu* (Skyhorse Publishing, 2018). For another version of this story, see Michael Kinsey, "How Can I Be Happy When Others Are Suffering?," *Mindsplain*, March 14, 2018, https://mindsplain.com/how -can-i-be-happy-when-others-are-suffering/.

15. An excellent essay on courage and the willingness to pay a price for exercising it can be found in, Robert J. Sternberg, "The Most Important Gift of All? The Gift of Courage," *Roper Review* 44, no. 2 (2022): 73–81.

16. Erving Goffman, *The Presentation of Self in Everyday Life* (Anchor, 1959).

17. Clayton M. Christensen, Taddy Hall, Karen Dillon, and David S. Duncan, *Competing Against Luck: The Story of Innovation and Customer Choice* (Harper Business, 2016).

18. Goffman, *The Presentation of Self in Everyday Life.*

19. Sports fans will recognize this.

20. Simon Baron-Cohen, *The Pattern Seekers: How Autism Drives Human Invention* (Basic Books, 2020). See especially chapter 2, pp. 14–44.

21. Dana Coester, *A Matter of Space: Designing Newsrooms for New Digital Practice* (American Press Institute, 2017), chapter 3, "How to Design Workspaces That Spur Collaboration," https://www.americanpressinstitute.org/publications/reports/strategy-studies/spaces-collaboration/.

22. Wendy Ross and Mike Groves, "Let's Just See What Happens: A Qualitative Case Study of Risk and Uncertainty in the Creative Process," *Journal of Creative Behavior* 57, no. 2 (2023): 305–18.

23. Peter M. Senge, *The Fifth Discipline: The Art and Practice of the Learning Organization* (Random House, 2006), 240.

24. Harald Warmelink, "Towards a Playful Organization Ideal-Type: Values of a Playful Organizational Culture," in *Proceedings of DiGRA 2011 Conference: Think Design Play*, ed. Marinka Copier, Annika Waern, and Helen W. Kennedy (Digital Games Research Association, 2011).

25. David D. Preiss, "Metacognition, Mind Wandering, and Cognitive Flexibility: Understanding Creativity," *Journal of Intelligence* 10, no. 3 (2022): 69.

Chapter 3

1. Alvin Powell, "Harvard Scientist Gary Ruvkun Awared Medicine Prize for microRNA Insights," *Harvard Gazette*, October 7, 2024, italics added.

2. Some scholars propose a special discipline, agnotology, that recognizes that ignorance is far more than simply not knowing. See, for instance, Robert N. Proctor and Londa Schiebinger, eds., *Agnotology: The Making and Unmaking of Ignorance* (Stanford University Press, 2008).

3. Recall Juliet's line in William Shakespeare's *Romeo and Juliet*: "That which we call a rose by any other name would smell as sweet."

4. Jennifer Logue, "Teaching Ignorance: On the Importance of Developing Psychoanalytic Sensibilities in Education," *Philosophical Studies in Education* 50 (2019): 108.

5. Joanne Roberts, "Organizational Ignorance," in *Routledge International Handbook of Ignorance Studies*, 2nd ed., ed. Matthias Gross and Linsey McGoey (Routledge, 2024), 374.

6. Ignorance appears to be uniquely tethered to the spatial. See for instance, Scott Frickel and Abby Kinchy, "Lost in Space: Place, Space, and Scale in the Production of Ignorance," in Gross and McGoey, *Routledge International Handbook of Ignorance Studies*.

7. See Joseph Chancellor and Sonja Lyubomirsky, "Humble Beginnings: Current

Trends, State Perspectives, and Hallmarks of Humility," *Social and Personality Psychology Compass* 7, no. 11 (2013): 819–33.

8. See, for instance, Mei Elansary et al., "Maternal Stress and Early Neurodevelopment: Exploring the Protective Role of Maternal Growth Mindset," *Journal of Developmental and Behavioral Pediatrics* 43, no. 2 (2022): e103–e109.

9. Jerome Kagan, *An Argument for Mind* (Yale University Press, 2006); Alison Gopnik, *The Philosophical Baby* (Farrar, Straus and Giroux, 2009); Jerome Kagan, *On Being Human: Why Mind Matters* (Yale University Press, 2016).

10. Mark Pagel, *Wired for Culture: Origins of the Human Social Mind* (W. W. Norton & Company, 2012).

11. David Epstein, *Range: Why Generalists Triumph in a Specialized World* (Riverhead Books, 2019).

12. Gerald Zaltman and Lindsay Zaltman, *Marketing Metaphoria: What Deep Metaphors Reveal About the Minds of Consumers* (Harvard Business Press, 2006). Also see Christine Moorman, Gerald Zaltman, and Rohit Deshpande, "Relationships Between Providers and Users of Market Research: The Dynamics of Trust Within and Between Organizations," *Journal of Marketing Research* 29, no. 3 (1992): 314–28.

13. We greatly exceed monkeys in this respect.

14. Essays on this important topic can be found in Janet Kourany and Martin Carrier, *Science and the Production of Ignorance: When the Quest for Knowledge Is Thwarted* (MIT Press, 2020). See also, Daniel R. DeNicola, *Understanding Ignorance: The Surprising Impact of What We Don't Know* (MIT Press, 2017); Steven Pinker, *The Blank Slate: The Modern Denial of Human Nature* (Penguin Books, 2002).

15. Kitty J. Jäger et al., "Where to Look for the Most Frequent Biases?," *Nephrology* 25, no. 6 (2020): 435–41; see also Mahzarin R. Banaji and Anthony G. Greenwald, *Blindspot: Hidden Biases of Good People* (Bantam, 2016).

16. Keith E. Stanovich, *The Bias That Divides Us: The Science and Politics of Myside Thinking* (MIT Press, 2021).

17. See, for example, the strange case of Phineas Gage in Antonio Damasio, *Descartes' Error: Emotion, Reason, and the Human Brain* (G. P. Putnam's Sons, 1994). See also Antonio Damasio, *Feeling and Knowing: Making Minds Conscious* (Pantheon, 2021); Craig Wright, *The Hidden Habits of Genius: Beyond Talent, IQ, and Grit, Unlocking the Secrets of Greatness* (Harper Collins, 2020); Gary Klein, *Seeing What Others Don't* (Public Books, 2013); Francesca Gino, *Rebel Talent: Why It Pays to Break the Rules at Work and in Life* (Dey Books, 2018).

18. Lee McIntyre, *Respecting Truth: Willful Ignorance in the Internet Age* (Routledge, 2015), 3–7. See also Stanovich, *The Bias That Divides Us.*

19. Xiao-Li Ming, "Statistical Paradises and Paradoxes in Big Data," *Annals of Applied Statistics* 12, no. 2 (2018): 685–726; see also Valerie C. Bradley et al., "Unrepresentative Big Surveys Significantly Overestimated US Vaccine Uptake," *Nature* 600, no. 7890 (2021): 695–700.

20. Susan A. J. Birch and Paul Bloom, "The Curse of Knowledge in Reasoning About False Beliefs," *Psychological Science* 18, no. 5 (2007): 382–86. Jumping to conclusions is more frequently studied as a problem among those with medically compromised decision-

making skills, but it has relevance for the general public as well. See, for example, Carmen Sanchez and David Dunning, "Jumping to Conclusions: Implications for Reasoning Errors, False Beliefs, Knowledge Corruption, and Impeded Learning," *Journal of Personal and Social Psychology* 120, no. 3 (2021): 789–815.

21. Adrian F. Ward et al., "People Mistake the Internet's Knowledge for Their Own," *PNAS* 118, no. 43 (2021), https://doi.org/10.1073/pnas.2105061118.

22. J. Kruger and D. Dunning, "Unskilled and Unaware of It: How Difficulties in Recognizing One's Own Incompetence Lead to Inflated Self-Assessments," *Journal of Personality and Social Psychology* 77, no. 6 (1999): 1121–34.

23. Jay P. Carlson et al., "Objective and Subjective Knowledge Relationships: A Quantitative Analysis of Consumer Research Findings," *Journal of Consumer Research* 35, no. 5 (2009): 864–76. (I've dubbed this the teenager effect.)

24. Christine Moorman et al., "Subjective Knowledge, Search Locations, and Consumer Knowledge," *Journal of Consumer Research* 31, no. 3 (2004): 673–80.

25. For bike riding, see Matthew Hutson, "Why You Don't Really Know What You Know," *MIT Technology Review*, October 21, 2020; for snapping fingers, see Acharya et al., "The Ultrafast Snap of a Finger Is Mediated by Skin Friction," *Journal of the Royal Society Interface* 18, no. 184 (2021), https://doi.org/10.1098/rsif.2021.0672.

26. Kenneth Koedinger, cited in Annie Murphy Paul, *The Extended Mind: The Power of Outside the Brain* (Mariner, 2021), 181.

27. See Kenneth R. Koedinger et al., "Learning Is Not a Spectator Sport: Doing Is Better Than Watching for Learning from a MOOC," *L@S '15: Proceedings of the Second (2015) ACM Conference on Learning @ Scale*, March 2015, 111–20.

28. For an interesting account of good and bad surprises see Basile Zimmermann, "Expect the Unexpected," in Gross and McGoey, *Routledge International Handbook of Ignorance Studies*, 127–35.

29. This is also discussed in Michelle F. Weinberger and Robert F. Lusch, "The Cultural Knowledge Perspective: Insights on Resource Creation for Marketing Theory, Practice, and Education," *Journal of Macromarketing* 43, no. 1 (2022): 1–13.

30. Stefan Schwarzkopf, "Sacred Excess: Organizational Ignorance in an Age of Toxic Data," *Organizational Studies* 41, no. 2 (2019): 197–217, https://doi.org/10.1177/01708406188 15527.

31. Dell Technologies, "The Data Paradox: Research Findings," 2021, https://www.delltechnologies.com/asset/en-ie/solutions/infrastructure-solutions/industry-market/data-paradox-research-findings.pdf.

32. Gerald Zaltman, "Daring to Understand and Change Thinking," in *Handbook of Advances in Marketing in an Era of Disruptions: Essays in Honor of Jagdish Sheth*, ed. Atul Parvatiyar and Rajendra Sisodia, 7–24 (Sage, 2019).

33. Zaltman and Zaltman, *Marketing Metaphoria*. My Olson Zaltman colleagues often use these with clients and with participants in ZMET research to encourage breakthrough thinking. For instance, "What if you could wave a magic wand and the concern you have would disappear? What would look or be different as a result?" or "Let's say you wake up tomorrow and the problem is now a benefit? What change might have taken place to explain that?"

34. See Judea Pearl and Dana Mackenzie, *The Book of Why: The New Science of Cause and Effect* (Basic Books, 2018); and Ian Mitroff, *The Subjective Side of Science: A Philosophical Inquiry into the Psychology of the Apollo Moon Scientists* (Elsevier, 1974).

35. Jerrold Rosenbaum, "Are Psychedelics an Effective Treatment for Mood Disorders?" *Harvard Magazine*, November 2021; R. L. Carhart-Harris and K. J. Friston, "REBUS and the Anarchic Brain: Toward a Unified Model of the Brain Action of Psychedelics," *Pharmacological Reviews* 71 (2019): 316–44.

36. Frank C. Keil, *Wonder: Childhood and the Lifelong Love of Science* (MIT Press, 2022), 7, 19–20.

37. Gopnik, *The Philosophical Baby.*

38. Keil, *Wonder*, 49.

39. Lindsay Zaltman and Gerald Zaltman, "What Do 'Really Good' Managers and 'Really Good' Researchers Want of One Another?," in *The Handbook of Market Research: Uses Misues and Future Advances*, ed. Rajiv Grover and Marco Vriens, 33–48 (Sage, 2006).

40. Malcolm Gladwell, *Outliers: The Story of Success* (Back Bay Books, 2011).

41. Thomas J. Harper, afterword to *In Praise of Shadows* by Jun'ichiro Tanizaki (Leete's Island Books, 1977), 45.

42. Raymond Pettit, *Learning from Winners: How the ARF Ogilvy Award Winners Use Market Research to Create Advertising Success* (Advertising Research Foundation, 2007).

43. Christine Moorman, Rohit Deshpande, and Gerald Zaltman, "Factors Affecting Trust in Market Research Relationships," *Journal of Marketing* 57, no. 1 (1993): 81–101; Leinan Zhang et. al., "Can Psychological Contracts Decrease Opportunistic Behaviors?" *Frontiers in Psychology*, June 2, 2022, 10.3389/fpsyg.2022.911389.

Chapter 4

1. Some days in advance of their interview, participants are given an assignment they are required to complete prior to their interview. The ZMET question frames the assignment. For example, we might ask, "When you think or hear about the role of X in your child's life, what thoughts and feelings come to mind?" They are then asked to find pictures or objects that express these thoughts and feelings that exclude direct references to X.

2. This question was stimulated by René Rosfort and Giovanni Stanghellini, "In the Mood for Thought: Feelings and Thinking in Philosophy," *New Literary History* 43, no. 3 (2012): 395–417.

3. John Kounios and Mark Beeman, "The Cognitive Neuroscience of Insight," *Annual Review of Psychology* 65 (2014): 71–93.

4. Mark Solms, *The Hidden Spring: A Journey to the Source of Consciousness* (W.W. Norton, 2021), 100.

5. Solms, *The Hidden Spring*, 89, italics added.

6. Solms, 89. See especially chapter 7, "The Free Energy Principle."

7. Simone P. Nguyen and Catherine McDermott, "Holding Multiple Category Representations: The Role of Age, Theory of Mind, and Rule Switching in Children's Developing Cross-Classification Abilities," *Journal of Experimental Child Psychology* 237 (2024), https://doi.org/10.1016/j.jecp.2023.105716.

8. See for example David Lagnado, "Causal Thinking," in *Causality in the Sciences,* ed. Phyllis McKay Illan, 129–49 (Oxford University Press, 2011). This chapter assesses the multiple sources people use as evidence in their construction of causal mental models.

9. Kevin N. Laland, *Darwin's Unfinished Symphony: How Culture Made the Human Mind* (Princeton University Press, 2017); Simon Baron-Cohen, *The Pattern Seekers: A New Theory of Human Invention* (Allen Lane, 2020).

10. Cecilia Heyes, *Cognitive Gadgets: The Cultural Evolution of Thinking* (Harvard University Press, 2018). A supporting position is offered in Laland, *Darwin's Unfinished Symphony.*

11. To be clear, while I am speaking of transfers between generations, changes in gadgets generally require many, many generations.

12. Dayna Baumeister, *Biomimicry Resource Handbook: A Seed Bank of Best Practices* (Biomimicry 3.8, 2014).

13. Lisa Feldman Barrett, *Seven and a Half Lessons About the Brain* (Houghton Mifflin Harcourt, 2020).

14. Stephen King, *On Writing: A Memoir of the Craft* (Scribner, 2000). See also Peter Mendelsund, *What We See When We Read* (Vintage Books, 2014).

15. James Lawley and Penny Tompkins, *Metaphors in Mind: Transformation Through Symbolic Modelling* (Developing Company Press, 2000); Gerald Zaltman, *How Customers Think: Essential Insights into the Mind of the Market* (Harvard Business School Press, 2003).

16. Jakob Hohwy, *The Predictive Mind* (Oxford University Press, 2014).

17. See Carol Tavris and Elliot Aronson, *Mistakes Were Made (but Not by Me)* (Houghton Mifflin Harcourt, 2007); Robert Burton, *On Being Certain: Believing You Are Right Even When You're Not* (St. Martin's Press, 2008).

18. Vincent P. Barabba was twice the director of the US Census Bureau and a longtime chief knowledge officer at General Motors and other leading companies. For a more complete discussion of human judgments about causality, see Judea Pearl and Dana Mackenzie, *The Book of Why: The New Science of Cause and Effect* (Basic Books, 2018).

19. Valerie Zeithaml, Bernard J. Jaworski, Ajay K. Kohli, Kapil R. Tuli, Wolfgang Ulaga, and Gerald Zaltman, "A Theories-in-Use Approach to Building Marketing Theory," *Journal of Marketing* 84, no. 1 (2020): 32–51.

20. Michael Strevens, *The Knowledge Machine: How Irrationality Created Modern Science* (Liveright, 2020), 82–83.

21. Vincent Barabba, *The Decision Loom: A Design for Interactive Decision-Making in Organizations* (Triarchy Press, 2011).

22. Vincent P. Barabba and Gerald Zaltman (1991), *Hearing the Voice of the Market: Competitive Advantage Through Creative Use of Market Information* (Harvard Business Press, 2011), 120–21.

23. Norbert Schwarz, "Self-Reports: How the Questions Shape the Answers," *American Psychologist* 54, no. 2 (1999): 96. Questionnaire design is a very important topic in most research areas; several excellent resources can be found searching online.

Chapter 5

1. Susan Engel, *The Hungry Mind: The Origins of Curiosity in Childhood* (Harvard University Press, 2015). There is considerable research about curiosity in the field of education. In my experience, the findings in that field, especially about the impact of learning environments, are highly relevant to the fields of management and organizational change.

2. Alexandr Ten et al., "Humans Monitor Learning Progress in Curiosity-Driven Exploration," *Nature Communications* 12, no. 1 (2021): 5972, https://doi.org/10.1038/s41467-021-26196-w; Maya Zhe Wang and Benjamin Y. Hayden, "Curiosity, Latent Learning, and Cognitive Maps," *BioRxiv*, June 1, 2020, https://doi.org/10.1101/2020.05.31.123380.

3. Adam Grant, *Think Again: The Power of Knowing What You Don't Know* (Viking, 2021).

4. See, for instance, Wendy Berliner and Judith Judd, *How to Succeed at School: Separating Fact from Fiction* (Routledge, 2020). See especially their discussion of myths about neuroscience, such as that we use only 10 percent of our brain. This spurious factoid apparently has its origins in early reports by neuroscientists suggesting they only knew how 10 percent of the human brain operates.

5. Cecilia Heyes, *Cognitive Gadgets: The Cultural Evolution of Thinking* (Harvard University Press, 2018).

6. Dan M. Kahan et al., "Science Curiosity and Political Information Processing," *Advances in Political Psychology* 38, no. S1 (2017): 197.

7. Jay H. Hardy, Alisha M. Ness, and Jensen Mecca, "Outside the Box: Epistemic Curiosity as Predictor of Creative Problem Solving and Creative Performance," *Personality and Individual Differences* 104 (2017): 230–37.

8. T. B. Kashdan et al., "The Five-Dimensional Curiosity Scale: Capturing the Bandwidth of Curiosity and Identifying Four Unique Subgroups of Curious People," *Journal of Research in Personality* 73 (2018): 130–49.

9. There is evidence that those practicing open-mindedness, i.e., who think about their thinking, have a greater feeling of control and are more effective in exercising control than those less open-minded. See, for instance, Jinyao Li, et al., "Beliefs About Self-Control," *Current Opinion in Psychology* 60 (December 2024).

10. Kimberlyn Leary, Julianna Pillemer, and Michael Wheeler "Negotiating with Emotion," *Harvard Business Review*, January/February, 2013.

11. Jennifer Stellar and R. Willer, "Unethical and Inept: The Influence of Moral Information on Perceptions of Competence," *Journal of Personality and Social Psychology* 114, no. 2 (2018): 195–210.

12. To be clear, I am not referring to using expert insight to help challenge one's own thinking, expand our useable pool of knowledge, or identify new decision options to evaluate. Those are the actions of an open mind attempting to open up even more.

13. When thinking by proxy leads to these three things, it is not only a poor substitute for curiosity, it also spells trouble for democracy.

14. Valerie A. Zeithaml, Bernard J. Jaworski, Ajay K. Kohli, Kapil R. Tuli, Wolfgang Ulaga, and Gerald Zaltman, "A Theories-in-Use Approach to Building Marketing Theory," *Journal of Marketing* 84, no. 1 (2020): 32–51.

15. Charlan Nemeth, *No! The Power of Disagreement in a World That Wants to Get Along* (Atlantic Books, 2018).

16. Diane Hamilton, "Developing and Testing Inhibitors of Curiosity in the Workplace with the Curiosity Code Index (CCI)," *Heliyon* 5, no. 1, https://doi.org/10.1016/j.heliyon.2019.e01185.

17. SAS Institute, "Curiosity@Work Report 2021," https://www.sas.com/content/dam/SAS/documents/corporate-collateral/brochures/en-curiosity-at-work-112457.pdf, 5.

18. SAS Institute, 5.

19. SAS Institute, 4.

Chapter 6

1. Isaiah Berlin, *The Hedgehog and the Fox: An Essay on Tolstoy's View of History* (Weidenfeld & Nicholson, 1953).

2. Evan F. Risko and Megan O. Kelly, "Thinking in the Digital Age: Everyday Cognition and the Dawn of a New Age of Metacognition Research," *Applied Cognitive Psychology* 37, no. 4 (2023): 785–88. A promising application of AI involves its potential to identify and thereby reduce human biases. See for example, Kejia Hu, Bowen Lou, and Bilai Baloch, "Reducing Human Bias in Decision Making and Improving Customer Satisfaction Through Artificial Intelligence," 2023, SSRN 4436554.

3. To be clear, few interviewees mentioned such a rule explicitly, but most provided clear evidence of its presence and use. In subsequent group meetings with participants, all readily agreed with this more formalized description of their thinking and actions.

4. Douglas Hofstadter and Emmanuel Sander, *Surfaces and Essences: Analogy as the Fuel and Fire of Thinking* (Basic Books, 2013), 4.

5. Hofstadter and Sander, *Surfaces and Essences*, 19.

6. An excellent discussion touching on several forms is found in Alan Wilson, *Being Interdisciplinary: Adventures in Urban Science and Beyond* (UCL Press, 2022). His discussion of going from data to AI is particularly instructive.

7. Frédéric Darbellay, "Creativity and Interdisciplinarity," *European Psychologist* 27, no. 3 (2022): 209.

8. Parenthetically, my work included the world population of these physicists and included personal interviews with many of the field's leaders. To this day I remain greatly impressed by their fluency in using metaphors.

9. Brian Sternthal and Gerald Zaltman, *Broadening the Concept of Consumer Behavior* (Associations for Consumer Research, 1975).

10. Susan Drake and Joanne Reid, "Thinking Now: Transdisciplinary Thinking as a Disposition," *Academia Letters*, article 387, 2021, https://doi.org/10.20935/AL387.

11. The importance of being inventive with new ideas is discussed by Frederic Darbellay, "The Gift of Interdisciplinarity: Toward an Ability to Think Across Disciplines," *International Journal for Talent Development and Creativity* 3 (2015): 201–11.

12. See Daniel J. Finkenstadt and Tojin T. Eapen, *Bioinspired Strategic Design: Nature-Inspired Principles for Dynamic Business Environments* (Routledge, 2024); Michael Pawlyn, *Biomimicry in Architecture* (RIBA, 2016); and Dayna Baumeister *Biomimicry: Resource Handbook: A Seed Bank of Best Practices* (Biomimicry 3.8, 2014).

13. Amin Al-Habaibeh, professor of intelligent engineering systems at Nottingham Trent University, coined the term *biospiration* in his article "Five Human Technologies Inspired by Nature—From Velcro to Racing Cars," *The Conversation*, December 30, 2022, https://theconversation.com/five-human-technologies-inspired-by-nature-from-velcro -to-racing-cars-195593. I'm going to let you match up the problem area with a particular animal. Hint: Air filtration scientists found novel solutions by learning about mollusks.

14. Victor E. Sower, Jo Ann Duffy, and Gerald Kohers, "Ferrari's Formula One Handovers and Handovers from Surgery to Intensive Care," American Society for Quality, August 2008, https://gwern.net/doc/technology/2008-sower.pdf.

15. Emre Soyer and Robin M. Hogarth, *The Myth of Experience* (Public Affairs, 2020). See especially chapter 2.

16. World Economic Forum, "Global Risks Report, 2023," https://www.weforum.org/ publications/global-risks-report-2023/.

17. I authored one of the first publications on this topic and perhaps the first book in the marketing discipline to address it: Gerald Zaltman, *Marketing: Contributions from the Behavioral Sciences* (Harcourt, Brace & World, 1965).

18. Several sources address this type of issue. Policymakers will find helpful J. Gareth Polhill and Bruce Edmonds, "Cognition and Hypocognition: Discursive and Simulation-Supported Decision-Making Within Complex Systems," *Futures* 148 (April 2023), https:// doi.org/10.1016/j.futures.2023.103121. Other informative sources include Kaidi Wu and David Dunning, "Hypocognition: Making Sense of the Landscape Beyond One's Conceptual Reach," *Review of General Psychology* 22, no. 1 (2018): 25–35. See also by the same authors "Unknown Unknowns: The Problem of Hypocognition," *Scientific American: Observations* (blog), August 9, 2018, https://www.scientificamerican.com/blog/observa tions/unknown-unknowns-the-problem-of-hypocognition/.

19. See, for example, Dedre Gentner and Julie Colhoun, "Analogical Processes in Human Thinking and Learning," in *Towards a Theory of Thinking* ed. Britt Glatzeder, Vinod Goel, and Albrecht Müller, 35–38. (Springer, 2010). See also Bernard Choi and Anita Pak, "Multidisciplinarity, Interdisciplinarity and Transdisciplinary in Health Research, Services, Education and Policy," *Clinical and Investigative Medicine* 29, no. 6 (2006): 351–64.

20. World Economic Forum, "Manage Risk More Effectively: A Risk Expert Shares What's Needed Most," *Meet the Leader* (podcast), July 27, 2023. Transcript available at https://www.weforum.org/podcasts/meet-the-leader/episodes/clifford-chance-bahare -heywood-risk.

21. Hofstadter and Sander, *Surfaces and Essences*; Gerald Zaltman, "Consumer Researchers: Take a Hike," *Journal of Consumer Research* 26, no. 4 (2000): 423–28.

22. An example is Philip Kotler and Gerald Zaltman, "Social Marketing: An Approach to Planned Social Change," *Journal of Marketing* 35, no. 3 (1971): 3–12. This article, one of the most highly cited in the marketing discipline, identified an entire set of new tools for advocates of social change and led to a new subdiscipline within the marketing profession.

23. Zoltan Kovecses, *Metaphor: A Practical Introduction* (Oxford University Press, 2002).

24. A classic source for this is George Lakoff and Mark Johnson, *Metaphors We Live By* (University of Chicago Press, 2003).

25. An excellent book on the impact of physical activity, including gesture, on thinking and the use of metaphor is Barbara Tversky, *Mind in Motion: How Action Shapes Thought* (Basic Books, 2019). One of the critical steps in ZMET involves asking people to describe what is and is not the sound, touch, scent, etc. of the topic being explored. Participants are then asked to explain their answers and often do so with surprising ease.

26. Mahzarin R. Banaji and Anthony G. Greenwald, *Blindspot: Hidden Biases of Good People* (Random House, 2016).

27. Paul H. Thibodeau and Lera Boroditsky, "Metaphors We Think With: The Role of Metaphor in Reasoning," *PLOS One* 6, no. 2 (2011), https://journals.plos.org/plosone/article?id=10.1371/journal.pone.0016782.

28. An excellent place to start is John Pollack, *Shortcut* (Random House, 2014); George Lakoff and Mark Johnson, *Philosophy in the Flesh: The Embodied Mind and Its Challenge to Western Thought* (Basic Books, 2009); Keith J. Holyoak and Paul Thagard, *Mental Leaps: Analogy in Creative Thought* (MIT Press, 1996); Zoltan Kovecses, *Metaphor in Culture: Universality and Variation* (Cambridge University Press, 2007).

29. For additional insight see Jennifer Clinehens, "The Gruen Effect: How IKEA's Store Design Makes You Buy More," *The Choice Hacking Newsletter*, 2023, https://www.choicehacking.com/2021/01/02/gruen-effect-ikea/.

30. Gregory S. Carpenter, "Market Driving, Market Driven, or Both? Toward a Concept of Dual Market Orientation," *Industrial Marketing Management* 113, no. 3/4 (2023): 357–59.

31. Eileen Fischer, "Mining the Metaphor of Market Driving to Propel Productive Research," *Industrial Marketing Management* 113, no. 3/4 (2023): 345–47.

32. Keith Sawyer, *Zig Zag: The Surprising Path to Greater Creativity* (Jossey-Bass, 2013), 158.

33. Gerald Zaltman and Lindsay Zaltman, *Marketing Metaphoria: What Deep Metaphors Reveal About the Minds of Consumers* (Harvard Business Press, 2008).

Chapter 7

1. Thomas Albright, "On the Perception of Probable Things: Neural Substrates of Associative Memory Imagery and Perception," *Neuron* 74, no. 2 (2012): 227–45.

2. The terms *risk*, *uncertainty*, and *ambiguity* are often conflated in everyday conversation. Risk involves a known probability—for example, of auto accidents occurring among a specific population. Uncertainty exists when the probability of such an event is unknown or unknowable—for example, if no historical accident data exists for the population in question. The contrast of these two terms with *ambiguity* and the contrast among different definitions of *ambiguity* can be found in David McLain, Efstathios Kefallonitis, and Kimberly Armani, "Ambiguity Tolerance in Organizations: Definitional Clarification and Perspectives on Future Research," *Frontiers in Psychology* 6, no. 344 (2015).

3. Roy F. Baumeister and William von Hippel, "Meaning and Evolution: Why Nature Selected Human Minds to Use Meaning," *Evolutionary Studies in Imaginative Culture* 4, no. 1 (2020): 1–18.

4. Iain McGilchrist, *The Matter with Things: Our Brains Our Delusions and the Unmaking of the World* (Perspectiva, 2021), 179.

5. For example, see Jason Hancock and Karen Mattick, "Tolerance of Ambiguity and Psychological Well-Being in Medical Training: A Systematic Review," *Medical Education* 54, no. 2 (2020): 125–37.

6. Vincent P. Barabba and Gerald Zaltman (1991), *Hearing the Voice of the Market: Competitive Advantage through Creative Use of Market Information* (Harvard Business Press, 2011).

7. Louise Goupil et al., "Listeners' Perceptions of the Certainty and Honesty of a Speaker Are Associated with a Common Prosodic Signature," *Nature Communications* 12, no. 1 (2021).

8. This list is drawn from Nadia M. Brashier and Elizabeth J. Marsh, "Judging Truth," *Annual Review of Psychology*, 71 (2020): 499–515.

9. O. H. Turnbull, R. B. Worsey, and C. H. Bowman, "Emotion and Intuition: Does Schadenfreude Make Interns Poor Learners?" *Philoctetes* 1, no. 1 (2007): 5–43.

10. J. Wang, H. Otgaar, and M. L. Howe, "Creating False Rewarding Memories Guides Novel Decision Making," *Journal of Experimental Psychology: Learning Memory and Cognition* 50, no. 1 (2023): 52–67.

11. Using an MRI machine, it is possible to identify the moment just prior to when we become aware of the second image.

12. Adapted from William W. Gaver, Jake Beaver, and Steve Benford, "Ambiguity as a Resource for Design," in *Proceedings of the SIGCHI Conference on Human Factors in Computing Systems* (Association for Computing Machinery, 2003), 233–40.

13. The discussion of imagination and creativity draws partly on Gerald Zaltman, "Marketing's Forthcoming Age of Imagination," *AMS Review* 6, no. 3 (2016): 99–115.

14. See McLain, Kefallonitis, and Armani, "Ambiguity Tolerance in Organizations."

15. Norbert Schwarz, "Feelings-as-Information Theory," in *Handbook of Theories of Social Psychology*, ed. P. Van Lange, 289–308 (Sage, 2012).

16. Baumeister and von Hippel, "Meaning and Evolution," 1–18.

17. Lisa Feldman Barrett, *How Emotions Are Made: The Secret Life of the Brain* (Marina Books, 2017).

Chapter 8

1. A good discussion of the history of practical wisdom can be found in Kristjan Kristjansson and Blaine J. Fowers, *Phronesis: Retrieving Practical Wisdom in Psychology Philosophy and Education* (Oxford University Press, 2024).

2. Maksim Rudnev et al., "Dimensions of Wisdom Perceptions Across Twelve Countries on Five Continents," *Nature Communications* 15 (2024): 1–13.

3. Kaili Zhang et al., "Wisdom: Meaning, Structure, Types, Arguments, and Future Concerns," *Current Psychology* 42 (2023): 15030–51; Igor Grossmann et al., "The Science of Wisdom in a Polarized World: Knowns and Unknowns," *Psychological Inquiry* 31, no. 2 (2020): 103–33.

4. Grossmann et al., "The Science of Wisdom in a Polarized World."

5. An excellent contemporary review of the concept of wisdom can be found in Dilip V. Jeste and Ellen E. Lee, "Emerging Empirical Science of Wisdom: Definition, Measure-

ment, Neurobiology, Longevity, and Interventions," *Harvard Review of Psychiatry* 27, no. 3 (2019): 127–40.

6. Balazs Aczel et al., "What Is Stupid? People's Conception of Unintelligent Behavior," *Intelligence* 53 (2015): 51–58.

7. E. H. Erikson, *Identity and the Life Cycle* (W. W. Norton, 1994). Originally published in 1980.

8. Dilip V. Jeste et al., "Expert Consensus on Characteristics of Wisdom: A Delphi Method Study," *Gerontologist* 50, no. 5 (2010): 668–80.

9. R. J. Sternberg and S. Karami, "What Is Wisdom? A United 6P Framework," *Review of General Psychology* 25, no. 2 (2021): 134–51.

10. S. J. Lopez et al., *Positive Psychology: The Science and Practical Explorations of Human Strengths*, 3rd ed. (Sage, 2015), 224–37.

11. P. B. Baltes and U. M. Staudinger, "Wisdom: A Metaheuristic to Orchestrate Mind and Virtue Toward Excellence," *American Psychologist* 55, no. 1 (2000): 122–36.

12. Baltes and Staudinger, "Wisdom," 132.

13. T. W. Meeks and D. V. Jeste, "Neurobiology of Wisdom: A Literature Review," *Archives of General Psychiatry* 21 (2009): 355–65.

14. A special issue of the *Journal of Intelligence* in 2018 addresses this point. See Robert J. Sternberg, ed., *The Emerging Role of Intelligence in the World of the Future* (MDPI, 2018), https://doi.org/10.3390/books978-3-03897-263-1.

15. See, for example, Carol S. Dweck, *Mindset: Changing the Way You Think to Fulfill Your Potential*, updated ed. (Robinson, 2017).

16. Robert J. Sternberg, *Adaptive Intelligence: Surviving and Thriving in Times of Uncertainty* (Cambridge University Press, 2017), 4, italics added.

17. Joseph E. LeDoux, *The Four Realms of Existence: A New Theory of Being Human* (Harvard University Press, 2023), 36.

18. Dweck, *Mindset*. See also Carol S. Dweck, "Beliefs That Make Smart People Dumb," in *Why Smart People Can Be So Stupid*, ed. Robert J. Sternberg, 24–41 (Yale University Press, 2002). For counterevidence suggesting both forms of praise may work equally well, see Jaap Glerum et al., "The Effects of Praise for Effort Versus Praise for Intelligence on Vocational Education Students," *Educational Psychology* 40, no. 10 (2020): 1270–86.

19. This is also described being educable. See Leslie Valient, *The Importance of Being Educable: A New Theory of Human Intelligence* (Princeton University Press, 2024).

20. Andrew Van de Ven and Paul E. Johnson, "Knowledge for Theory and Practice," *Academy of Management Review* 31 (2006): 802–21. There are many excellent discussions of complex adaptive systems and their importance. For those less familiar with this field, I recommend Peter M. Senge, *The Fifth Discipline: The Art and Practice of the Learning Organization* (Doubleday, 2006); Roger L. Martin, *A New Way to Think* (Harvard Business Review Press, 2022); and Meghan Carmody-Bubb, *Cognition and Decision Making in Complex Adaptive Systems: The Human Factor in Organizational Performance* (Springer, 2023). See also Tim Sullivan, "Embracing Complexity," *Harvard Business Review*, September 2011; and D. J. Snowden and M. E. Boone, "A Leader's Framework for Decision Making," *Harvard Business Review*, November 2007.

21. Gerd Gigerenzer, "When All Is Just a Click Away," in *Critical Thinking in Psychol-*

ogy, 2nd ed., ed. Robert J. Sternberg and Diane F. Halpern (Cambridge University Press, 2020), 97–223.

22. Daniel C. Dennett, *I've Been Thinking* (Norton, 2023), 384.

23. Harri Raisio et al., "The Concept of Wicked Problems: Improving the Understanding of Managing Problem Wickedness in Health and Social Care," in *The Management of Wicked Problems in Health and Social Care*, ed. W. Thomas et al. (Routledge, 2018). An excellent source on the use of improvisation is Stephen Nachmanovitch, *Free Play: Improvisation in Life and Art* (Putnam, 1990); see also Alfonso Montuori, "The Complexity of Improvisation and the Improvisation of Complexity: Social Science, Art and Creativity," *Human Relations* 56, no. 2 (2003): 237–55.

24. This is not unique to management settings. It is also common in legal proceedings, scientific research, and events involving expert panels as decision makers.

25. Judea Pearl and Dana Mackenzie, *The Book of Why: The New Science of Cause and Effect* (Basic Books, 2018). George Marcus notes that which of our mutually exclusive viewpoints comes to the fore "is a function of both political and personality dispositions and contemporaneous understandings of whatever is being faced." George E. Marcus, "Open-Mindedness and Dogmatism in a Darwinian World," in *Divided: Open-Mindedness and Dogmatism in a Polarized World*, ed. Victor Ottati and Chadly Stern (Oxford University Press, 2023), chapter 12, 247.

26. Donald Hoffman, *The Case Against Reality: Why Evolution Hid the Truth from Our Eyes* (W. W. Norton, 2019).

27. The importance of these client-centered virtues in practitioner wisdom is noted in other contexts as well, see for example, Jack M. C. Kwong and Peter R. Fawson, "Practitioner Wisdom: A Conceptual Approach," *British Journal of Social Work* 5, no. 52 (2022): 4721–37.

28. A Harvard Kennedy School task force on learning to disagree found that keeping the number of people interacting low in numbers was important and valuable (personal communication).

29. Bruce G. Charlton, "Clever Sillies: Why High IQ People Tend to Be Deficient in Common Sense," *Medical Hypotheses* 73, no. 6 (2009): 867–70.

30. Robert J. Sternberg, ed., *Why Smart People Can Be So Stupid* (Yale University Press, 2002).

31. Akila Raoul and Jeffrey Huntsinger, "Feeling Open- or Closed-Minded: The Role of Affective Feelings in the Closing or Opening of the Mind," in Ottati and Stern, *Divided*, 253–57.

32. Robert M. Sapolsky *Behave: The Biology of Humans at Our Best and Worst* (Penguin Books, 2023).

33. Heather A. Butler and Diane F. Halpern, "Critical Thinking Impacts Our Everyday Lives," in Sternberg and Halpern, *Critical Thinking in Psychology*, 152–72.

34. Adapted from Donald P. Warwick and Herbert C. Kelman, "Ethical Issues in Social Intervention," in *Processes and Phenomena of Social Change*, ed. Gerald Zaltman (Wiley, 1973), 377–418.

35. I recommend reading Joseph L. Badaracco, *Your True Moral Compass: Defining Reality Responsibility and Practicality in Your Leadership Moments* (Springer, 2023).

36. Jeste and Lee, 25.

Chapter 9

1. Valerie A. Zeithaml, Bernard J. Jaworski, Ajay K. Kohli, Kapil R. Tuli, Wolfgang Ulaga, and Gerald Zaltman, "A Theories-in-Use Approach to Building Marketing Theory," *Journal of Marketing* 84, no. 1 (2020): 32–51.

2. Recently I came upon an interesting statement by a professional trapeze performer: "The flying trapeze act is an incredible amount of work. It's an hour to warm up and then the act is 10 to 15 minutes long." Izzy Patrowicz, Harvard University graduate, quoted in Nikki Rojas, "When the Circus Called, She Took the Leap," *Harvard Gazette*, May 15, 2024.

3. Leslie Valient, *The Importance of Being Educable: A New Theory of Human Uniqueness* (Princeton University Press, 2024).

4. Daniel L. Schacter, *The Seven Sins of Memory: How the Mind Forgets and Remembers* (Houghton Mifflin, 2002); Charan Ranganath, *Why We Remember: Unlocking Memory's Power to Hold on to What Matters* (Doubleday, 2024), 194.

5. Ranganath, *Why We Remember.*

6. Andy Clark, *The Experience Machine: How Our Minds Predict and Shape Reality* (Pantheon Books, 2023), 76.

7. Christopher Engel and Wolf Singer, *Better Than Conscious?: Decision Making the Human Mind and Implications for Institutions* (MIT Press, 2008), 381.

8. Robin M. Hogarth, *Educating Intuition* (University of Chicago Press, 2010), 21.

9. Hogarth, *Educating Intuition*, 214–47.

10. Hogarth, 246. In this regard he is in agreement with Iain McGilchrist's descriptions of science, reason, imagination, and intuition as the four and mutually dependent pathways to knowledge. Iain McGilchrist, *The Matter with Things: Our Brains Our Delusions and the Unmaking of the World*, vol. 1 (Perspectiva Press, 2021).

11. Adam Frank, Marcelo Gleiser, and Evan Thompson, *The Blind Spot: Why Science Cannot Ignore Human Experience* (MIT Press, 2024).

12. James Geary, *I Is an Other: The Secret Life of Metaphor and How It Shapes the Way We See the World* (Harper Perennial, 2012), 9.

13. McGilchrist, *The Matter with Things*, vol. 1, chapter 8. See also Eric R. Kandel, *The Age of Insight: The Quest to Understand the Unconscious in Art Mind and Brain from Vienna 1900 to the Present* (Random House, 2012), especially chapter 28, 449–60; George Lakoff and Mark Johnson, *Philosophy in the Flesh: The Embodied Mind and Its Challenge to Western Thought* (Basic Books, 1999).

14. C. Salvi et al., "Insight Solutions Are Correct More Often Than Analytic Solutions," *Thinking & Reasoning* 22, no. 4 (2016): 443–60. See also Amory H. Danek and Carola Salvi, "Moment of Truth: Why Aha! Experiences Are Correct," *Journal of Creative Behavior* 54, no. 2 (2020): 484–86.

15. Miguel Pina e Cunha, Joao Vieira da Cunha, and Ken N. Kamoche, "Organizational Improvisation: What, When, How and Why," in *Organizational Improvisation*, ed. Ken N. Kamoche, Miguel Pina e Cunha, and Joao Vieira da Cunha (Routledge, 2002), 99. The authors draw on more than fifty different ways in which improvisation has been used by management scientists.

16. See McGilchrist, *The Matter with Things*, vol. 1; and Kandel, *The Age of Insight.*

17. Guy Claxton, *Intelligence in the Flesh: Why Your Mind Needs Your Body Much More Than It Thinks* (Yale University Press, 2015).

18. See Christoph Engel and Wolf Singer, eds., *Better Than Conscious? Decision Making the Human Mind and Implications for Institutions* (MIT Press, 2008). See also Farah Bader and Martin Wiener, "Neuroimaging Signatures of Metacognitive Improvement in Sensorimotor Timing," *Journal of Neuroscience* 44, no. 9 (2024): 1–11, an interesting neuroimaging study that describes the brain's finely tuned updating mechanism for correcting motor actions.

19. I am indebted to conversations with Jason Apollo Voss, author of *The Intuitive Investor: A Radical Guide for Manifesting Wealth* (Select Books, 2010), for this insight.

Appendix 1

1. For those interested in how right and left brain hemispheres collaborate in this process see Annukka K. Lindell "Lateral Thinkers Are Not So Laterally Minded," *Laterality* 16, no. 4 (2011): 479–98.

2. There is a growing literature on the impact of physical settings on patient recovery from a variety of physical and mental health conditions. This work both informs and is informed by several ZMET studies Olson Zaltman has undertaken on the design of various children's hospitals. A sample of the literature includes: Juan Luis Higuera-Trujillo et al., "The Cognitive-Emotional Design and Study of Architectural Space: A Scoping Review of Neuroarchitecture and Its Precursor Approaches," *Sensors* 21, no. 6 (March 21, 2021); Cleo Valentine, "Health Implications of Virtual Architecture: An Interdisciplinary Exploration of the Transferability of Findings from Neuroarchitecture," *International Journal of Research on Public Health* 20, no. 3 (2023), https://doi.org/10.3390/ijerph20032735; Weihong Guo et al., "Research on the Psychologically Restorative Effects of Campus Common Spaces from the Perspective of Health," *Frontiers in Public Health* 11 (2023), https://doi.org/10.3389/fpubh.2023.1131180.

3. Charalampos Mainemelis and Sarah Ronson, "Ideas Are Born in Fields of Play: Towards a Theory of Play and Creativity in Organizational Settings," *Research in Organizational Behavior* 27 (2006): 81–131. See John Kounios and Mark Beeman, "The Cognitive Neuroscience of Insight," *Annals of the Review of Psychology* 65 (2014): 71–93. See also Jennifer S. Beer and Michelle A. Harris, "The Advantages and Disadvantages of Self-Insight: New Psychological and Neural Perspectives," *Advances in Experimental Social Psychology* 60 (2019): 121–73, and Valerie A. Zeithaml, Bernard J. Jaworski, Ajay K. Kohli, Kapil R. Tuli, Wolfgang Ulaga, and Gerald Zaltman, "A Theories-in-Use Approach to Building Marketing Theory," *Journal of Marketing* 84, no. 1 (2020): 32–51.

4. Joan Meyers-Levy and Rui Zhu, "The Influence of Ceiling Height: The Effect of Priming on the Type of Processing That People Use," *Journal of Consumer Research* 34, no. 2 (2007): 174–86.

5. Sally Augustin, "Perspective: Designing for Collaboration and Collaborating for Design," *Journal of Interior Design* 39, no. 1 (2014): ix–xviii.

6. Stuart Brown, *Play: How It Shapes the Brain Opens the Imagination and Invigorates the Soul* (Penguin Books, 2024), 20–21. See also, Jon Otis and Eve A. Edelstein, "Engaging the Mind: Neuroscience in the Design Process," *Journal of Interior Design* 47, no. 1 (2022): 3.

7. Niamh Merriman, Jan Ondřej, Eugenie Roudaia et al., "Familiar Environments Enhance Object and Spatial Memory in Both Younger and Older Adults," *Experimental Brain Research* 234, no. 6 (2016): 1555–74.

8. Juhani Pallasmaa, *The Thinking Hand: Existential and Embodied Wisdom in Architecture* (Wiley, 2009).

9. Jonathan C. Molloy, "Can Architecture Make Us More Creative?," *Arch Daily* April 3, 2013, https://www.archdaily.com/353496/can-architecture-make-us-more-creative.

10. Christopher Alexander, Sara Ishikawa, Murray Silverstein, et al., *A Pattern Language: Towns Buildings Construction* (Oxford University Press, 1977).

Appendix 2

1. See for example, Douglas Hofstadter, and Emmanuel Sander, *Surfaces and Essences: Analogy as the Fuel and Fire of Thinking* (Basic Books, 2013); Iain McGilchrist, *The Matter with Things: Our Brains Our Delusions and the Unmaking of the World* (Perspectiva Press, 2021); Dedre Gentner et al., eds., *The Analogical Mind: Perspectives from Cognitive Science* (MIT Press, 2001); Eric R. Kandel, *The Age of Insight: The Quest to Understand the Unconscious in Art Mind and Brain* (Random House, 2012); George Lakoff, *Philosophy in the Flesh: The Embodied Mind and Its Challenge to Western Thought* (Basic Books, 1999).

2. Three recent sources are Chen-Yao, "How Broad Cognitive Abilities Contribute to Traditional Analogies, Creative Analogies, and General Creativity, *Thinking Skills and Creativity* 45 (2022), https://doi.org/10.1016/j.tsc.2022.101068; D. L. Chiappe et al., "The Role of Working Memory in Metaphor Production and Comprehension," *Journal of Memory and Language* 56, no. 2 (2007): 172–88; and Paul Thibodeau et al., "The Mind Is an Ecosystem: Systemic Metaphors Promote Systems Thinking," *Metaphor and the Social World* 6, no. 2 (2016): 225–42.

3. Liad Mudrick and Leon Y. Deouell, "Neuroscientific Evidence for Processing Without Awareness," *Annual Review of Neuroscience* 45 (2022): 403–23.

4. Sam Glucksberg, *Understanding Figurative Language: From Metaphors to Idioms* (Oxford University Press, 2001); Gerald A. Goldin and James J. Kaput, "A Joint Perspective on the Idea of Representation in Learning and Doing Mathematics," in *Theories of Mathematical Learning*, ed. Leslie P. Steffe, Pearla Nesher, Paul Cobb, Bharath Sriraman, and Brian Greerp, 397–430 (Routledge, 1996); Consuela C. Casula, "Stimulating Unconscious Processes with Metaphors and Narrative," *American Journal of Clinical Hypnosis* 64, no. 4 (2022): 339–54; Peter Mendelsund, *What We See When We Read* (Vintage, 2014).

5. Thomas J. Reynolds and Jerry C. Olson, *The Means-End Approach to Marketing and Advertising Strategy* (Erlbaum, 2001); Tânia Modesto Veludo-de-Oliveira et al., "Discussing Laddering Application by the Means-End Chain Theory," *The Qualitative Report* 11, no. 4 (2006): 626–42.

6. Raymond W. Gibbs Jr. et al., "Metaphor Is Grounded in Embodied Experience," *Journal of Pragmatics* 36, no. 7 (2004): 1189–1210.

7. Jennifer Edson Escalas, "Self-Referencing and Persuasion: Narrative Transportation Versus Analytical Elaboration," *Journal of Consumer Research* 33, no. 4 (2007): 421–29; Ivor F. Goodson, *Developing Narrative Theory: Life Histories and Personal Representation* (Routledge, 2012).

8. Tom van Laer et al., "The Extended Transportation-Imagery Model: A Meta-Analysis of the Antecedents and Consequences of Consumers' Narrative Transportation," *Journal of Consumer Research* 40, no. 4 (2014): 797–817.

9. Carolyn B. Mervis and Eleanor Rosch, "Categorization of Natural Objects," *Annual Review of Psychology* 32 (1981): 89–115.

10. George Kelly, *The Psychology of Personal Constructs*, 1st ed. (Norton, 1955); Fatema Kawaf and Stephen Tagg, "The Construction of Online Shopping Experience," *Computers in Human Behavior* 72 (2017): 222–32.

11. Donna A. Henderson and Samuel T. Gladding, "The Creative Arts in Counseling: A Multicultural Perspective," *The Arts in Psychology* 25, no. 3 (1998): 183–87.

12. Francisco J. Varela et al., *The Embodied Mind: Cognitive Science and Human Experience*, rev. ed. (MIT Press, 2017).

13. Aradhna Krishna, "An Integrative Review of Sensory Marketing: Engaging the Senses to Affect Perception, Judgment, and Behavior," *Journal of Consumer Psychology* 22 (2012): 332–51.

14. Ana Cruz et al., "The Core Techniques of Morenian Psychodrama: A Systematic Review of Literature," *Frontiers in Psychology* 9 (2018), article 1263.

15. Anita Eerland et al., "Leaning to the Left Makes the Eiffel Tower Seem Smaller: Posture-Modulated Estimation," *Psychological Science* 22, no. 12 (2011): 1511–14; Olaf Blanke, "Multisensory Brain Mechanisms of Bodily Self-Consciousness," *Nature Reviews Neuroscience* 13, no. 8 (2012): 556–71; George Lakoff, "Explaining Embodied Cognition Results," *Topics in Cognitive Science* 4, no. 4 (2012): 773–85.

16. Samuel T. Gladding, "The Impact of Creativity in Counseling," Journal of Creativity in Mental Health 3, no. 2 (2008): 97–104; Ravi Mehta and Darren W. Dahl, "Creativity: Past, Present, and Future," *Consumer Psychology Review* 2, no. 1 (2018): 30–49.

17. Jonathan Gottschall, *The Storytelling Animal: How Stories Make Us Human* (Mariner Books, 2013), 56.

INDEX

Note: Page numbers in italic type indicate figures.

adaptation, ix, x, xii, 91, 142, 146, 152, 162–63

Advertising Research Foundation, 119

Aha! Spas, 18, 165–71, *166*. *See also* brainstorming; epiphanies; insights

AI. *See* artificial intelligence

Albright, T., "On the Perception of Probable Things," 124, *125*, *126*

ambiguity, 123–42; Am I? questions regarding, 124, 133, 141, 142; Are we? questions regarding, 142; avoidance of, 132–33, 137; case examples involving, 127–28, 133–34, 140–41; creativity elicited by, 136; curiosity and, 95; decision-making and, 137–39; defining, 127; desire to be right vs. fear of being wrong in situations of, 134–35; embracing, 22, 127, 130–32, 135–36; emotions associated with, 95, 130–32, 141; imagination elicited by, 127–29, 136; metaphors for, 130; positive signs for interpreting, 130; risks for misinterpreting, 128–30

Am I? questions: on adaptation, 163; on ambiguity, 124, 133, 141, 142; on curiosity, 88, 90, 93, 96, 102, 103; in decision-making, 157–58; on environments for thinking and insight, 170; on ignorance, 47, 49, 67; on imaginative and metaphorical thinking, 160–61; on improvisation, 161–62; inner voice as prompt to, x, 22–23, 25; on insights, 161; on intuition, 160; on metaphors, 121; on open-mindedness, x, 13–14, 143–44; on questions, 69–70, 85; self-awareness arising from, 23; on serious play, 25–26, 45; value of, 158; on wisdom, 154

analogies and analogical thinking, 93, 108, 111–12, 114–15, 173. *See also* metaphors

anomalies, 98, 137

curiosity, 87–104; ambiguity and, 95; Am
I? questions regarding, 88, 90, 92, 93,
96, 102, 103; Are we? questions regarding, 103–4; avoidance/encouragement
of, 99–101; barriers to, 97–100, *98*;
breadth-oriented, 95–96; case examples involving, 90–91, 94–95, 99–100;
defining, 90; depth-oriented, 95–96;
economic impact of, 92; emotions
associated with, 88, 90, 94, 95; how it
works, 91–92; ignorance as prompt for,
60; as natural trait, 88, 91; questions'
role in, 73; serious play in relation to,
42; technology and, 100–101; types
of, 91, 93–96; Wizard approach to, 36;
wondering compared to, 62–63, 93–94

Darbellay, Frédéric, 108
data: differences of opinion over, 149;
ignorance resulting from overreliance
on, 58, 60; questioning of, 81–82. *See
also* information
decision-making: ambiguity and, 137–39;
emotion in, 14, 57; questions' role in,
74–75. *See also* mind/thinking
deep metaphors, 120
Dell Technologies, 60
Dennett, Daniel C., 148
ding alarm, 148
disciplinarity, willingness to transcend,
105, 107–9, 121
discipline, 40
discovery and invention, 36, 53, 60–61, 130,
132–33
"di-stance," 64
diversity, 149–50
diversive curiosity, 93
Dunning-Kruger Effect, 58
embodied cognition, 178–79
emotion: ambiguity and, 95, 130–32, 141;
associated with foolishness, 152; associated with questions, 72; curiosity and,
88, 90, 94, 95; ignorance concerning,
56–57; metaphors for, 12, 14; in re-

sponse to problems/challenges, 2, 12,
14; serious play and, 38–39; in thinking
and decision-making, 14, 57
empathic curiosity, 96

Engel, Christopher, 159
Engel, Susan, 90
epiphanies, 62. *See also* Aha! Spas; insights
epistemic curiosity, 93
errors: questions for detecting, 80–82;
serious play as source of, 39. *See also*
failure, fear of; foolishness

failure, fear of, 99, 134–35. *See also* errors
false confidence, 58
feelings. *See* emotion
Fernbach, Philip, 8
Feynman, Richard, 148
flow, 39–41
fluid thinking, 155–63, *156*
Flynn effect, 13
foolishness, 151–52. *See also* errors; ignorance
forbidden knowledge, 57
Formula One auto racing, 110
fox thinking, 106–7, 113, 115
frames. *See* mental models
Freud, Sigmund, 4
Friston, Karl, 23
Frito-Lay, 118–20
Fry, Art, 36

Gates Foundation, 179
Gladwell, Malcolm, 63
global risks, 11–12
Goffman, Erving, 40
Gottschall, Jonathan, 181
Graff, Garrett M., 9
Grand Ogilvy Award, 119
Great Ormond Hospital, London, En-
gland, 110
groupthink, 98–99, 137
Gutenberg, Johannes, 118